Political Philosophy and Public Purpose

Series Editor
Michael J. Thompson, William Paterson University, New York, NY, USA

This series offers books that seek to explore new perspectives in social and political criticism. Seeing contemporary academic political theory and philosophy as largely dominated by hyper-academic and overly-technical debates, the books in this series seek to connect the politically engaged traditions of philosophical thought with contemporary social and political life. The idea of philosophy emphasized here is not as an aloof enterprise, but rather a publicly-oriented activity that emphasizes rational reflection as well as informed praxis.

Mattia Di Pierro

Claude Lefort's Political Philosophy

Democracy, Indeterminacy, Institution

Mattia Di Pierro
Philosophy
University of Milan
Milan, Italy

ISSN 2524-714X   ISSN 2524-7158   (electronic)
Political Philosophy and Public Purpose
ISBN 978-3-031-36377-1   ISBN 978-3-031-36378-8   (eBook)
https://doi.org/10.1007/978-3-031-36378-8

© The Editor(s) (if applicable) and The Author(s), under exclusive license to Springer Nature Switzerland AG 2023

This work is subject to copyright. All rights are solely and exclusively licensed by the Publisher, whether the whole or part of the material is concerned, specifically the rights of translation, reprinting, reuse of illustrations, recitation, broadcasting, reproduction on microfilms or in any other physical way, and transmission or information storage and retrieval, electronic adaptation, computer software, or by similar or dissimilar methodology now known or hereafter developed.
The use of general descriptive names, registered names, trademarks, service marks, etc. in this publication does not imply, even in the absence of a specific statement, that such names are exempt from the relevant protective laws and regulations and therefore free for general use.
The publisher, the authors, and the editors are safe to assume that the advice and information in this book are believed to be true and accurate at the date of publication. Neither the publisher nor the authors or the editors give a warranty, expressed or implied, with respect to the material contained herein or for any errors or omissions that may have been made. The publisher remains neutral with regard to jurisdictional claims in published maps and institutional affiliations.

Cover illustration: Jose A. Bernat Bacete/Moment/Getty Images

This Palgrave Macmillan imprint is published by the registered company Springer Nature Switzerland AG
The registered company address is: Gewerbestrasse 11, 6330 Cham, Switzerland

To Sara

Foreword

Before examining the originality of Di Pierro's monograph, which currently stands as the most comprehensive and reliable introduction to Lefort's work, let us explore for a moment the recent interest in this author. My impression is that Lefort fills a gap in political thought that no other contemporary philosopher has been able to address. If we compare it to that of the three greatest political philosophers of the twentieth century—Carl Schmitt, Hannah Arendt, and Michel Foucault—we might recognize that while they inaugurated research pathways that remain of great importance today, Lefort nevertheless offers something that they lack. Schmitt's reflections on the political, Arendt's thoughts on the action, and Foucault's consideration of power are of great value, but none of them offer a theory of democracy and its institutions capable of responding to our present needs. Di Pierro's thesis, based on a meticulous reading of Lefort's texts, asserts that at the heart of the Frenchman's work is the relationship between democracy and institution. This does not mean that Lefort's analysis should be reduced to political science or political sociology. On the contrary, it is firmly grounded in the philosophical experience, and, in particular, in his relationship with Merleau-Ponty. Lefort was not only the latter's most faithful pupil, but perhaps also the only one capable of translating his phenomenological assumptions into the language of politics.

In this sense, Lefort's work lays the foundation for what has been termed the instituting paradigm, and as such marks a highly innovative contribution to the structure of contemporary political thought compared to the most influential strands in the philosophical-political debate. Far from both the destituent conceptions inspired by Heidegger, which theorize the deactivation of institutions, and the theories of constituent power that equate revolution with the productive power of being, Lefort's ontology and politics articulate a form that acknowledges their relationship while recognizing their distinction. This dialectic, which intertwines conjunction and disjunction, unity, and division, creates the possibility of thinking about democracy in institutive terms.

Lefort's political engagement, alongside Castoriadis, in the French heterodox left of the 1950s and 1960s is well known, as is his intellectual journey into anthropology and ethnology, which broadened his perspective on the diachronic and synchronic planes. By studying archaic rites and non-Western peoples, following the example of Pierre Clastres, he acquired hermeneutical tools that were more penetrating than those typically possessed by political philosophers. However, Lefort's encounter with Merleau-Ponty, which Di Pierro reconstructs analytically, remains the decisive experience in his formation. Above all, Lefort absorbed two notions from the French phenomenologist in an original way that detaches them both from Husserlian semantics still predominantly anchored in a philosophy of consciousness: the notion of the "chiasm" and that of the "field". Both have a strong ontological emphasis, in a key that today would be called "postfoundationalist" but cannot be reduced to Heidegger and Deleuze's conceptual lexicon. For Lefort, being and difference both take on a peculiar character that articulates ontology and phenomenology in a novel way. Being is neither an unfathomable abyss nor an infinitely productive power, but the place where human beings come into a relationship with each other. Difference is thus not the margin that separates Being from being, nor even that which continually proliferates on the plane of immanence, but the original conflict that cuts through the social, establishing it politically. Lefort is neither a philosopher of origin, following the line connecting Heidegger to Derrida or Nancy, nor a philosopher of immanence in the mold of Bergson or Deleuze.

Di Pierro explains that the concept of chiasm means that everything, every element of reality, is included in being, in an interwoven fabric whose beginning is impossible to identify and which never fully coincides with itself. The result of this is that presence is never full, but is marked by a latency that means it is removed from all empirical determination and is not even fully visible, but appears to be in the shadows. In this sense, Lefort's perspective cannot be classified as either dualist or monist, nor is it univocal or plurivocal. It is instead characterized by the dominant figure of the relation, or co-implication, which precedes the elements of relation and robs them of the purity of determination. But to fully understand the instituting dynamic that Lefort inherits from Merleau-Ponty, one must consider not only the concept of the chiasm but also that of the field. Rather than arising from subjectivity, the phenomenon of instituting is constituted at the intersection of the active and the passive, of the individual and the collective, and of past and future experiences. The institution is this constantly evolving field that articulates permanence and innovation. Merleau-Ponty also leaves behind the Husserlian dialectic of *Urstiftung* and *Endstiftung*, which remains tied to the semantics of conscience, and opens up a field where the subject is itself altered, removed from itself, and engaged in a continuous confrontation not only with others, but with its own internal otherness. This means that in Merleau-Ponty phenomenological reduction remains incomplete and partial, and no subject can fully account for itself. Our experience is always separated from itself in some way, or covered by a veil that prevents its integral recognition.

The great book on Machiavelli, which Di Pierro examines in depth, should be viewed in this phenomenological perspective, which permeates Lefort's entire oeuvre. In this regard, I share the view that breaking his itinerary in two is incorrect. It is certainly true that at the end of the 1960s Lefort's work takes on certain new elements, but his basic orientations do not change. Thus, rather than a point of rupture, as it has sometimes been considered, his *Machiavel* should be understood as a point of junction that accounts for the preceding phase while also inaugurating the next one. The category of opacity, which characterizes not only the interpretation of texts but also social reality, which is never fully conscious of itself, is the element of continuity between the two periods and is most thoroughly elaborated in the volume on Machiavelli. The instituting role of politicians is to bring awareness to a society divided from the beginning, although this is an awareness which it fails to elaborate. In this sense the institution, much more than an internal moment within the political sphere, is its very mode of being. In Lefort, politics involves establishing relationships that are never quite complete, and always open to change.

This is not to say that Lefort values the event more than the form or sets the one against the other. On this point, Di Pierro rightly asserts his sharp disagreement with philosophical neo-anarchism, whether that influenced by Heidegger (like Schürmann) or by Arendt (like Abensour), which are related to Lefort in several ways. The central point of difference between Lefort's views and theirs concerns the question of power. While Abensour follows the young Marx in asserting the opposition between democracy and the state, Lefort's thesis is that no society can exist without power. However, power should not be viewed as something tangible that can be possessed by someone. Indeed, democracies are characterized by the fact that within them power can never be grasped or occupied in a protracted way. Rather, it is the elusive point around which the democratic process revolves. Not only that, but it serves as the mechanism by which society communicates symbolically. Establishing a society means accessing a symbolic dimension that implies a certain level of detachment from its immediacy and a relationship with otherness that is never severed.

From this point of view, the negative returns play a role in Lefort's thinking that sets him apart from all philosophies of immanence. Through power, society establishes a relationship with its own exterior, to a point that necessarily transcends it, while also situating itself within it. This is a crucial point that is often difficult to comprehend. What sets democratic societies apart from those of the *ancien régime*, or even from totalitarian ones, is that the transcendence of power is not external. Otherwise, the people would not be able to call themselves sovereign, as they do. Rather, the transcendence of power is internal to that which does not coincide with it. After all, even for Machiavelli, the prince is never fully independent of the different gazes focused on him. Therefore, Machiavelli is not a backward thinker of absolute sovereignty, as Foucault claimed, but rather the originator of modern politics. As Merleau-Ponty had already realized, before Lefort developed his own original insights, the role of appearance, which is constitutive of Machiavellian representation, concerns phenomenology as much as ontology. As Castoriadis would do with even more conviction, Lefort identifies the instituting role of the social imaginary in the power of appearance.

Based on these observations, we can now return to the question of democracy that forms the epicenter of Lefort's entire body of work. His focus on democracy places him firmly at the forefront of the contemporary debate, removing him from the discussion of totalitarianism that in many ways we have left behind. Although Lefort worked on both totalitarianism and democracy, this is not to say that he develops his analysis of one from the other. Claiming that Lefort is a theorist of democracy as an institution as well as an instituting energy does not mean that his analysis is entirely satisfactory. Di Pierro himself acknowledges certain internal inconsistencies in Lefort's work, particularly his sometimes unconvincing way of relating the social and the political, and his conception of rights, which does not fully acknowledge the instituting role played by legal praxis today. Nevertheless, this is not to agree with the idea that the "second" Lefort should be placed on the liberal horizon, as some have suggested. His special relevance, which makes him a significant author not only for his own time, but also for our own, stems precisely from his ability to escape such categorizations. Di Pierro's book makes a powerful contribution to recognizing the irreducible specificity of Lefort's thought.

Naples, Italy   Roberto Esposito

Acknowledgments

This book is the latest result of a broader and longer research project, conducted in many moments of solitude but also through multiple opportunities for meetings and discussions. My first thanks go to Andrea Lanza, who has followed the evolution of this work and carefully read each chapter. His patience, advice, and my countless discussions with him have been truly invaluable. I also owe much to the suggestions of Dick Howard and Stéphane Vibert and thank them for their attentive examination of the text. This work would never have succeeded or even come to light without the teaching and support of Marco Geuna, Mauro Simonazzi, and Annalisa Ceron, who form the research group I work with at the University of Milan.

I also need to mention that my research owes much to Roberto Esposito—who kindly wrote the preface to this volume and whose lesson innervates these pages—and to a group of colleagues and friends with whom I had the fortune to work at the Scuola Normale Superiore in Pisa and with whom I am still in regular contact. In particular: Francesco Marchesi, Elia Zaru (who also read and commented on parts of the work), Andrea Di Gesu, Paolo Missiroli, and Claudia Terra. Since the beginning of my research on Claude Lefort I have had many encounters and discussions that have flowed more or less directly into the following pages, especially with Mirko Alagna, Gilles Bataillon, Simona Forti, Judith Revel, Nadia Urbinati, and Miguel Vatter who kindly helped me sort through my ideas for the original project. Michael Thompson generously agreed to include the book in the series that he edits. Finally, I am grateful to Matthew Armistead, who edited my English with professionalism and extreme helpfulness, preventing me from making terrible mistakes.

I am very thankful for the financial support of the Philosophy Department of the University of Milan and the ATLAS research grant awarded to me by the Université Franco-Italienne, as well as the help provided by the Fondation Maison des Sciences de l'Homme, which made it possible to conduct my research between Milan and Paris.

Claude Lefort's Essential Bibliography

Listed below are the major works of Claude Lefort, and their English translations. For a more detailed bibliography see:

Molina, Esteban. 2005. *Le défi du politique. Totalitarisme et démocratie chez Claude Lefort*. Paris: L'Harmattan.
Poltier, Hugues. 1998. *Passion du politique. La pensée de Claude Lefort*. Genève: Labor et Fides.
Lefort, Claude. 2021. *Lectures politiques. De Dante à Soljenitsyne*. Paris: Puf.
Lefort, Claude. 2007. *Le temps présent. Écrits 1945–2005*. Paris: Belin.
Lefort, Claude. 1999. *La complication. Retour sur le communisme*. Paris: Fayard. English translation by J. Bourg. 2007. *Complications: Communism and the Dilemma of Democracy*. New York: Columbia University Press.
Lefort, Claude. 1994. *L'invention démocratique. Les limites de la domination totalitaire*. Paris: Fayard.
Lefort, Claude. 1993. *La modernité de Dante*. In *La monarchie*, Dante 9–91. Paris: Belin. English translation by J. Rushworth. 2020. *Dante's Modernity. An Introduction to the Monarchia*. Berlin: ICI Berlin Press. Also in Lefort 2021.

Lefort, Claude. 1992. *Écrire. A l'épreuve du politique*. Paris: Calmann-Lévy. Eng. Translatation by D.A. Curtis. 2000. *Writing. The Political Test*. Durham and London: Duke University Press.

Lefort, Claude. 1990. Flesh and Otherness. In *Ontology and Alterity in Merleau-Ponty*, (ed.) G.A. Johnson and M.B. Smith 3–13. Evanston: Northwestern University Press.

Lefort, Claude. 1986. *Essais sur le politique. XIXe et XXe siècles*. Paris: Seuil. English translation by D. Macey. 1988. *Democracy and Political Theory*. Cambridge: Polity Press.

Lefort, Claude. 1986. *The Political Forms of Modern Society: Bureaucracy, Democracy, Totalitarianism*. Cambridge: MIT Press. With partial translation of Lefort 1994, 1979 and 1978.

Lefort, Claude. 1979. *Éléments d'une critique de la bureaucratie*. 2nd edition. Paris: Gallimard.

Lefort. Claude. 1978. *Les formes de l'histoire. Essais d'anthropologie politique*. Paris: Gallimard.

Lefort, Claude. 1978. *Sur une colonne absente. Écrits autour de Merleau-Ponty*. Paris: Gallimard.

Lefort, Claude. 1976. *Un homme en trop. Réflexions sur «l'Archipel du Goulag»*. Paris: Seuil.

Lefort, Claude. 1972. *Le travail de l'œuvre Machiavel*. Paris: Gallimard. Partial english translation by M.B. Smith. 2012. *Machiavelli in the Making*. Evanston: Northwestern University Press.

Lefort, Claude. 1971. *Éléments d'une critique de la bureaucratie*. Paris: Droz.

Lefort, Claude and Gauchet, Marcel. 1971. Sur la démocratie : le politique et l'institution du social. *Texures* 2/3: 7–78.

Lefort. Claude. 1968. Le désordre nouveau. In *Mai 1968 : la Brèche. Premières réflexions sur les événements*, (ed.) E. Morin, C. Lefort and J.-M. Coudray, 35–62. Paris: Fayard.

Contents

1 **Introduction** 1
   Event and Form 3
   What About Lefort? 7
   References 16

2 **Socialisme ou Barbarie** 19
   The Chaulieu–Montal Tendency 19
   Socialisme ou Barbarie 25
   A Phenomenology of the Proletarian Experience 31
   The Role of Theory 36
   Lefort or Castoriadis: The Proletariat, the Party, and the Organization 40
   References 45

3 **The Symbolic Dimension of the Social** 51
   Phenomenological Marxism 51
   The Social as Culture 57
   A Political Issue at the Bottom of the Social 61
   The Social Is the Real, or Marx's Mistake 66
      The Symbolic and the Political 74
   The Symbolic Institution of the Social 79
   References 84

4	**A Sociology of a Divided Society: Alienation, Ideology and a Project for a Study of Democracy**	89
	Alienation, or a Sociology of the Division of the Social	89
	Ideology	94
	From the Proletariat to the People	99
	References	108
5	**The Modern Symbolic Change**	111
	The Image of the Body and Heteronomy	111
	Ancien Régime Societies and the Theological-Political	118
	The State, Disincorporation, and the Modern Form of Society	124
	Dante, Civic Humanism and the Birth of Modernity	132
	References	142
6	**Niccolò Machiavelli**	147
	The Critique of Tradition, or the Loss of Foundation	147
	The Conspiracy: A New Politics	155
	The Conflict	161
	The Role of the People	166
	Power, Imaginary and the Foundation	173
	The Original Division of the Social	181
	References	187
7	**The Political and the Institution of the Social**	191
	Structure or Institution	191
	Interpretation or Archaeology: Lefort and Foucault	199
	Against Theories of Immanence	209
	References	215
8	**Democracy**	219
	The Democratic Form of Society	219
	Modernity and Democracy	225
	Totalitarianism	232
	On Revolution: Change and Foundation in Democratic Society	241
	References	248
Index		253

CHAPTER 1

Introduction

If, as we hear these days, history has returned after its supposed end, armed with tanks and nostalgic imperial ambitions, it is worth asking where it had gone. Moreover, if the end of history was inextricably linked to the uncontroversial advance of democracy, or at least its Western model, it might be necessary to revisit a reflection on the meaning and essence of the democratic form of society. This book aims to meet these requirements by presenting the reflections of a philosopher who has reflected extensively on the issues of history, democracy, and politics. It proposes an as yet unexplored approach that may offer innovative tools for theory and criticism, providing new references that can clarify the ontology of our present while abandoning certain patterns that have proved, if not erroneous, at least inadequate.[1]

I am not referring solely to normative theories of politics, such as neo-contractualism, which endlessly analyze the enigma of human coexistence as the outcome of rational calculation and the interaction between moral and autonomous individuals who participate in a universal reason in a Kantian sense. Nor is my allusion limited to research that seeks to reduce society and human actions to their physical causes, to the result

---

[1] This work was preceded by another book (Di Pierro 2020) in which I presented my interpretation of Lefort's thought to the Italian public. This second volume is a revision, a continuation, and a closure of that research.

of neuronal processes. Instead, I refer also to post-structuralist theory, which has dominated the field of critical theory and certain strands of political philosophy for decades, as well as to recent developments in post-operaist theory, to new materialisms and vitalisms that inform current reflections on the ecological crisis (Bennet 2010) and the debate on identities, including sexual and gender identities. Finally, I also refer to attempts to conceptualize a plebeian politics or a "radical democracy".

If we accept Claude Lefort's notion of democracy as the quintessential form of political society because, lacking certain points of reference, it rests on a foundation that is continually renewed and at the same time constantly challenged, it becomes clear that the aforementioned theories reason differently and, in effect, "undemocratically". They attempt, more or less surreptitiously, to establish a stable and indisputable foundation by referring to the rational individual, to neurons, matter, birth, the unending productivity of life, the agency of nature, the social as an affirmative immanent force, and to politics as the human ability to introduce novelty: components that impart order and direction to the democratic chaos and are designed to restore a foundation. Indeed, these theories squeeze the symbolic and the real, the analysis and the object of analysis, into one another, eliminating indeterminacy and the dimension of interpretation. As we will see, following Lefort's lead, it must be said that such theories do not grasp the political dimension and are thus essentially ideology, hiding the contingency of the foundation, the emptiness that lies at the heart of society.

In fact, following this pattern of thought, an important and potentially highly productive part of the contemporary theory has landed on diplopic thinking that recovers a surreptitious foundation by interpreting the social and political dimensions as the opposition between event and form, power and resistance, politics and institution.

In the following pages, I will try to challenge this tradition by drawing on Lefort's thinking to obtain new insights and perspectives on the present. This endeavor is complicated, however, by the fact that Lefort's own ideas have often been seen as part of the same paradigm that I intend, and he intended, to criticize. To provide clarity, it is essential to start at the beginning.

Event and Form

In France, the entry of the tanks into Budapest in 1956 marked the collapse of an entire structure of belief, of a framework through which to interpret the world that had seemed set in stone until that point. After being the homeland of socialism, the Soviet Union became first a power like any other, and then a totalitarian society, thus leaving scores of intellectual *engagés* orphaned. Structuralism then took the place of Marxism as the hegemonic cultural phenomenon, and Lévi-Strauss became the champion of the era. The new science aimed to analyze the social as an object in order to identify its elemental and universal structures and set forth a truth capable of replacing that of the party and the Diamat.

However, the universalism and *longue durée* associated with structuralism soon become the target of critique, and an internal twist led to the emergence of the "post" version of that new theory. Political disillusionment brought with it suspicion toward homogeneity and transparency, as these were viewed as masks of power, devices of government and control, and elements of totalitarianism. To understand the structure, one must destroy the grand narratives, the universal and timeless structures, and focus on the contradictions that constitute it: the difference underlying continuity, the madness lurking beneath or alongside Reason. The subject must be deconstructed, history destroyed, and the fiction of the social unmasked. The subjectivities beneath the proletariat must be unveiled, beyond the mediation of the party, to reveal the purity, multiplicity, difference, and contradictory nature of humanity exploited for progress or left on the margins.

These approaches were anticipated somewhat by the Johnson–Forest Tendency and by the Socialisme ou Barbarie theory of worker autonomy, and later by the analyses of early *operaismo* in Italy. In this case the subject to be reached was the Fordist factory worker, the unskilled mass-worker previously in thrall to the Communist Party.

However, through a kind of heterogenesis of ends, the refusal of mediation and objectivity of universal structures ends up recovering a plane of stability and a latent foundation, and reaching a politically autonomous and structurally progressive plane. Under the guise of grand narratives, Foucault (2002) then discovers the immanence of dispersed discursive practices. Beneath the fiction of the proletariat, another equally stable and continuous subject is revealed: an autonomous subjectivity that is resistant to institutional mediations, possesses its own voice, and adheres to its own irrepressible desire. The destruction of representation takes place alongside the emergence of an affirmative, productive, and immediately political plane of immanence. This background occasionally takes on the appearance of desire, life, or the social. In this context, the works of Gilles Deleuze become an indispensable point of reference. Through his interpretation of the texts of Baruch Spinoza and Henri Bergson, and against phenomenology, Deleuze inaugurates a conception of reality as full affirmation, a continuous flow that proceeds through perpetual differentiation (2009).

The renewal of theory was happening at the same time as a significant change in the production model in the 1960s, the eruption of revolts in 1968, and the violent endeavor to integrate them in the following decade. The factory model spread out to the rest of society and the extraction of value started to occur in unprecedented and widespread ways. The growth of exploitation now involved subjects who were no longer immediately identifiable with the figure of the mass, of the Fordist worker.

In this context, theories of immanence take on a clear political dimension. The affirmative unity of the social desire corresponds to the negativity of institutions that seek to control this positivity, impeding its flow, and imposing definitions. The immediately political activity of a dynamic, vibrant society corresponds to the repression of institutional apparatuses. The social represents a constituent power that stands in opposition to constituted power, manifesting as a multitude with an ever-present possibility of revolt. The most radical forms identify an affirmative, vital *élan* that bubbles beneath the surface of every human society, denying any attempt at containment, stable definition, or boundary.

Here we again see a subtle twisting of thought that seeks to restore transparency and grounding to the discussion. The social realm is seen as the whole truth, to be attained by stripping away the layers of ideology and repression of that obscure politics behind the veil of false representations. Genuine politics, in this view, serves to liberate or channel the affirming, autonomous, and spontaneous aspects of the social. It involves the continuous creation of difference and the eruption of vitality that resists all constituted power. Flow is thus seen as the opposite of institution, resistance as the opposite of power, and event as the opposite of form. Democracy can be understood as a sign of abundance, as a continuous affirmation of the social, the plebs, desire, nature, and life (Breaugh 2013; Tønder and Thomassen 2005; Negri 1999). The social is constituent power, an event, an action without representation. On the one hand, there is *le politique*, which questions the established order of identities, roles, and hierarchies; on the other there is *la police*, which imposes order, identifies, and gives form (Rancière 2004), and which cannot be escaped. The theory of immanence thus leads to a diplopic view of the social that conceals the dimension of the political.

While I have thus far traced the trajectory of structuralism and post-structuralism, it would be a mistake to confine the analysis to the walls of the École Normale. Far from being the only landing place of French theory, the notion of the immediate affirmative of the social and the resulting dichotomy between event and form is reflective of a broader zeitgeist that goes far beyond the boundaries of post-structuralism and its influence on so-called French Theory.

One can therefore not fail to notice the sense of kinship that emerges in Sheldon Wolin's statement that "Politics is continuous, ceaseless, and endless. In contrast, the political is episodic, rare" (Wolin 2016, p. 100). Wolin's influences may not be primarily Deleuze or Foucault, however, but Hannah Arendt and Claude Lefort himself.

In 1966 Hannah Arendt (2018a, p. 384) examined the conditions and significance of revolution, and stated: "the meaning of revolution is the actualization of one of the greatest and most elementary human potentialities, the unequaled experience of *being* free to make a new beginning, from which comes the pride of having opened the world to a *Novus Ordo Seclorum*".

Arendt believed that the key to political change and foundation was an "essential" human capacity: action. This faculty was given an ambiguous role by the thinker, who placed it in an almost pre-political and at the same time already political space. Indeed, on the one hand, action, as the ability to initiate a new series of events, served as the condition of possibility for politics. On the other hand, action always takes place in intimate connection with discourse, and is in this sense appearance or meaning, and thus something always linked to the public sphere, to acting together, to power, and, in short, to politics. Action is such if it is recognized, discussed, and interpreted. This tension reverberates in some of the key concepts of Arendt's thought, such as politics, which is both an event and a discourse on the existing, and foundation, which on the one hand is an *ex nihilo* novelty and on the other a novelty that is always impossible, discursive, and linked to elements prior and external to it (Arendt 2006, 2018b).

This tension within Arendt's thought was often resolved by collapsing politics onto action, which was then collapsed onto the event. The price to be paid for resolving the aporia was a partial reading, the disavowal of many pages of her work and their productive contradiction. Nevertheless, politics becomes no more than a disruptive and causeless episode, an *ex nihilo* explosion that arose from humanity's remarkably endless ability to destroy a given situation, distrust the established, and introduce the new by interrupting the repetition of the already given. Politics, as an event without cause or project, can be thought of in terms of its autonomy and the semantics of freedom.

Arendt's enemy, and that of some of her interpreters, was above all totalitarianism, but also a certain Marxist economicist and determinist thought. However, in the face of the eternal present ushered in by the fall of the Berlin Wall and the USSR, and of the end of history tinged with neoliberal globalization, the interpretation of the Arendtian theory of politics has taken on a messianic perspective. Today we have *politics*, the management of the present, governmentality, and technology, but one day politics will come. And this will be an eruption that will destroy current institutions and establish a space of freedom. This space, however, will quickly be closed by new institutions that will assign it a name, impose definitions, and establish a political discourse. The irruption of the political will inevitably be followed by the management, interpretation, and containment of this propulsive force. The event will be followed by the form that only another event can challenge.

According to many interpreters of Arendt, politics is thus understood as a possibility that can undermine every project and construction. In the meantime, all that remains is to stand by and be ready to decipher the anticipatory signs of the event: a demonstration, a revolt. Action will present itself, perhaps following a series of struggles, but in reality always suddenly, like a volcanic eruption. Thus all that remains is to manage the present, perhaps retreating into anarchic individualism and self-care, while waiting in hope for the event.

In this theoretical framework, politics and democracy are often confused. Democracy is seen as the explosion of the *demos* and the demos as the name given to the human potentiality of the new, of the event. It represents the driving force of politics and the possibility of freedom. In other words, democracy becomes another way of referring to an immediately political and fully affirmative social, as the immediate power of the politics of being in common.

Once again, politics is understood as an immanent and affirmative plane that is inherently positive, progressive, and democratic. It is a surging and performative force that emerges in the streets when people come together and recognize each other among the barricades. Before this moment, it is merely a potentiality. After it, when the event invariably passes, it anchors itself not to minds and ideologies but to bodies. Not to speech but to voice. It is the direct expression of identities and values that are not proposed but acted upon (Cavarero 2021; Butler 2018).

Here, the two paths we have been following converge and combine. Both view the social dimension as a split between event and form, constituent power and constituted power, life and process. Therefore, both paths interpret form, institution, and identity as elements that curb the freedom and spontaneous affirmativity that shape politics. They identify an immanent and immediately productive plane from which politics arises, merging with democracy.

It is at precisely this point that the possibility and originality of Claude Lefort's theses emerge.

What About Lefort?

Lefort's work has also mostly been interpreted within the theoretical framework outlined above, or at least through its relation to it. While his detractors have reduced his work to an essentially liberal theory, his apologists have frequently placed it in continuity with Arendt's theories or with post-structuralism. Almost as if he were acquiring proof of criticality, his theory has been read through the categories of event and form, and of a politics as a continuous deconstruction of the instituted. Through the mediation of Miguel Abensour in particular, and to some extent Pierre Clastres, Lefort became the theorist of *démocratie sauvage* pitted against the state, advocating for an idea of politics understood as the possibility of the new, of freedom, of event versus form, and questioning of all that is instituted (Abensour 2011; Clastres 1987). Also, through the common theme of councils, his texts have increasingly been associated with those of Arendt, and his categories conflated with those of the more famous author of *On Revolution* and *The Human Condition* (Ask Popp-Madsen 2021).

However, beyond the undoubtedly interesting aspects that have emerged from these readings, the most significant and peculiar core of the author's theory has been misunderstood, depowered, and concealed.

The first aim of this book is therefore to extract Lefort's work from this context of interpretation in order to grasp its difference and productive core. It will then become clear that it moves in the opposite direction from structuralism, post-structuralism, the Arendtian idea of politics, and the conception of the relationship between event and form that I have briefly described above. In this way, it offers some useful tools for critiquing the idea of philosophy and the relationship between theory and society that underpin what I have called, with some approximation, theories of the immanence of the political. It exposes some of their contradictory and ideological effects.

The first step to teasing out this potential interpretation is to understand the close relationship, or even continuity, that exists between Lefort's reflections and those of Maurice Merleau-Ponty. One could even argue, provocatively, that Lefort's entire body of work can be seen as an attempt to "apply" Merleau-Ponty's phenomenological method to the analysis of society and politics. This connection is not simply historical and biographical. While it is true that Lefort was a young student of Merleau-Ponty's, collaborated with him on "Les Temps Modernes", and edited several of his posthumous works, what matters more is the structure of Lefort's reflection, which allows for this argument.

For Lefort, the main merit of Merleau-Ponty's work is his promotion of a new indirect ontology that voids any pure element and can therefore account for the interweaving and co-implication of all the elements that make up reality or being. This is not coincidental, since in *Phenomenology of Perception* his primary polemic target is the dualistic scheme of classical and Cartesian philosophy, as well as empiricism (Merleau-Ponty 2012). This is the *diplopia*, a dual vision that separates subject and object, perceiver and perceived, being and beingness. Merleau-Ponty, on the other hand, proposes a thought freed from the categories of subject and object. Lefort describes it as a thought of latency that wants to approach without ever grasping, to illuminate without ever fully bringing out of the shadows that which always eludes all determination; that which exceeds every sensible or intelligible datum but is nevertheless responsible for everything that takes place and is in Being. Merleau-Ponty's reflection thus inaugurates a thought of chiasma that gives reason to the intertwining of all the elements of reality, rejecting any illusion of *surplomb*, or the existence of a perspective from which it is possible to grasp Being in its totality and objectivity.

The stages of the prematurely interrupted elaboration of this chiasm thinking, which seeks to understand being as an interweaving (*entrelacs*) of experienced phenomena, are presented first in *Phenomenology of Perception* and then in *The Visible and the Invisible* (Merleau-Ponty 1969, 2012). In these works, Merleau-Ponty argues that being is always enveloped in a "fog" composed of a "promiscuity of visage, words, actions, with, between them all, that cohesion which cannot be denied them since they are all differences, extreme divergencies of the same something" (84). Therefore, Being is not a pure ontological background, nor is it something external to the subject or to thought: it is always in relation, it is always situated, related to the act, and it always demands a creation for it to be experienced. Through the concepts of "chiasma", "flesh", and "institution", Merleau-Ponty attempts to decipher this continuous exchange, this fundamental interweaving of the real.

Thought thus finds itself immersed in the entanglement of being, situated within it. Its contact with being, however, also establishes the impossibility of coinciding with it. It is part of the same "flesh", yet also separated by a caesura. This condition of thought, Lefort notes, is precisely what differentiates Merleau-Ponty's approach from that of Edmund Husserl, and it is here that the novelty and merit of his work reside: phenomenological reduction turns out to be incomplete, consciousness is neither a starting nor ending point, the very thought that enunciates phenomenology is subject to the phenomenological method. Thus Merleau-Ponty's phenomenology does not sever the links between self and the thing that is thought, but rather takes on the task of thinking them. As an interrogation, it first and foremost asks questions about the meaning of the interrogation itself.

But if the visible is what relates and at the same time differentiates what sees and what is seen, if the "flesh" is the fabric in which phenomena appear simultaneously aggregated and different, then there can be no possible coincidence between seeing and seen, perceiver and perceived, or thought and being. Between these elements, which only make sense in their mutual relationship, there therefore emerges a division which in turn is the condition for the possibility of the relationship itself. That is, it is only through the invisible that sight and the seen can make sense. However, the invisible is not external to the relationship, but is the relationship itself. The concept of *chair* involves highlighting a gap, a productive division.

Lefort's thought moves within these main coordinates, and is indebted to his interpretation of his master's phenomenology. This is indispensable to understanding Lefort fully without connecting him to the diplopia between event and form, between constituent and instituted, that he actually rejects, and without considering him merely a contingent and occasional critic of the Soviet regime and totalitarianism. On the contrary, I define Lefort's thought as a phenomenology and ontology of the political that attempts to analyze societies without presupposing pure foundations, subjects, or events, and overcomes the simplistic scheme that separates immanence and transcendence in order to grasp the interweaving and chiasma that constitutes the social and its political. His thought is itself political: the result of contingent experience, traversed by the relations and contradictions of a given "institution of the social".

Thus, just as Merleau-Ponty sought to avoid any sense of overarching thought by establishing a reflection that was first and foremost an investigation of its own presuppositions, Lefort proposes a philosophy as an "experience of the world". He aims to analyze society by discarding all illusions of objectivity, rejecting any belief in a reality to be discovered beneath social or political discourse, discarding all mechanism and economism, and abandoning all foundations, whether they be nothingness or the immanent productivity of the social. Lefort's reflection is first and foremost an investigation of its own presuppositions. It seeks to grasp itself as part of the same object it analyzes. It acknowledges its complicity in the distortions it seeks to judge or challenge, without abandoning critique as a result. It is a thought of *the* political and *in the* political that confronts the indeterminacy that emerges from the background of the interweaving of all the elements and meanings that constitute the social and determine reflection itself. That indeterminacy makes the political possible.

Only from this starting point, while keeping the theoretical framework I have schematically presented above in mind, is it possible to fully understand the fundamental concepts of Lefort's philosophy, such as his conception of the relationship between theory and politics, the idea of the institution of the social, the centrality of the notion of interpretation, the theory of the symbolic, the critique of totalitarianism, and his definition of democracy.

The pages of *Le travail de l'oeuvre*, the 1972 work devoted to Machiavelli, and the theory of democracy developed in the following decade offer the best examples of this political phenomenology, of the analysis of the web of relations and conflicts pervaded by an otherness that constitutes the political institution of the social (Lefort 1972, 2012). Furthermore, precisely the democratic social form reflects the movement of being and thought described by Merleau-Ponty, his idea of *institution*. Democracy, in fact, develops through a perpetual questioning of the legitimacy of power and a constant reexamination of the assumptions of community, out of which new oppositions, new identities as well as a common context and meaning are being created continuously and simultaneously.

This phenomenological approach is not only one possible interpretation of Lefort's work, but is the one that highlights its greatest potential and reveals the internal coherence of his reasoning. This does not mean, of course, that every other reading should be considered incorrect, mystifying, or invented. On the other hand, Lefort's work is not a systematic and coherent totality of thought. Instead, it must be admitted that his grand project of a political phenomenology, of an ontology of the institution, is shot through with an internal tension. This becomes most apparent in his reflections on proletarian and workers' autonomy in the late 1940s and during the period of Socialisme ou Barbarie, in his analysis of the 1968 uprisings, and even in the antinomies that run through his definitions of modernity and democracy, as well as in the theory of the symbolic itself. As I will show in the last chapter, for example, Lefort's definition of democracy rests on ambivalence and does not always seem consistent with the idea of the political institution of the social on which, however, all his work rests. Thus, it is precisely these internal tensions that offer footholds for dualistic interpretations *à la* Abensour (2011, pp. 102–124), and for the interpretation of politics as an event as opposed to form.

However, these internal tensions do not call into question the coherence of the path characterized by what I have called the phenomenology of the social or the ontology of the political, which marks the entire arc of Lefort's reflection. As I state in the first two chapters, it is already recognizable in the background of the research on the proletariat, in the critique of philosophies of history in the 1950s, and in the period of militancy in Socialisme ou Barbarie. This same phenomenological structure of thought then emerges more clearly in the notion of "proletarian experience" in 1955 and is the basis for the definition of totalitarianism. Not only that but, as I show in the second chapter, in the 1950s the phenomenological method leads Lefort toward his confrontation with ethnology and the elaboration of the idea of the political institution of the social. Moreover, as I demonstrate in Chapter 6, this same approach explicitly underlies the distinction between the political (*le politique*) and politics (*la politique*), as well as the critique of structuralism and post-structuralism, including the critique of the work of Lévi-Strauss, Louis Althusser, Gilles Deleuze, and Michel Foucault, that Lefort undertook in the 1970s.

The continuity of the French thinker's reflection thus emerges from the phenomenological perspective. However, it is a coherence that has never been sufficiently emphasized. On the contrary, in an attempt to bring order to work that was decidedly unsystematic and closely linked to contingent events, Lefort's thought was mostly presented as divided into two distinct phases. The first, youthful phase was internal to Marxism and characterized by political militancy, and supposedly corresponded to his years in Socialisme ou Barbarie, in which his political commitment and belief in the necessity of revolution guided his theoretical positions (Flynn 2005; Poltier 1998). By contrast, his abandonment of the group in 1958 supposedly led to a more mature and personal phase in which his "real" theory developed. This second period would be characterized by a critique of Marxism and the abandonment of revolution in favor of a democratic approach imbued with liberalism. With this distinction in mind, some interpreters have identified a certain continuity in the critique of totalitarianism, which became the guiding light of Lefort's reflection, the deepest core of his work (Molina 2005). If during his time with Socialisme ou Barbarie his work, still operating in a Marxist paradigm, was directed toward a critique of the USSR as a bureaucratic society, his abandonment of Marx and the revolutionary perspective supposedly led to a redefinition of the totalitarian society on which his interest in democracy and its revaluation would depend.

Moreover, the phenomenological perspective I have chosen not only highlights the continuity of Lefort's reflection beyond the significant changes, but also proposes a reversal of perspective: democracy, not totalitarianism was the fulcrum of his work. Following the pathway that I will set out in the next few pages, it will in fact be evident that, from the 1950s, on the basis of an understanding of the symbolic institution of the social, the intention guiding the Parisian philosopher's reflection was the investigation of a contemporary democratic society and, consequently, of modernity. Although a 1966 text, which I will analyze in

Chapter 3, clearly presents his plan to develop a sociology of democracy in the following years, the core of this interest can already be found in his interventions on the historicity of the previous decade.

The anthropological studies of the 1950s, and in particular the emergence of the notion of the symbolic I analyze in the second chapter, provided Lefort with valuable tools to articulate his phenomenology of the social more precisely. He realized that at the foundation of every society and its relationship with otherness, the world, division, change, time, and history lies a kind of "choice", a political question. This choice determines the internal organization and relationships of each society with its elements, including the economy. As I illustrate in Chapter 2, at this point the tools offered by Marx and Marxism obviously appeared insufficient and Lefort therefore sought to overcome them. However, he did not reject the hypothesis of the primacy of relations of production, but rather the primacy of the economic in general, positing instead a more complicated relationship between the various dimensions that constitute the social. Lefort, in short, believed that the relationship between structure and superstructure should not be overturned. The symbolic is not an autonomous and primary dimension that determines the productive structure, as the matter is rather more complicated. Economy and social meanings must be understood together, in their mutual relationship and within the broader context of the symbolic and political institution of the social. Marx is not to be abandoned, he should be made more complicated.

Thus even Lefort's relationship with the Trier philosopher cannot be seen as a straightforward abandonment. While his writings of the 1960s certainly contained a direct critique of Marxism, which he always experienced in an unorthodox way, he never fully rejected it. On the contrary, Marx continued to be an essential point of reference for his reflection on temporality, modernity, and, therefore, democracy.

At this point, it is important to emphasize that due to the influence of his anthropological studies and his shift away from Marxism, Lefort's work became more explicitly focused on comprehending the symbolic institution of a democratic society. However, this research project took him into a much broader field than expected, and in fact it soon became apparent to him that in order to understand the meaning of democracy, it was first necessary to understand modernity. Still keeping Marx's work as a reference point, the French thinker then attempted to retrace the analysis of the birth of capitalism, which in *Capital* and the *Grundrisse* was conducted in symbolic terms, but within the framework of a theory of the symbolic institution of the social.

It is only within this framework that Lefort's research on the work of Niccolò Machiavelli, Florentine humanism, and the figure of Dante Alighieri, which I detail in the fourth chapter, gains its full significance. By reading the documents preserved in the archives of the EHESS, the lectures delivered at this institution in the 1960s and 1970s, and their accompanying notes, I was able to fully appreciate the scope of these studies and Lefort's interest in defining modernity, which had previously been underestimated as a mere corollary. On the contrary, through careful reading, it becomes clear that Lefort's work is first and foremost a major inquiry into the meaning of the modern.

Only from this perspective is it possible to fully understand Machiavelli's interpretation without reducing it to instrumental use. In *Le travail de l'œuvre*, Lefort does not simply take six-century-old texts and apply contemporary categories to them in order to find elements to support his definition of democracy (Lefort 2012). Machiavelli is not, for him, an *ante-litteram* democrat, a staunch advocate of the government of the people and their tumults. Lefort's approach is instead genealogical: his goal is to unearth in *The Prince* and the *Discourses* the first signs of a momentous change that opened the door to the democratic form of society. Machiavelli, following on from Coluccio Salutati and Leonardo Bruni in his unique way, was for Lefort one of the first thinkers to observe the symbolic mutation that invests modern politics and to adapt to it a special mode of thought that, conscious of being part of the political dimension it analyzes, rejects every *surplomb*, every universal truth, every unquestionable foundation. Through the study of Machiavelli and Florentine humanism, Lefort discovers a different modernity, one not built on the foundation of reason or the body politic—on Hobbes, Descartes, or Rousseau—but on the absence of foundation. Beyond the modernity of the moderns and post-moderns there emerges a modernity of the era of the political institution of the social, of democracy.

In this sense, *Le travail de l'œuvre*, to which I devote Chapter 5, presents one of the most significant points in Lefort's phenomenology of the social. In it he lays out an articulate theory about political subjectivities and the "flesh of the social". The analysis of the imaginary and symbolic dimension of the prince's power, the examination of the reciprocal link between the latter and the desire of the people, and the highlighting of the knot that binds law and turmoil describe a scene in which there are no pure subjectivities. Each element is defined by the intertwining of the flesh of the social and in the relationship with otherness, in which everything is taken into the symbolic and political institution. The same conception of the "original division of the social", addressed on several occasions in the 1972 work devoted to Machiavelli, translates the impossible coincidence between thought and being, between being and experience, placing it at the foundation of modern politics and the modern form of society.

Descended from studies on modernity and the political institution of the social is a unique conception of democracy viewed not as the society of equality, isegory, or isonomy, but as the society of indeterminacy and groundlessness. Democracy is not the name of the form of government created by the members of a community who, gathered in the agora, recognize themselves as equals. Rather, it is the historically verifiable social form that arises from the absence of communities and from the abyss opened at the center of community with modernity.

From this perspective, it is perhaps possible to overcome the criticism that Lefort's theory of the political is merely a dated critique of totalitarian societies and a warning against drifting into totalitarianism and authoritarianism in our own contemporary societies, a warning which would prove to be almost entirely useless by now (Poltier 2015). While such criticisms rightly point out the problematic deficiency of the economic analysis in Lefort's work, I believe that by following the interpretation I propose, Lefort's thought and theory of the political can still teach us a great deal. At the very least, they offer us useful tools to rethink the meaning of modernity and democracy, to reconsider the relationship between theory and politics, to detect and critique contemporary forms of ideology, to assess how any autonomization of the economic or the technological is politically instituted, to question any end of history and politics or easy solution to the issue of emancipation, and to fully understand the necessity of politics and division in their instituting function, now more than ever. They confront us with the tragic nature of the political and the vacuum in which it exists, forcing us to act and think politically, beyond any schematic division between event and form, beyond any appeasing affirmative and immediately political and progressive conception of democracy and the social.

References

Abensour, Miguel. 2011. *Democracy Against the State: Marx and the Machiavellian Moment*. Malden: Polity.
Arendt, Hannah. 2006. *On Revolution*. New York: Penguin.
Arendt, Hannah. 2018a. *Thinking Without a Banister. Essays in Understanding, 1953–1975*. New York: Schocken Books.
Arendt, Hannah. 2018b. *The Human Condition*. Chicago: University of Chicago Press.
Ask Popp-Madsen, Benjamin. 2021. *Visions of Council Democracy. Castoriadis, Arendt, Lefort*. Edinburgh: Edinburgh University Press.
Bennet, Jane. 2010. *Vibrant Matter: A Political Ecology of Things*. Durham: Duke University Press.
Breaugh, Martin. 2013. *The Plebeian Experience: A Discontinuous History of Political Freedom*. New York: Columbia University Press.
Butler, Judith. 2018. *Notes Toward a Performative Theory of Assembly*. Cambridge: Harvard University Press.
Cavarero, Adriana. 2021. *Surging Democracy. Notes on Hannah Arendt's Political Thought*. Redwood City: Stanford.
Clastres, Pierre. 1987. *Society Against the State: Essays in Political Anthropology*. New York: Zone Books.
Deleuze, Gilles, and Guattari, Felix. 2009. *Anti-Oedipus. Capitalism and Schizophrenia*. New York: Penguin.
Di Pierro, Mattia. 2020. *L'esperienza del mondo: Claude Lefort e la fenomenologia del politico*. Pisa: ETS.
Flynn, Bernard. 2005. *The Philosophy of Claude Lefort: Interpreting the Political*. Evanston: Northwestern University Press.
Foucault, Michel. 2002. *The Archaeology of Knowledge*. London-New York: Routledge.
Lefort, Claude. 1972. *Le Travail de l'œuvre Machiavel*. Paris: Gallimard.
Lefort, Claude. 2012. *Machiavelli in the Making*. Evanston: Northwestern University Press.
Merleau-Ponty, Maurice. 1969. *The Visible and the Invisible*. Evanston: Northwestern University Press.
Merleau-Ponty, Maurice. 2012. *Phenomenology of Perception*. London: Routledge.
Molina, Esteban. 2005. *Le défi du politique: totalitarisme et démocratie chez Claude Lefort*. Paris: L'Harmattan.
Negri, Antonio. 1999. *Insurgencies: Constituent Power and the Modern State*. Minneapolis: University of Minnesota Press.
Poltier, Hugues. 1998. *Passion du politique. La pensée de Claude Lefort*. Genève: Labor et Fides.

Poltier, Hugues. 2015. La question de la politique dans la pensée du politique de Claude Lefort. In *Cornelius Castoriadis et Claude Lefort: l'expérience démocratique*, ed. N. Poirier, 84–94. Lormont: Le bord de l'eau.

Rancière, Jacques. 2004. *Disagreement. Politics and Philosophy*. Minneapolis: The University of Minnesota Press.

Tønder, Lars, and Thomassen, Lasse. 2005. *Radical Democracy: Politics Between Abundance and Lack*. Manchester: Manchester University Press.

Wolin, Sheldon. 2016. *Fugitive Democracy And Other Essays*. Princeton: Princeton University Press.

CHAPTER 2

Socialisme ou Barbarie

THE CHAULIEU–MONTAL TENDENCY

Claude Lefort, born Claude Cohen in 1924 to Rosette Cohen and Charles Flandin, took an early interest in politics. Prompted to read Marx and Trotsky by Maurice Merleau-Ponty, his professor at the Lycée Carnot in Paris between 1941 and 1942, he frequented Trotskyist circles as early as the period of Nazi occupation and joined the *Parti Communiste Internationaliste* (PCI) in 1943 (Poirier 2020; Poltier 1997). His membership of that party was driven by an aversion to Soviet bureaucratization and militarization and by strong anti-Stalinist convictions, supported by his readings of André Gide and the testimonies of early Soviet dissidents.[1] Lefort's political activism and intellectual energy in these years are thus focused on a specific target, namely the economism and materialism reflected in the politics of the USSR and the French Communist Party (PCF). In a number of articles published between 1945 and 1947 by *Les Temps Modernes*, an important journal of the French intellectual left directed by Merleau-Ponty and Jean-Paul Sartre, Lefort engages in a critique of what he calls "crass materialism", a term he uses to describe certain interpretations of Marxism, widespread among

---

[1] See Gide (1936), Ciliga (1979). For Lefort's references to Ciliga see Lefort (1979, pp. 145–154).

© The Author(s), under exclusive license to Springer Nature Switzerland AG 2023
M. Di Pierro, *Claude Lefort's Political Philosophy*, Political Philosophy and Public Purpose, https://doi.org/10.1007/978-3-031-36378-8_2

French communist intellectuals and members of the PCF, that considered Marx' philosophy a "scientific method" able to establish an objective understanding of society and the laws of its development (Lefort 1979, 2007). Such readings discern the reality of any society in its economic infrastructure, which changes according to essential and knowable laws. History is consequently a process made up of stages that are as objective as they are inevitable, and revolution is nothing more than the mechanical outcome of an economic conjuncture. In Lefort's view, this kind of "crass materialism" completely ignores the human component and debases the meaning of Marx's work. According to him, it is necessary instead to understand that human and proletarian productivity are at the heart of Marx's materialism; that history is not a necessary process but one that is in human hands; that revolution is not a foregone conclusion but depends on the political capacity of the working class; and that any idea that the objective laws of historical and social development can be grasped objectively is illusory and erroneous (Lefort 2007, p. 73).

At a PCI meeting held in 1946 to prepare for the second congress of the Fourth International, Lefort was left deeply impressed by the contribution of Cornelius Castoriadis, a new party member who had recently arrived in Paris from Greece. Castoriadis issued a stinging rebuke of Soviet bureaucratism and of the positions of the PCI, arguing that the party needed to change its attitude toward the Soviet Union.[2] The USSR could no longer be seen as the home of the proletariat and indeed had to be understood as the proletarian revolution's principal enemy.

Trotsky (1972), of course, had also severely criticized Stalin's regime, referring to it as a form of Bonapartism that arose from the antagonism between the people and the bureaucracy. The latter lived on the exploitation of proletarian labor and on its role in the distribution of material goods, thus guaranteeing itself power and prosperity. However, despite this bleak picture, in the eyes of the father of the Fourth International overall the USSR remained a progressive force devoted to economic and social development. The working-class character of the Soviet state was safeguarded by its economic structure, and could not be challenged by bureaucratic degeneration that was in any case destined to a quick

---

[2] In 1946 Castoriadis (1922–1997) had recently left Greece, where he had lived until then, for France and Paris. For an in-depth discussion of his political and intellectual journey, see Dosse (2014).

end. Soon, Trotsky (1972) predicted, this corrupt regime, this "degenerated workers' state", would sink into its own contradictions. The leaders of the Soviet bureaucracy were proceeding in a direction at odds with the progressive economic order of the country and would soon be overwhelmed by events, by new waves of revolution or capitalist counterrevolution. Within the Fourth International, these considerations were translated into a precise political objective: the defense of the USSR against Western capitalist imperialism. Although a proletarian revolution against the bureaucratic apparatus was desirable, defeat to the capitalist countries would have meant the loss of all revolutionary hope and any prospect of economic and social improvement for the masses.

It is precisely the approach taken by Trotsky and the PCI that, in his speech, Castoriadis suggests should be abandoned, because it has become necessary to comprehend fully the innovative nature of what has developed behind the Iron Curtain: not the degeneration of a workers' state, but rather the birth of a new type of society, a "new historical formation" (Castoriadis 1988a, p. 41). The Soviet regime is neither capitalist nor socialist, nor is it even on the march toward either of these forms, but rather is something entirely different (Castoriadis 2018, p. 592).[3] The Trotskyist position has been overtaken and contradicted by events such as the consolidation of the regime after the victory over Nazism, its expansion into Western Europe, and the permanence of Stalin in power make it necessary to revise and renew the analysis. At this point in its development and consolidation, the Stalinist apparatus can no longer be seen as a momentary and contradictory perversion. Soviet society has reached full maturity and its functioning has to be understood without reference to its revolutionary origin. Judging the USSR to be a workers' state because of the collectivization of the economy and the ending of private property is a serious mistake. Indeed, a Marxist analysis involves looking more deeply at the relations of production hidden behind the veil of legal formalism. The Soviet regime has of course suppressed private property, the free market,

---

[3] Castoriadis wrote in 1946: "The key issue here can be expressed as follows. Social democracy, created in a period in which the proletariat and the bourgeoisie were the only forces of polarization, the only sources of autonomous power on the political scene, could betray the former only by passing into the latter's camp, only by following a more and more overtly bourgeois politics. Inasmuch as it has monstrously betrayed the proletarian revolution, Stalinism, in contrast, follows an equally independent political line and autonomous strategy opposed to that of the bourgeoisie no less than to that of the proletariat" (Castoriadis 1988a, p. 37).

and the search for profit of individual enterprises, which is a fundamental condition for the Marxian law of value. However, beyond this legal structure, Castoriadis notes, one discovers the existence of a genuine class that, while not participating in production, arbitrarily regulates the distribution of goods. Just like proletarians in capitalist countries, the labor power of Soviet workers is exploited by a class of owners, the bureaucracy, and the class relationship has therefore by no means disappeared (Castoriadis 2018, pp. 615–624; 1988a, pp. 37–43).[4]

As well as taking a tough stance against Trotskyist theory, Castoriadis' analysis also points the finger at Western communist parties, and the PCF in particular, which, having been dazzled by the past, insist on defending the Soviet Union. Theirs is not merely an error, however. In addition to merely representing an emanation of Moscow's wishes, their existence and structure is an expression of the same Soviet bureaucratic logic, in the division between the rulers and the ruled. Consequently, the proletarian movement has to aim not only at the reversal of power relations in Western capitalist countries, but must also turn against Stalinism and the parties that represent the Soviet bureaucracy in the West. The proletariat, in short, must understand that its first enemy is the global spread of Stalinism. Socialism, the class struggle of the international proletariat, has to respond to this new form of bureaucratic barbarism.

> Only a short time ago revolutionary politics consisted essentially of the struggle against the overt instruments of bourgeois domination (State and bourgeois parties). For a long time, however, it has been complicated by the appearance of a new and no less fundamental task: the struggle against the working class's own parties. The working class had created these parties for its liberation, but, one way or another, they have been betrayed by them. (Castoriadis 1988a, p. 37)

The intervention of his comrade helped Lefort to organize certain ideas that had already been in his mind, but which had struggled to acquire a clear form (Lefort 2007, pp. 223–260). The shared working hypothesis of the need for a profound critique of bureaucratic society

---

[4] Castoriadis's analysis of bureaucratic society, which would later be shared by Lefort and the SouB group, is rooted in a broader debate already diffused in Trotskyist circles since at least the 1930s by authors such as Rizzi (1985) or Burnham (1941). See Murphy (2020).

and global Stalinism led the two men to establish the so-called Chaulieu–Montal Tendency within the PCI, with a membership of around ten militants.[5]

Lefort made explicit his position toward the USSR and Trotskyism in a series of essays published in *Les Temps Modernes*.[6] One particularly long article that appeared in February 1947 (Lefort 1979, pp. 117–144)[7] offers an analysis of the Soviet Union that builds on Victor Kravchenko's book *I Chose Freedom*, one of the earliest accounts of the Soviet system of forced labor and prison camps and a work that exposes the contradictions of the Soviet regime (Kravchenko 1946).[8] According to Lefort, the picture painted in the book not only reveals a standard classist social structure, but also a new kind of society. Exploitation seems to have its own particular meaning, and the labor camps represent a new social formation whose paradigmatic features are the arbitrary violence meted out to the peasants and the form of terror inherent to the bureaucratic class that structure social relations. A specific element then appears to characterize this society, namely the ideology of history. The idea of a progressive history, guided by a logic developed independently of men, acts as the ideological apparatus that conceals the mechanisms of exploitation and division of the Soviet bureaucratic regime and justifies contemporary acts

---

[5] The tendency was named after the pseudonyms of Castoriadis (Pierre Chaulieu) and Lefort (Claude Montal). In immediate postwar France, where the International Communist Party had recently emerged from illegality and at a time when Stalinism was at the height of its power, the use of pseudonyms was widespread and based on understandable caution.

[6] Founded in 1944 by Jean-Paul Sartre, Simone de Beauvoir, and Merleau-Ponty himself, *Les Temps Modernes* occupied a dominant position in the part of the French intellectual left not directly aligned with the PCF. From 1945 Lefort regularly published reviews and articles in the journal. This collaboration continued until 1953, when a bitter dispute with Sartre forced him to leave. Among Lefort's contributions, published even in the early issues of the journal, see, for example: Lefort (1979, pp. 33–58, 117–144, 145–154; 2007, pp. 31–36, 37–47, 48–76).

[7] A partial translation can be found in Castoriadis et al. (2019, pp. 109–122).

[8] In France the book was published in 1946. It presented for the first time the testimony of a person directly involved in the life of the bureaucratic class. An engineer by profession, Kravchenko had been the head of a major metallurgical enterprise and, during World War II, had represented the USSR at the Soviet Chamber of Commerce in Washington. The considerable interest of his testimony thus lay in the fact that his criticisms of the Soviet economic model were made from the point of view of a technician and not a politician. Lefort's judgment also leans toward Charles Bettelheim's *La Planification soviétique* (Bettelheim 1945).

of terror and sacrifice. This is carried out in the name of the development of forces of production, of a future reward that will be reached by following a predetermined path.

In 1948, in an article with the significant title "La contradiction de Trotsky", Lefort continued his critique of the USSR, adding to it a critique of Trotskyism (Lefort 1986, pp. 31–51). Two contradictions are imputed to the father of the Fourth International. The first is theoretical and concerns his judgment of the Stalin regime: on the one hand, Trotsky thought that the Soviet system was a moment in the dictatorship of the proletariat, and on the other he argued for the need for a revolutionary uprising by the proletariat against the bourgeoisie. The second contradiction, however, concerns political activity and its role in the party. Lefort highlights Trotsky's own responsibilities for the bureaucratic degeneration of the Bolshevik Party by noting how the goal of party unity always guided his political action, to the detriment of the interests of the revolution and of the masses. Trotsky's defense of the party, which he saw as a divine aspect of historical development regardless of its content and approach, explains the tactics of compromise employed by the Trotskyite opposition, which contributed to the rise of Stalin and his bureaucracy.[9] By adhering to the Bolshevik conception of the party, the theorist of permanent revolution was imprisoned by the illusory idea of a proletarian leadership extrinsic to the party and created in the image of a leader who, with his ability to grasp the bigger picture and the interests of the future, could even act against the immediate interests of the masses. In short, despite all his declarations, Trotsky was not a victim of the rise of bureaucracy but one of its architects. Moreover, was he himself not one of the protagonists of the Kronstadt massacre (Lefort 1979, p. 54)?

Together with Castoriadis, Lefort thus pursues a radical critique of the image and history of the USSR, revealing the true face of the regime while paving the way for the emergence of a new revolutionary consciousness and true socialism. A socialism that would not be built on the backs of the proletariat but, on the contrary, would be realized in a society without rulers and followers.

---

[9] Lefort's (1986, pp. 31–51) critique focuses on the continuing concessions to bureaucracy that underpinned the conciliation adopted by Trotsky and the opposition. The pages written by Esteban Molina (2005) clearly describe Lefort's position on these issues.

Socialisme ou Barbarie

The rift with the positions of the PCI was inevitable, as the path laid out by the two militants demanded a new commitment and project. In 1949 the Chaulieu–Montal Tendency separated from the party and established the *Socialisme ou Barbarie* group (henceforth SouB) and a journal with the same name.[10] The intention was to adapt Marx to the changing labor and production conditions of the era, to the overbearing emergence of bureaucratic society, in opposition to the analyses of the pro-Soviet communist parties. This effort was by no means isolated and rather should be understood within a broader framework of relations linking various similar theoretical experiences, like the Johnson–Forest Tendency or early Italian workerism (*operaismo*).[11]

As the editorial that opens the first issue of the journal states, the goal was first and foremost to manage the fettering of the revolutionary energy and the withering of Marxist thought. A new political and social framework required a reconsideration of Marx's concepts, a theoretical leap forward that would free them from outdated and untenable theses. Faced with the defeat of the European labor movement and the situation in the Soviet Union, and confronted by the progress of capitalism and the

---

[10] For a history of the *Socialisme ou Barbarie* group, the journal, the personalities associated with it, and its role in the French scene, see: Dosse (2018, pp. 250–251; 2014), Frager (2021), Hastings-King (1997, 1999, 2015), P. Caumières et al. (2012), Gottraux (1997), Raynaud (1989). The reasons for the split from the PCI are expressed in "Lettre ouverte aux militants du P.C.I. et de la 'IVᵉ Internationale,'" 1949. *Socialisme ou Barbarie* 1: 90–102.

[11] Theories decidedly close to those of Lefort and Castoriadis were also put forward by the Johnson–Forest Tendency, which arose in the 1940s out of an internal conflict within the *Socialist Workers Party*, America's leading Trotskyist organization. A few years before, the French comrades C.L.R James, Raya Dunayevskaya, and Grace Lee Boggs, the founders of the group, criticized the Soviet regime by focusing on its process of bureaucratization and developed a theory of class as an autonomous and affirmative subject. The group's founders had direct links with members of *Socialisme ou Barbarie* and Castoriadis in particular, at least until the early 1950s. The clearest sign of these exchanges is the publication in *SouB* of *The American Worker*. It was the first attempt to investigate worker subjectivity conducted by the JFT group. The text was later also published in 1954 in Italy in the magazine *Battaglia comunista*. The translation from the French version was carried out by Danilo Montaldi, a key figure in the birth of Italian *operaismo*, who brought to the peninsula the ideas of the French group, with which he had come into contact on a trip to Paris in 1953. For an in-depth study of the relations between *SouB* and French and international radical politics see Gottraux (1997, pp. 199–254), P. Caumières et al. (2012, pp. 175–225). On Italian *operaismo* see at least Wright (2002).

process of European reconstruction, the need arose to articulate a new vocabulary and reinvigorate theory (Castoraidis 1988a, pp. 76–106).

> A century after the *Communist Manifesto* was written and thirty years after the Russian Revolution, the revolutionary movement, which has witnessed great victories and suffered profound defeats, seems somehow to have disappeared. Like a river approaching the sea, it has broken up into rivulets, run into swamps and marshes, and finally dried up on the sands. Never has there been more talk of "Marxism", of "socialism", of the working class, and of a new historical era. And never has real Marxism been so distorted, socialism so abused, and the working class so often sold out and betrayed by those claiming to represent it. (Castoriadis 1988a, p. 76)

The starting point of the entire analysis is obviously a review and definition of the bureaucratic society, which should be understood within the broader context of a new phase of capitalism and in the clear light of the ever-increasing exploitation of labor power. Indeed, at this time the bureaucratic model appears to be expanding far beyond Soviet borders and into the entire organization of world capitalism. Increased state intervention in the economy, the creation of large monopolies, and the new Taylorist system usher in a phase in which the fundamental opposition between the haves and the have-nots is replaced by that between management and workers, directors and executants. Within this framework, the antagonism between the United States and the USSR has reached an unprecedented point: the two systems have both come to represent stages in the process of increasing concentration of productive forces and division between workers and managers.[12] Like beyond the Iron Curtain, in the West capitalism is clearly revealing a new trend toward bureaucratic structuring and thus toward an ever increasing and more widespread exploitation of labor (Hastings-King 2015, p. 38). This fundamental similarity between the two regimes, the SouB theorists argue, will lead them to develop a global system of exploitation and bring about a new total

---

[12] "The bureaucracy was the social expression of these new economic forms. As traditional forms of property and the bourgeoisie of the classical period are pushed aside by State property and by the bureaucracy, the main conflict within society gradually ceases to be the old one between the owners of wealth and those without property and is replaced by the conflict between directors and executants in the process of production. In fact, the bureaucracy justifies its own existence (and can be explained in objective terms) only insofar as it plays a role deemed essential to the 'management' of the productive activities of society and, thereby, of all other forms of activity" (Castoriadis 1988a, p. 79).

war (Guillaume 1949, 1950; Castoriadis 1988a, p. 102).[13] The only bulwark against impending barbarism is the effort of the exploited masses to establish a socialism that outlaws the division between managers and workers and ushers in a society administered by the workers themselves. In an explicit reference to the ideas of Rosa Luxemburg and to council communism, for the SouB group communism therefore means direct democracy, the management of production and society by the producers themselves, the annulment of class division and working-class control of the economy. Only the rejection of all social division and the placing of power genuinely in the hands of the workers could overcome the contradictions of bureaucratic society without leading to the same perversion of revolution witnessed in the Soviet Union.

Within this context, communist parties and trade unions cannot be seen as potential allies. As agents of the bureaucratic ruling class they merely reproduce, through their governing bodies and organizational structure, the same mechanisms of division that lay at the foundations of bureaucratic rationality. SouB, at least at its inception, thus does not seek to present itself as the "real" revolutionary party, but rather constitutes itself as a useful space in which to connect many and varied experiences of struggle: an instance of theoretical and practical engagement through which the working class could achieve a new consciousness of its revolutionary role. The intent is to unmask the counter-revolutionary role of parties and trade unions in order to open a new path toward proletarian revolution. Pursuing this aim above all entails the rejection of Leninist-style party organization and any separation between theory and praxis, consciousness and action, intellectual and manual labor, leaders and militants. SouB should therefore not take on the role of a Leninist vanguard, of the leadership of the proletariat from its outside, but serve as a revolutionary organ that overcomes all divisions, an instrument for the development of theory carried out directly by workers.[14]

---

[13] The prospect of a new global war is not an incidental aspect of group theory. It is precisely the concentration of capital and the new bureaucratic management of it that lead in this direction, and to the increasingly sharp choice between socialism and the barbarism of war. In this regard, see also the numerous interventions published in the journal's notes under the title "La situation intérnationale", found in all issues from the second to the eighth and then in several subsequent issues.

[14] In the last lines of the group's introduction in the first issue of the journal Castoriadis writes: "But from this point of view, the essential thing for a political vanguard organization to do, once it has become aware of the need to abolish the distinction

The premise for this theoretical and practical engagement is the idea of "workers' autonomy", and SouB members in fact do not see the proletariat as a passive subject. Rather than being mechanically determined by the relations of production it instead possesses an autonomous capacity for thought and experience capable of moving beyond the apparatus of subjectification established by capital and the division of labor. Its actions are capable of being affirmative, productive, and independent, and it participates actively in production by continuously finding alternative solutions to capitalist and bureaucratic logic, solutions that are essential to the production process itself. Consequently, the idea of autonomy also describes the theoretical self-sufficiency of the proletariat. The working class possesses its own voice, its own theory, and is therefore not forced to accept a consciousness and direction imposed from outside and from above. It does not require the mediation of the party, the vanguard, or external theory to act and transform society. Autonomy is thus the attempt to think collectively, in a Marxist framework, about theory and praxis and about manual and intellectual labor, and thus to dismantle bureaucratic-capitalist reason in favor of a workers' reason capable of designing a society in its own image. To repeat, autonomy is the precondition that makes it possible to conceive socialism taking the shape of proletarian self-government (Lefort 1979, pp. 76–77; Castoriadis 1988b, pp. 90–192).

By contrast, Bolshevism, Leninism, Stalinism, dialectical materialism, and the ideology of the pro-Soviet communist parties turn the proletariat into an object and instrument of external wishes, devoid of any consciousness and autonomy of its own, and incapable of action and of fighting for its own emancipation. From this point of view, only external will, consciousness, and theory—embodied by the party or vanguard—are able

in society between directors and executants, is to seek from the outset to abolish this distinction within its own ranks. This is not just a simple question of better by-laws, but involves above all raising the consciousness and developing the talents of its militants through their ongoing and permanent theoretical and practical education along these lines. Such an organization can grow only by preparing to link up with the process by which autonomous mass organs are created. In this very limited sense, it might be correct to say that the organization represents the ideological and political leadership of the working class under the conditions extant in the present exploiting society. It is essential to add, however, that it is a 'leadership' that is constantly preparing its own dissolution through its fusion with the working class's autonomous organs" (Castoriadis 1988a, p. 105). The reader may notice some tension between the project seeking autonomy and these comments. I will clarify this aspect further on.

to understand the historical process, perceive its direction of movement, and therefore guide the masses toward their own future, giving them form and identity. The result is a division between those who know and those who obey, between leaders and militants. The result is the bureaucratic society.

In opposition to these degenerations, the SouB group argues that it is necessary to turn the image of the proletariat upside down and recognize its positive activity and progressive energy. Indeed, it is precisely the autonomous action of the proletariat, its ability to overcome and pick apart the ganglia of bureaucratic society, that is in evidence in some of the most significant strikes and upheavals of those years. The June 1953 rebellion in Berlin, the 1955 strikes in France, and the Budapest uprising of the following year not only confirmed the deceitfulness of socialism beyond the Iron Curtain, but also provided evidence of the proletariat's immediate organizational capacity as well as its maturity (Castoriadis et al. 2019, pp. 189–244; Lefort 1994, pp. 193–234; Castoriadis 1988b, pp. 57–89; Guillaume 1956–1957; Mothé 1956–1957, Simon 1956).[15]

This theoretical framework fueled the commitment of SouB militants inside the factories and their continuous effort to involve workers in the group and the journal. Investigations and the publication of articles written directly by workers recounting their experience in the factories were the main tools used to document the activity and autonomy of the proletariat and to capture its unfiltered, "pure" voice without any prior interpretation (Hastings-King 2015, pp. 165–234).[16] This approach was also being trialed in the same period by members of the Johnson–Forest Tendency (JFT) and was embodied above all in the publication in the *Socialisme ou Barbarie* journal of the translation of *The American Worker*, a diary of daily experience in American industry published in 1947 by JFT and in particular by Paul Romano (pseudonym of Phil Singer) and Ria Stone (pseudonym of Grace Lee Boggs).[17] Through the mediation of

---

[15] Issue 13 of *Socialisme ou Barbarie*, released in 1954, contains an in-depth look at the East German uprisings. Issue XX of the journal, published in 1956–1957, delves into the Hungarian and Polish uprisings. Lefort's text, originally published in issue 20, was partially translated in Castoriadis et al. (2019, pp. 216–235).

[16] In this context see also Mothé (1959) and Hastings-King (2015, pp. 235–320).

[17] The excerpts, published under the title "L'ouvrier américain", are found in issues I (pp. 79–89), II (pp. 83–94), III (pp. 68–81), IV (pp. 45–57), and V–VI (pp. 124–135). Ample space is then given to articles informing readers about strikes, French and

the SouB, the same methodologies and the same text would also be taken up and translated in Italy, thanks to Danilo Montaldi and a group of militants and theorists who can be considered the forerunners of *operaismo*, or at least of some elements of it.[18] On the other hand, obtaining the "true" word of the worker, and giving voice without mediation to those who were relegated to the margins of development by modernization and capital appears to have been a requirement shared by most of the political theories of that time. This was an aspiration that, from different and sometimes contradictory perspectives, would be developed in the following decades. One thinks of the work of Foucault, the archival research carried out by Jacques Rancière, the work of Pier Paolo Pasolini, but also the heresies of Menocchio recounted by Carlo Ginzburg.

However, this project, the creation of a group lacking a party structure but capable of fostering the encounter between theory and praxis, workers and intellectuals, was never really accomplished. Beyond the relative significance of SouB in the French political landscape, the direct involvement of workers in the development of theory and in publishing also encountered considerable difficulties and was ultimately rather mediocre (Dosse 2014, p. 90; Escobar 2012; Gottraux 1997, pp. 255–314). The period of the group's greatest success and expansion was instead characterized by the influx of university and middle school students. These practical difficulties were reflected in an underlying theoretical tension that ran through SouB's entire history and was a key aspect in the image of the proletariat and how to relate to it, or in other words to issues of organization. This was a conflict evident above all in the positions of the two main exponents: Castoriadis and Lefort.[19]

As has been noted, the latter's participation in SouB was characterized by a certain isolation in a group dominated by the charisma and positions of the Greek-French thinker (Chollet 2019; Dosse 2014, pp. 117–136). While the analysis of bureaucratic society, the criticisms of

---

otherwise, as well as to speeches examining labor and working-class conditions more or less theoretically.

[18] On Danilo Montaldi see Amico (2022) and Capuzzo (2021). SouB members were also in contact with the Italian journal *Battaglia Comunista*, linked to the Italian Communist Internationalist Party.

[19] On the relationship between Lefort and Castoriadis there is now rather extensive literature. See Poirier (2010, 2015, 2019, 2022), Dosse (2014; 2021, pp. 205–248), Chollet (2019), Legros and Rothnie (2017), Thompson (2008).

Soviet communism and of Trotskyism, had brought Lefort and Castoriadis closer together, they diverged on several issues relating to the conception of the proletariat and the relationship that the group could and should maintain with it. Among the elements at the root of these divisions one can discern the phenomenological approach that characterizes Lefort's thinking and separates him from his comrade. The article "L'expérience prolétarienne" published in the tenth edition of *Socialisme ou Barbarie* in 1952 is one moment when this difference emerges most clearly and, not coincidentally, is also a fundamental point in the development of Lefort's work.

A Phenomenology of the Proletarian Experience

The aforementioned "L'expérience prolétarienne", and the article "Le proletariat et sa direction", published in the tenth and eleventh issues of *Socialisme ou Barbarie*, in 1952, clearly demonstrate Lefort's peculiar phenomenological method and present some of the themes that marked the entire arc of his thought (Lefort 1979, pp. 59–70 and pp. 71–97).[20] Once again, the author's polemical objective is the critique of what he called "pseudo marxisme": the mechanistic and economistic interpretations of Marx's work that turn the class struggle into a purely economic matter. This economic materialism, which fueled Stalinism and the bureaucratic ideologies that came to permeate the communist parties, interprets history as a course of events that is mechanically determined and proceeds independently of the will of men. From such a perspective it would be possible to recognize objective laws similar to natural laws capable of explaining both the characteristics of the ideological superstructure and the behavior of classes themselves. Guided in its development by an objective process foreign to it, and trapped in a pattern with no way out, the proletariat thus becomes a completely passive force, condemned to exist as a pure reaction to external economic factors, shaped by the action of capital (Lefort 1979, p. 72).

Although Marx himself repeatedly criticized these kinds of interpretations of materialism, Lefort concedes that certain ambiguities in his theory provided pseudo-Marxism with a number of footholds. In fact, the author

---

[20] For an examination of Lefort's intervention and its importance in the philosopher's overall thinking, see Cash (2019), Gambarotto (2019) and Labelle (2015).

of *Capital* failed to outline in a sufficiently concrete way the physiognomy and role of the proletariat, whose definition appears to be built on the continuous tension between a complete loss and total reconquest of its humanity. The importance of the proletariat gaining consciousness in order to seize its role as the leader of humanity is matched by a description of it cast in such obscure terms that it is difficult to understand how it could possibly fulfill this destiny (73). Lefort refers in particular to the passages in the *Economic and Philosophical Manuscripts* and the *The German Ideology* in which Marx sets out his theory of alienation. These present the worker as a kind of sub-human, deprived of all human characteristics, physical and moral. Estranged in the object of his labor, reduced to a commodity, annulled, he is completely passive, devoid of consciousness, incapable of reaction, and totally possessed by his own labor. It is a negativity in the face of the activity of capital. From this description comes the idea, held by Marx himself, that the overthrow of the bourgeoisie is sufficient to guarantee the victory of socialism. However, in other parts of Marx's work the proletarian revolution is not presented as an instantaneous transformation of society but rather is described as a process. It is the conquest of social control by the exploited class, which, having become conscious of its own role through the revolutionary movement, liberates itself from the capitalist system, and acquires the leadership of society. And yet, Lefort asks, how is it possible for the proletariat to transform itself into the ruling class if it remains completely alienated and radically excluded from social life right up to the eve of the revolution? How can the worker, reduced to a sub-human condition, and defined and nullified by the productive apparatus that shapes him as an object, rise to a productive role and assume responsibility for the destiny of humanity?

Here we see one of those pseudo-Marxist footholds: if the proletariat is completely subjugated to capital, if it is only able to react, if it lives merely in denial, then only a force external to it can lead it to emancipation. This opens up space for the economistic interpretation, which sees the contradiction between the development of productive forces and relations of production as the only element needed to herald the victory of the proletariat over bourgeois capitalism. Similarly, the bureaucratic ideologies that propagandize the need for a party or vanguard capable of providing the positive impetus which the proletariat is itself incapable of generating creeps into this same crack in Marx's theory.

Lefort argues, however, that these theories were rejected by Marx and refuted by history. First, the outcome of the Russian Revolution and the emergence of bureaucratic society revealed the falsity of any theory that considers the elimination of the bourgeoisie to be the sufficient condition for the establishment of socialism. They showed that the storming of the Winter Palace did not lead automatically to a socialist society, and that in fact bourgeois rule can be replaced by even more severe types of subjugation. Moreover, the "practical existence" of the proletariat makes it clear that it does not merely react to economically defined external factors but is also able to act, having "intervened in a revolutionary manner based not on some schema provided by the objective situation, but on its total, cumulative *experience*" (73).[21]

It is therefore necessary to understand that the working class is not just an economic category. To do so, Lefort once again suggests following Marx himself. Indeed, it would be wrong to react to the ambiguities encountered in Marx's theory by simply abandoning it, as the texts themselves offer valuable pointers leading to a different conception of the proletariat. The memorable sentence that opens the *Manifesto*, in which it is stated that "the history of all hitherto existing society is the history of class struggles" (Marx and Engels 2002, p. 219) exemplifies this. Here Marx and Engels not only liken the creativity of history to that of the labor movement but in fact place the whole of historical progress into the hands of proletarian productive power. The proletariat, far from being described as a passive element whose experience is limited by the action of capital, is rather characterized by its own activity, its creativity, and its ability to produce history. It emerges here from its state of sub-humanity to become the source of all social life. Its class dimension does not appear in the negative in relation to the action of capital but reveals itself when it challenges the power of the bourgeoisie and denies the economic order in order to establish a new and different one (Lefort 1979, p. 75).

The proletariat, Lefort thus asserts, is not objective and cannot be reduced to its economic role. Its conduct is not merely the consequence of its conditions of existence and it therefore does not conform to any objective law. On the contrary, in order to express itself as a class it is forced to disengage from its conditions of existence and to interpret and oppose them. Only the ensuing struggle to change these conditions reveals its physiognomy as a class, a kind of identity that emerges from an "experience" in which "the economic and the political have no separate

---

[21] Unless specified, all translations that refer to texts not translated into English are those of this author.

reality": the working class is defined only by the theoretical and practical action that it takes to shape its own conditions (66). As a result, the proletariat should be understood in terms of the continuous relationship between its conditions of existence and its own reflection on these conditions. In other words it is the product of an economic situation, of the thoughts that individual subjectivities develop regarding that condition, and of the history that aggregates these multiple reflections into a common experience of struggle. Only the accumulation of past experiences based on individual personal experiences makes it possible to speak about the common experience of the proletarian class. On the other hand, the economic situation is itself silent and only an examination based on individual knowledge and a collective history can make it speak. The objective challenge of economic laws cannot be the starting point for action and opposition to the given conditions, as this is the preserve of the subjective experience of exploitation and the act of placing this into a historical and ideological context that is continually reinterpreted through daily actions and the everyday perception of exploitation.

The claim regarding the proletariat's productivity, about its role as the source of universal production, and as the custodian of the culture of the whole of society, is confirmed by the analysis of real production, in the merely relative autonomy of technical progress and its rationalization.[22] Indeed, a thorough investigation of industrial production reveals the active role of workers in a process that they must withstand but which they also help to modify and improve. Through the solutions they find on a daily basis to the many problems that arise in specific elements of production and elude capitalist rationality, workers make technical invention possible by actively participating in it (81). Capitalist rationality, therefore, does not work alone: productive capacity is highly dependent on the contribution of the workers, which at the same time modifies relations of production.[23] It is here, even during the capitalist phase, through the daily experience of the workers themselves, through their action,

---

[22] In Lefort's eyes, the motivations driving capital are not sufficient to account for technological progress and rationalization. These aspects of social development have consequences that transcend the dimension of class struggle and can only be understood through the intervention of worker rationality.

[23] It has been pointed out (Hastings-King 2015, p. 120) that this analysis refers to a precise figure of the average, skilled worker, who would later be replaced during the 1960s.

and through their reworking of labor and exploitation, that something resembling an alternative class identity and a rationality capable of challenging bourgeois rule arises. The transition to socialism is therefore not a mechanical event, the sudden explosion of the contradiction between productive force and the relations of production. Rather, revolution is conceivable as the outcome of the maturation of a workers' experience that becomes aware of its own capacity to produce social progress. Men, not conditions, are revolutionary (80).

The concept of "experience" is a key element if one wishes to understand Lefort's reflection, its method, its continuity, and its internal differences. It is in experience that, first of all, the phenomenological approach of the author's thought and the debt he owed to Maurice Merleau-Ponty emerge quite clearly. As I have shown, Lefort rejects any attempt to reduce the proletariat to its economic dimension, to see it as the outcome of relations of production. On the contrary, for him the proletariat must be understood in its ability to produce society, in its autonomy from its given material conditions, which it is able to oppose. The working class, in short, can be such because it *interprets* its own material conditions, detaches itself from them and fights them. The result of the struggle is therefore not a foregone conclusion, and its outcomes are not predictable. The concept of experience is thus first and foremost of use in demonstrating the impossibility of realizing the objectivity, inextricability, and dynamic recursiveness between reality and its interpretation, between the economic and the political. In short, just as Merleau-Ponty had proposed in the *Phenomenology of Perception*, the task is to overcome the dichotomy between subject and object in order to consider the ever-present co-involvement, or praxis. In such a context, a social subject is not an objective fact, but the outcome of the contingent encounter between a series of intimately related planes that develop with reference to each other: the economic situation, the political interpretation, one's own history and its reworking, ideology, and so forth.

Clearly Lefort's polemical targets are once again the mechanistic and economistic interpretations of Marx's work and the attempts to turn Marxism into a rigorous science. But more generally, he directs his criticisms to what Merleau-Ponty had called *pensée de surplomb* (overhanging thought), i.e. any theory that seeks to analyze its object from an external position, without modifying it or being modified by it, without being involved in a particular environment, in a complex fabric that is impossible to ignore, that is to say in a "world". Again, by this term Merleau-Ponty meant to refer to any thought which considers itself capable of observing its object from above, from such a distance as to be able to grasp it in its entirety (Merleau-Ponty 1969). It can thus be understood how the concept of "experience" is also the attempt to give a name to a theory that does not consider itself external to its object of analysis but emerges in contact with it. Thus Lefort tries to avoid imposing a definition on the proletariat, instead attempting—not without some difficulty—to make it emerge from the everyday aspect of the workers' own lived experience. This is a research method that in this period Lefort refers to as "realist" (Lefort 1979, pp. 89–90), and which the author developed through obvious references to the phenomenological method and sought to address in the final pages of "L'expérience prolétarienne".

The Role of Theory

Lefort uses the concept of "proletarian experience" as part of an attempt to "exercise" a theory that arises in the arena of praxis. Against any philosophy of history and all forms of mechanism, his aim is to conceive a materialism built on human activity and production. According to him, this "realist" approach was already outlined in the passages of *The German Ideology* devoted to Feuerbach, in which the nexus between criticism and the material environment, between theory and real individuals in their actual living conditions is defined. In short, the matter at hand is that of rejecting economic materialism and the idea of a progressive and deterministic dialectic in order to understand how men developing their material production and material relations transform their reality and their thinking. This means first of all avoiding fixing the proletariat as an abstraction and instead investigating how it "actually" arises from the lives of specific individuals (Lefort 1979, p. 79). This is what gives rise to Lefort's effort in the 1952 article and in the pages of *Socialisme ou Barbarie* to reach the "voice" of the workers, an autonomous proletarian expressiveness that comes before any conditioning and mediation, through a series of testimonies and inquiries.

The second part of "L'expérience prolétarienne" is thus devoted to establishing a proper research methodology, in other words one that manages to grasp the workers' experience and to convey it without betraying it, without any external or top-down imposition. In a move reminiscent of Merleau-Ponty's method, Lefort first of all rejects the objective and subjective criteria. The former only considers the economic context while the latter aims to understand proletarian consciousness through an examination of the succession of ideologies. The historical method, which involves looking for continuity in the major manifestations of class as moments within a progressive experience, is the third to be discarded. Finally, the author outlines a fourth methodology. This, which he defines as "concrete", sets out to analyze the relationship between the proletarian and his labor by avoiding any external evaluation and instead limiting itself to explicating what is implicit in the experience itself (91). The role of theory, in this instance, is merely to seek the manifestation of the worker's capacity for invention and power of social organization in his everyday actions.

The intervention of theory is necessary, Lefort explains, because workers are immersed in the dominant capitalist rationality where they are defined by relations of production and the mechanism of exploitation. In this context, the alternative rationality that presents itself through the conflict experienced at the level of production emerges only in a fragmented way. The theory thus has to limit itself to recomposing these dispersed fragments of information in order to link them together in the form of a unique workers' rationality. Its role is therefore not external. The theorist does not possess knowledge through which he might shape the workers' experience; he does not impose any identity, direction, or form. On the contrary, he relies on the workers' narrations to supply the alternative rationality of which he himself is incapable in order to recreate a descriptive order different from the capitalist and bourgeois one. He must question and interpret the direct testimony of individual workers, their real experiences, while remaining as faithful as possible to it.[24] The journal is the link between these two perspectives, that of theory and that of proletarian experience. It is the medium through which the worker is represented with his own narrations, freed from contingency and recomposed in a fully working-class perspective.

---

[24] For a more detailed analysis see Hastings-King (2015, p. 110). This mode of research is reminiscent of what in Italy has taken the name of "worker inquiry", developed especially by Romano Alquati (2019), which characterized the workerist experience, especially in the late 1950s and early 1960s. The affinities are obviously not coincidental but related to that series of relationships (first and foremost with Danilo Montaldi) already highlighted above.

However, the description of this concrete and internal method is only the beginning of the author's reflection. Certain difficulties soon emerge, and the path to the proletarian reality remains blocked. Indeed, Lefort notes toward the end of the article that even the concrete approach is abstract as it is only capable of reaching the proletariat indirectly, and thus alters it. Similarly, avoiding this impasse by asserting that the proletariat cannot be reached by theory but only by practice could only be an illusory shortcut, as such an assertion would in fact disregard the role of knowledge and ignore the fact that this is just as much an integral aspect of the proletariat's identity as labor and struggle. Any direct path to the *true* existence of the proletariat thus appears to be cut off. In experience, Lefort seems to assert, mediation is implicit. It would be illusory to believe that we can reach the proletariat in its reality, that is, stripped of all the representations of its condition and of the historical framework in which it is embedded, which lie beyond the bourgeois society and the communist parties that have claimed to define it. There is always an unbridgeable gap between action and narration. Any type of reality always depends on a representation, and any testimony, even the most spontaneous, inevitably remains at some remove from the action itself, being caught up in a contingent historical context from which it cannot abstract itself.

Looking more closely, for Lefort the concrete method thus appears as limited as any other. In order to try to grasp the meaning of the workers' experience, the *essence* of the proletariat as an alternative organization, attitude, and mentality to those of the bourgeoisie, it is necessary for all the aforementioned methods to work together. It is necessary to consider the historical, ideological, and economic context as well as their mutual relations. Only this tangled web allows a perpetually changing and contingent identity to emerge and permits something akin to a workers' experience to stand out.

At the article's climax, therefore, the attempt to find a path, that of inquiries, toward the proletarian voice seems to crash against its own aporias, against the denunciation of the ideological status of any experience of the original. The essay thus ends with a series of questions which, while leaving the path of inquiry open, ask who would be the subjectivity legitimately given the task of interpretation. And that this might be the members of SouB seems far from obvious to Lefort (96).

To these difficulties is added another that the author does not consider, which concerns the unity of the proletarian subject. As I have said, Lefort uses the concept of experience to justify the actual autonomous existence of the working class by rooting it in the daily work of the factory. Yet this unique subject does not at all seem self-evident. How can one actually ignore the multiple divisions within the labor movement? How can one overlook the very fact that there is no single shared history? How can one fail to see that by tracing back the most varied positions (of the PCI members, Stalinists, anarchists, Trotskyists) to moments in a single proletarian experience, one risks falling back into the teleological history that Lefort had wanted to abandon?[25]

I do not want to make an attempt to answer these questions. It is sufficient here to note how this difficulty already reveals the points of tension between Marx's proletarian theory and Lefort's analysis which, as I shall show later, will lead the French phenomenologist away from the theory of the proletariat and revolution.

Before concluding this section, it is also important to highlight how the debate on the concrete method, the attempt to outline a theory that is not thought to be external to the reality it describes, again makes evident the phenomenological roots of Lefort's thought and the debt he owed to the work of Maurice Merleau-Ponty. This is not because of the affinity between the critique of economism and the most widespread "scientific" materialisms. Above all, it is important to point out how the peculiar phenomenology that Merleau-Ponty was outlining in those same years— the emphasis on thought and the subject being situated, the consequent need to go beyond the difference between subject and object, the impossibility of finishing the *epoché*—clearly shapes Lefort's analysis of social and political dimensions.[26] The result is a politics and analysis of a Merleau-Ponty type that does not, however, correspond to those proposed by Merleau-Ponty himself (Monferrand 2018).

---

[25] Monferrand (2018) and Gilles Labelle (2015) make this difficulty clear.

[26] Hastings-King emphasizes the convergence between Lefort's analysis of the worker experience and phenomenology. In particular, Lefort's investigation of collective class behavior would extend and rethink the intentionality on which Merleau-Ponty had worked in *Phenomenology of Perception* (Merleau-Ponty 2012). See Hastings-King (2015, p. 116).

Lefort or Castoriadis: The Proletariat, the Party, and the Organization

On May 28, 1952, the PCF called a demonstration against the visit of General Matthew Ridgway of the United States. The day ended with heavy clashes, arrests, and the death of two protestors. The violence and the low worker participation in the strikes subsequently proclaimed by the party and the CGT[27] then fueled a chorus of criticism. In response to the authorities' attacks, Jean-Paul Sartre wrote a series of articles in *Les Temps Modernes* titled "The Communists and Peace", in which he took the side of the PCF against the "slimy rats" of the bourgeois right and the anti-communists (Sartre 1968).[28] In these contributions, the philosopher anchors his defense of the party to a precise conception of the proletariat as pure negativity, an action without history to which only the party can bestow unity, consciousness, memory, and direction. Only under the leadership of the party can the proletariat, which is itself formless, mere dust, act, and move toward its emancipation. Consequently, every accusation leveled against the PCF must be fought against, treated as a criticism of the only instrument available to the struggle being fought by the French proletariat, the only means through which it might exist and act politically.

Lefort responded with a strong rebuttal published in the April issue of the same journal (Lefort 1971, pp. 59–79).[29] The battleground was the interpretation of Marx and, of course, the conception of the proletariat. Lefort sets out his own interpretation of the proletariat as experience, in opposition to Sartre's depiction.

> While Sartre declares that "it matters little whether or not praxis is dialectically generated by the proletarian condition", I say on the contrary that this dialectical genesis of class is the key, that it is praxis itself. The experience of the proletariat, its praxis, is thus the historical movement by which it integrates its conditions of existence (in the sense of its mode of production

---

[27] *Confédération générale du travail*, one of the most important of the French trade unions, founded in 1895.

[28] The article marks Sartre's rapprochement with the PCF, which would end with the events in Budapest in 1956. See Dosse (2018).

[29] The article was published in Lefort (1971), along with another work directed at Sartre titled "De la repone à la question" (80–108). They no longer appear in the 1979 edition. This exclusion should not be interpreted as a distancing, as the author himself states in (1979, p. 7).

and corresponding social relations), it *realizes itself* as a class by organizing and fighting, and elaborates the meaning of its opposition to capitalism. (Lefort 1971, p. 69. My italics)

The autonomy and creativity of the proletariat anchor it in a history that Sartre surprisingly refuses to see. He distorts Marx's teaching, forgetting that the proletariat is a reality that is at once economic, social, and historical and that emptying it of all content turns it into a mere object shaped by the will of the party.

Sartre's retort was not long in coming and indeed followed Lefort's intervention in the same issue of the journal (1968, pp. 233–296). It was violent and did hold back on personal attacks.[30] In August Castoriadis also entered the fray, this time in the pages of *Socialisme ou Barbarie*. In his article, "Sartre, le stalinisme et les ouvriers", he accuses the existentialist philosopher of failing to understand the theses of both Marx and Lefort, and thus defends a conception of the proletariat as experience, as well as the workers' autonomy and creative capacity (Castoriadis 1988a, pp. 207–241).

However, if from the outside the SouB front appears to have been united in its opposition to Sartre, the internal situation does not seem to have been as clear. Castoriadis and Lefort's positions on the issues at stake—the conception of the proletariat, its autonomy, and its relation to a party vanguard—seem far from aligned, and even their visions of what the group itself should be are quite different. Not coincidentally, the debate around the organizational structure animates and divides SouB throughout the period from its split from the PCI to 1958, the year that Lefort and some of his comrades abandon it.[31]

---

[30] The controversy between the two did not end at this point but continued until 1954 when Lefort responded with the aforementioned essay (Lefort 1971, pp. 80–108). After Sartre's response, Lefort left *Les Temps Modernes*. For a further study of this debate, in which Castoriadis and Merleau-Ponty also played a certain role, see: Feron (2019), Dosse (2018, pp. 125–131), Molina (2005, pp. 61–85) and Gottraux (1997, pp. 256–261). This is intertwined with the controversy that in the same years pitted Sartre against Merleau-Ponty, as a result of which he resigned his editorship of the journal. See Dosse (2018, pp. 131–139; 2021, pp. 83–110), and Stewart (1998).

[31] The discussions that took place during these years are often reported in *Socialisme ou Barbarie* in the section "La vie de notre group". In particular see issues IV, V, and VI.

The standpoints are already clear in 1949, shortly after the publication of the journal's first issue, when a plenary meeting devoted entirely to the question of the revolutionary party is held. For Castoriadis (Chaulieu 1949), the goal of SouB has to be the seizure of the state, the overturning of power relations: revolution. However, such a project requires unity and organization, which are not spontaneously present in the proletariat. Class unity, for example, is veiled and obstructed in the daily experience of workers by a set of specific factors like economic stratification or corporate, regional, and national differences. Moreover, the alienation to which workers are subjected makes it impossible for them to emancipate themselves from the mechanism of production in order to achieve the ideological unity and organization necessary for revolutionary struggle. The development of proletarian consciousness, Castoriadis therefore asserts, has to be conceived as the result of the work of the most conscious and well-prepared workers' vanguards (99–103). They alone can fulfill the task of leading the class toward revolution, and they can only do so by organizing themselves into a party. Such a party, however, has to respond to these structural needs without becoming an external organ of direction and has to establish the unity denied at the level of the superstructure to facilitate a liberation from alienation that only revolution will fully resolve. Only a shared program can bring coherence to collective action, and only a party is capable of delivering the leadership and coordination needed to steer the alienated, divided, and exploited proletariat to revolution. Politics is a struggle for power, for the seizure of the institution of the state, and only a party can be equal to that struggle (100). Of course, such a party must be conscious of past history and mistakes, mobilize the majority of the proletariat on the basis of an anti-bureaucratic program, and structure itself so as to engineer its own dissolution. However, those who dispute its necessity, Castoriadis says, deny history by failing to recognize the preponderant role that organization has continually played in the development of working-class strength and the difficulties that have always forced spontaneous movements to dissipate (102).

The incompatibility with Lefort's ideas is evident and did not remain latent for long. Two years after the 1949 meeting, the question of organization exploded once again, and this time it was Lefort's turn to take the floor. The ninth issue of the journal appeared over a year after the previous one, with a brief note explaining that the delay was due to difficulties related to the general crisis in the workers' movement but especially to the fact that in June 1951 several comrades left SouB following a disagreement with the majority regarding the creation of the revolutionary party. The note went on to announce the forthcoming publication of the texts around which the discussion had taken place and the split consummated. A section entitled "Discussion sur le problème du parti révolutionnaire" thus appeared in the second issue of the same year.[32] This consisted of two articles, respectively signed by Castoriadis and Lefort, presenting the two points of view and the reasons for the split (Castoriadis 1988a, pp. 198–204; Lefort 1979, pp. 59–70).

The two positions expressed in the articles are far apart, to say the least. If for Castoriadis the question is how to rethink the theory of revolutionary leadership and develop a new type of party, for Lefort, one must instead understand that the proletariat does not need a theory, because the "proletariat *is* its own theory", while the party is an instrument irretrievably tied to the past (Lefort 1979, p. 59). In the present-day struggle, and with the maturation of proletarian experience that has developed up to this point, the party no longer makes any sense. The outcome of the Russian Revolution, the perversion of Bolshevik politics, and the emergence of the bureaucratic class showed the proletariat that it is impossible to alienate itself into stable forms of representation without these becoming autonomous. It is this lesson that the project of Castoriadis and the majority of the group seems to have failed to grasp: the party, even in its ambition to represent the demands of the proletariat, is by its very constitution inclined to define itself as the only form of power, to produce the very division which lies at the basis of bureaucratic society (67). If an organizational structure is needed, Lefort argues that it should be as fluid and open as possible, taking the form of a horizontal organization that rejects all hierarchy and merely connects militants and formations that identify with the socialist revolutionary project. It follows that if for Castoriadis SouB should constitute itself through clearly defined boundaries, an internal hierarchy, and collective discipline, for Lefort the only possible structure is mutable, inclusive, non-hierarchical and without strictly defined borders.

The perpetually unresolved disagreement continued to lurk in the background for some years. In 1958 the events in Algeria and the political crisis that opened up in France led some of the group's militants to

[32] See Chaulieu and Montal (1952). Explicit reference is made here to the fact that Lefort himself questioned the resolution voted on in 1949.

believe that the time for revolution had come. The question of organization then immediately detonated with a bang, leading to an unbridgeable rift within the group.[33] The old alignments reasserted themselves and the majority, led by Castoriadis along with Guillaume and Véga, ousted the minority, which once again rallied around Lefort's positions.[34] The latter was left with only enough time to make a final speech in which he reiterated his distrust of the party structure and signaled his final abandonment of SouB, which would continue without its co-founder until 1967.[35]

Even before this, Lefort's entire trajectory within the group appears to have been marked by a certain isolation (Chollet 2019; Mongin 1993), with his position seemingly always placing him in a minority in relation to Castoriadis's ideas and charisma. From the beginning, his rejection of party structures clashed with an opposing plan: while he wanted SouB to be an instrument for the elaboration of ideas placed in the hands of the proletariat, Castoriadis and the majority of the militants wanted it to become a revolutionary vanguard capable of organizing the masses and seizing power. Theirs was a project that, in Lefort's eyes, merely repeated the mistakes of the past, proposing once more a bureaucratic conception of theory and of the relationship with the working class. For Lefort, who was close to the positions held by Merleau-Ponty, the majority was pursuing a fallacious rationalistic design and applying the illusory knowledge of *surplomb*. The influence of the JFT, the arrival of Bordigist militants, of Jean-François Lyotard and Pierre Souyri, all of whom agreed

---

[33] See Chaulieu (1958). This is a typewritten internal document. After their abandonment of SouB, the minority members found the organization *Informations et liaisons ouvrières* (ILO). SouB continued its activities for almost a decade, until 1967.

[34] See "Résolution présentée à l'assemblée générale du 6 juin 1958", p. 3. The typewritten document, probably drafted by Lefort (Gottraux 1997, p. 90) is the minority's response to the resolution presented on June 6 by Chaulieu, Garros, Guillaume, Mothé, and Véga. I thank Philippe Gottraux for kindly providing me with the documentation.

[35] The text of this speech, which is unsigned, first appeared in the form of an internal document, an expression of minority positions with the title: "La question de l'organisation révolutionnaire et du fonctionnement du groupe: contribution à la discussion". The text later published in *Socialisme ou Barbarie* 26: 120–134 and in Lefort (1979, pp. 98–113) with the title "Organisation et parti. Contribution à une discussion" is essentially the same, although some corrections were made. For example, the most direct references to the internal life of the group were removed.

with the need for organization, helped exacerbate this difference (Chollet 2019, p. 45).[36]

However, it is bizarre to note that it is precisely Lefort's minoritarian position that actually reflects more accurately the history of SouB, which never got close to becoming either a vanguard or even a revolutionary party. Ultimately, its marginal role was to introduce some novel and innovative themes into the debate of the time—the critique of bureaucracy, the emphasis on the autonomy and creativity of the proletariat, workers' inquiries—that would, however, only gain weight and resonance after its dissolution.

Although Lefort always opposed the attempts at organization promoted by Castoriadis, the relationship between the two appears more complex than one of straightforward opposition. It was in fact marked by a series of ruptures and rapprochements which, as we shall see, would continue even after the end of SouB (Dosse 2014; 2021, pp. 205–247). These reveal a common ground of analysis and at the same time a profound difference in the outcomes of their reflection (Poirier 2022, p. 90). If the paths of the two thinkers converged in the critique of Stalinism, bureaucratic society, and scientific interpretations of Marxism, they would in fact not be slow to diverge around the conception of democracy. Thus it was that while Castoriadis came to interpret democracy in terms of the autonomy of the social (Castoriadis 1987) and through the idea of a radical imaginary, Lefort, again following the phenomenological method introduced by Merleau-Ponty, would define the shape of democratic society through the concepts of division and indeterminacy (92).[37]

References

Alquati, Romano. 2019. Co-Research and Worker's Inquiry. *South Atlantic Quarterly* 118/2: 470–478.

---

[36] It is no coincidence, as Howard (2019, p. 203) and Chollet (2019) note, that during the 1950s Lefort published many of his most important writings outside of SouB, in journals such as *Les Temps Modernes* or the *Cahiers internationaux de sociologie*.

[37] Poirier (2022, p. 90) states: "If Castoriadis and Lefort show a common interest for Merleau-Ponty's approach in his last texts, their interpretation of them will, however, take them in fairly different directions. [...] In this original source, Castoriadis highlights a dimension of creative activity where Lefort instead focuses on the passivity, which is an opening to, rather than an opening of".

Amico, Giorgio. 2022. *Danilo Montaldi. Vita di un militante politico di base (1929–1975)*. Roma: Deriveapprodi.
Bettelheim, Charles. 1945. *La Planification soviétique*. Paris: Rivière.
Burnham, James. 1941. *The Managerial Revolution or What Is Happening in the World Now*. New York: John Day Co.
Capuzzo, Paolo. 2021. Tra "comunismo eretico" e ricerca sociale. In *Lasciare un segno nella vita. Danilo Montaldi e il Novecento*, ed. G. Fofi and M. Salvati, 135–149. Roma: Viella.
Cash, Conall. 2019. Politique symbolique et expression. «L'expérience prolétarienne» entre Merleau-Ponty et le post-marxisme. *Rue Descartes* 46/2: 117–126.
Castoriadis, Cornelius. 1987. *The imaginary institution of the society*. Cambridge: Polity Press.
Castoriadis, Cornelius. 1988a. *Political and Social Writings Volume 1, 1946–1955: From the Critique of Bureaucracy to the Positive Content of Socialism*. Minneapolis: University of Minnesota Press.
Castoriadis, Cornelius. 1988b. *Political and Social Writings Volume 2, 1955–1960: From the Workers' Struggle Against Bureaucracy to Revolution in the Age of Modern Capitalism*. Minneapolis: University of Minnesota Press.
Castoriadis, Cornelius. 2018. *La Société bureaucratique. Écrits politiques, 1945–1997, V*. Paris: Éditions du Sandre.
Castoriadis, Cornelius, et al. 2019. *A Socialisme ou Barbarie Anthology: Autonomy, Critique and Revolution in the Age of Bureaucratic Capitalism*. London: Eris.
Caumières, Philippe, Klimis, Sophie, and Van Eynde, Laurent. 2012. *Socialisme ou Barbarie aujourd'hui. Analyses et témoignages*. Bruxelles: Presses de l'Université Saint-Louis.
Chaulieu, Pierre. 1949. Le parti révolutionnaire. Résolution. *Socialisme ou Barbarie* 2: 99. Now in Castoriadis 2012.
Chaulieu, Pierre. 1958. *Sur la minorité. Bulletin Intérieur*, September: 1–13.
Chaulieu, Pierre, and Montal, Claude. 1952. Discussion sur le problème du parti révolutionnaire. *Socialisme ou Barbarie* 10: 10–27.
Chollet, Antoine. 2019. Claude Lefort, un intrus à Socialisme ou Barbarie? *Rue Descartes* 96: 41–53.
Ciliga, Ante. 1979. *The Russian Enigma*. London. Ink Links.
Dosse, François. 2014. *Castoriadis: une vie*. Paris: La Decouverte.
Dosse, François. 2018. *La saga des intellectuels français 1944–1989. I. À L'Epreuve de l'histoire 1944–1968*. Paris: Gallimard.
Dosse, François. 2021. *Amitiés philosophiques*. Paris: Odile Jacob.

Escobar, Enrique. 2012. Sur l'«influence» de Socialisme ou Barbarie et, inévitablement, sur Castoriadis. In *Socialisme ou Barbarie aujourd'hui. Analyses et témoignages*, ed. P. Caumières, S. Klimis, and L. Van Eynde, 175–225. Bruxelles: Presses de l'université de Saint-Luois.

Feron, Alexandre. 2019. Sartre contre Lefort. De quoi l'expérience prolétarienne est-elle le nom? *Rue Descartes* 46/2: 65–79.

Frager, Dominique. 2021. *Socialisme ou barbarie: L'aventure d'un groupe (1946–1969)*. Paris: Syllepse.

Gambarotto, Yaël. 2019. La philosophie come interprétation du present: Claude Lefort et les années «Socialisme ou Barbarie». *Rue Descartes* 96/2: 54–64.

Gide, André. 1936. *Return from the U.S.S.R.* New York: Knopf.

Gottraux, Philippe. 1997. *Socialisme ou Barbarie. Un engagement politique et intellectuel dans la France de l'après-guerre*. Lausanne: Payot.

Guillaume, Philippe. 1949. La guerre et notre époque. *Socialisme ou Barbarie* 3: 1–21.

Guillaume, Philippe. 1950. La guerre et notre époque. Suite. *Socialisme ou Barbarie* 5–6: 77–123.

Guillaume, Philippe. 1956–1957. Comment ils se sont battus. *Socialisme ou Barbarie* 20: 117–123.

Hastings-King, Stephen. 1997. On the Marxist Imaginary and the Problem of Practice: Socialisme ou Barbarie, 1952–6. *Thesis Eleven* 46: 69–84.

Hastings-King, Stephen. 1999. L'Internationale Situationniste, Socialisme ou Barbarie and the Crisis of the Marxist Imaginary. *SubStance* 40: 26–54.

Hastings-King, Stephen. 2015. *Looking for the Proletariat. Socialisme ou Barbarie and the Problem of Worker Writing*. Chicago: Haymarket Books.

Howard, Dick. 2019. *The Marxian Legacy: The Search for the New Left*. 3rd edition. London: Palgrave Macmillan.

Kravchenko, Viktor. 1946. *I Chose Freedom: The Personal and Political Life of a Soviet Official*. New York: Charles Scribner's Sons.

Labelle, Gilles. 2015. Parcours de Claude Lefort: de l'«expérience prolétarienne» de l'«aliénation» à la critique du marxisme. *Politique et Sociétés* 34/1: 17–36.

Lefort, Claude. 1971. *Éléments d'une critique de la bureaucratie*. Paris: Droz.

Lefort, Claude. 1979. *Éléments d'une critique de la bureaucratie*. 2nd edition. Paris: Gallimard.

Lefort, Claude. 1986. *The Political Forms of Modern Society. Bureaucracy, Democracy, Totalitarianism*. Cambridge: MIT Press.

Lefort, Claude. 1994. *L'invention démocratique. Les limites de la domination totalitaire*. Paris: Fayard.

Lefort, Claude. 2007. *Le temps présent. Écrits 1945–2005*. Paris: Belin.

Legros, Robert, and Rothnie, Steve. 2017. Cornelius Castoriadis and Claude Lefort: The Question of Autonomy. *Social Imaginaries* 3/2: 181–189.

Marx, Karl, and Engels, Friedrich. 2002. *The Communist Manifesto.* London: Penguin Books.
Merleau-Ponty, Maurice. 1969. *The Visible and the Invisible.* Evanston: Northwestern University Press.
Merleau-Ponty, Maurice. 2012. *Phenomenology of Perception.* London: Routledge.
Molina, Esteban. 2005. *Le défi du politique. Totalitarisme et démocratie chez Claude Lefort.* Paris: L'Harmattan.
Monferrand, Frédéric. 2018. Politiser l'expérience Merleau-Ponty, Socialisme ou Barbarie et l'expérience prolétarienne. *Chiasmi International* 19: 87–100.
Mongin, Olivier. 1993. Un parcours politique. Du cercle des idéologies au cercle des croyances. In *La Démocratie à l'œuvre. Autour de Claude Lefort*, ed. C. Habib and C. Mouchard, 137–150. Paris: Éditions Esprit.
Mothé, Daniel. 1956–1957. Chez Renault on parle de la Hongrie. *Socialisme ou Barbarie* 20: 124–133.
Mothé, Daniel. 1959. *Journal d'un ouvrier.* Paris: Minuit.
Murphy, Peter. 2020. From 'Capitalism and Revolution' to 'Capitalism and Managerialism'. *Thesis Eleven* 161/1: 23–34.
Poirier, Nicolas. 2010. Division du social et auto-institution: le projet démocratique selon Castoriadis et Lefort. *Raison publique* 13: 243–260.
Poirier, Nicolas. 2015. *Cornelius Castoriadis et Claude Lefort: l'expérience démocratique.* Lormont: Le Bord de l'eau.
Poirier, Nicolas. 2019. Dépasser ou assumer la division sociale? Castoriadis et Lefort face à la révolution hongroise. *Rue Descartes* 46: 30–40.
Poirier, Nicolas. 2020. *Introduction à Claude Lefort.* Paris: La Découverte.
Poirier, Nicolas. 2022. Wild Being, Between Ontology and Politics: Merleau-Ponty, Lefort, Castoriadis. *International Journal of Social Imaginaries* 1: 84–106.
Poltier, Hugues. 1997. *Claude Lefort. La découverte du politique.* Paris: Michalon.
Raynaud, Philippe. 1989. Société bureaucratique et totalitarisme. Remarques sur l'évolution du groupe «Socialisme ou Barbarie». In *Autonomie et autotransformation de la Société: la philosophie militante de Cornelius Castoriadis*, ed. G. Busino, 255–268. Genève-Paris: Librairie Droz.
Rizzi, Bruno. 1985. *The Bureaucratization of the World.* New York: Free Press.
Sartre, Jean-Paul. 1968. *The Communists and Peace with a Reply to Claude Lefort.* New York: George Braziller.
Simon. J. 1956. Les grèves de l'été 1955. *Socialisme ou Barbarie* 18: 2–36.
Stewart, Jon. 1998. *The Debate Between Sartre and Merleau-Ponty.* Evanston: Northwestern University Press.
Thompson, John. 2008. Ideology and the Social Imaginary: An Appraisal of Castoriadis and Lefort. *Theory and Society* 21/5: 659–681.

Trotsky, Leon. 1972. *The Revolution Betrayed: What Is the Soviet Union and Where Is It Going?* New York: Pathfinder Press.

Wright, Steve. 2002. *Storming Heaven: Class, Composition and Struggle in Italian Autonomist Marxism.* London: Pluto Press.

CHAPTER 3

The Symbolic Dimension of the Social

Phenomenological Marxism

Lefort's departure from SouB in 1958 was a kind of liberation, the end of a self-imposed censorship (Lefort 2007, p. 236). From outside the group and its militancy, he felt free to develop a body of ideas that had been struggling to express itself through the apparatus of Marxist theory. This does not mean, however, that Lefort developed his "true" ideas only after this point.[1] On the contrary, it was precisely during his participation in SouB and in close confrontation with Marx that his distinctive ideas took shape, and it was only through continuous engagement with Marx's texts that he devised a personal method for analyzing social and political phenomena. This would come to characterize the full span of his work and involved the critique of all absolute knowledge, all illusions of objectivity, and all underlying foundations. We must therefore turn first to the 1950s to understand the fundamental structure of Lefort's thought.

The decade was marked by a particular intellectual ferment in French Marxism as the publication of the Trier philosopher's early works and the emergence of structuralism opened the way to new understandings of

---

[1] This seems to be the belief expressed in certain studies, such as Flynn (2005). Instead Chollet (2019), Labelle (2015), and Poirier (2020) highlight the continuity of Lefort's thought.

© The Author(s), under exclusive license to Springer Nature Switzerland AG 2023
M. Di Pierro, *Claude Lefort's Political Philosophy*, Political Philosophy and Public Purpose,
https://doi.org/10.1007/978-3-031-36378-8_3

Marx's work that opposed the interpretations based on historical materialism and the orthodoxy of the PCF.[2] The postwar period also saw the rise of a Hegelian interpretation of Marx's thought that aimed to reappraise its philosophical component, which had been neglected by official readings of dialectical materialism and by an understanding of Marxism as a "scientific worldview".[3] Marx the economist was replaced by Marx the philosopher, with his thought interpreted as the translation into materialist terms of the Hegelian *Phenomenology of Spirit* with which the structures of development (commodities, money, and capital) would maintain a direct correspondence. Some scholars thus went as far as to assert that the author of *Capital*, far from overthrowing the Hegelian rationalist project, actually intended to bring it to fruition, to go where Hegel had not dared to go: toward the complete translation of the real into the rational, toward the end of History. Jean Hyppolite (1955, p. 138), for example, argued that while Hegel rejected the possibility that the tragic nature of the human condition could come to an end and confined the manifestation of the idea to a few exceptional occasions, Marx's thought conceived it as an effective means of reconciliation. By finding actual resolutions to contradictions, and by theorizing the classless society, Marx ended Hegel's endless dialectic, finally making the suppression of the tragic dimension of History possible. Marx was therefore a metaphysical thinker, a proponent of a radical realism in which reason and reality reach their synthesis and fulfillment.

---

[2] There are several French intellectuals who, in order to address the crisis of Marxism connected to events in the Soviet Union and especially to the repression of the 1956 Hungarian uprising, turned to the work of Claude Lévi-Strauss and the structuralist movement. The aim was to overcome certain rigidities inherent in official Marxism, for example in the relationship between structure and superstructure. It is not irrelevant to note how Merleau-Ponty (1964a) himself became interested in the work of Marcel Mauss and Lévi-Strauss. See Dosse (1998, 2014, 2018), Geroulanos (2017), Breckman (2013, pp. 84–89), and Poltier (1998, pp. 21–38).

[3] Authors such as Alexandre Kojève, Jean Wahl, Jean Hyppolite, Henri Lefebvre, Pierre Bigo, Jean-Paul Sartre, and Merleau-Ponty were among the protagonists of this debate. It is through the relationship with Hegel that Marx the philosopher, who had been overlooked by dialectical materialism, was brought into the spotlight. Hyppolite is certainly a central figure for any attempt to understand Hegelian studies in France and the debate on the relationship between Hegel and Marx in this period. See at least Hyppolite (1979). On Marxism and the fortunes of the young Marx in France following World War II see Jay (1986), Pompeo Faracovi (1972), and Lichteim (1966).

Alienation theory constituted the very crux of this interpretation and others like it. It was the cornerstone of the possible correspondence between the development of the Spirit in Hegel and the historical-dialectical process in Marx. The process of becoming, understood as a path through successive forms of alienation, was the arena in which the effort to demonstrate the accordance between the two authors played out (Lefort 1978a, p. 86).[4] If in the Hegelian system Spirit proceeded through the various stages of alienation toward unity, in Marx history was merely the realization of man's essence, accomplished by overcoming consecutive forms of separation between dead and living labor. Marxism, interpreters who tended in this direction, like Hyppolite, concluded, is idealism. This was a theory that claimed to be able to identify the real and the rational, and the prerequisite for the conception of becoming that it attributed to Marx was an accessible, disclosable human nature capable of justifying and connecting the successive stages of alienation. Only this preliminary assumption made it possible for him to establish a contradiction between the socialization of labor and the private mode of production, between dead and living labor. And only this prior acceptance of the dichotomy between the real and the alienated could allow him to assert that politics, law, and religion are simply expressions of alienation. Given these assumptions, it was possible to argue that "[t]he idea of alienation entirely dominates this political economy" (Bigo 1954, p. 27), and that "with a slight modification, the first sentence of the Communist Manifesto could look like this: history is the history of the alienation of man" (Landshut and Mayer 1935, p. XLII).[5] The whole of Marx's work would then follow from this opposition between reality and alienation, on which the power of criticism would in fact be based.

Lefort's reflection enters this agitated political-intellectual framework through a peculiar path. Critical of all scientific interpretations of Marxism, he distances himself as much from structuralist interpretations, which do not renounce the objectivity of universal structures, as from Hegelian ones, and instead proposes a phenomenological approach in continuity with the endeavor undertaken by Merleau-Ponty in the same years. According to Lefort (1978a), it is first and foremost necessary to

---

[4] I am referring to the article "L'aliénation comme concept sociologique", which was first published in 1955 in the journal *Cahiers Internationaux de Sociologie* 8: 35–54.

[5] Landshut and Mayer were also the editors of the first edition of Marx's early works in 1923. See Marx (1923).

extricate Marx from all mechanistic, economistic interpretations, but also to rescue his texts from all forms of essentialism.

The first question to be resolved relates to the reality-alienation dichotomy that lies at the heart of both mechanistic and contemporary interpretations that bring Marx closer to Hegel (83–86). Lefort does not hesitate to recognize certain naturalistic and essentialist traits in Marx's work that might lead certain readers, like Hyppolite, to infer a reality from which to derive the alienated condition and the consequent possibility of critique. In the preface to *Capital*, for example, when referring to the analogy between social and natural laws, Marx surreptitiously introduces the idea of humanity and society in itself.[6] For Lefort (85) there is also no shortage of texts, such as the introduction to the *Critique of Political Economy*, in which the path of humanity is depicted as being inevitably progressive. A process of successive separations between living and objectified forces is in this case the prescribed path taken by a teleologically directed social body moving toward a necessary synthesis. However, Lefort (85–86) locates the main core of Marx's essentialism in the first section of *Capital*, and in particular in the famous pages in which he outlines his theory of fetishism. In them Marx analyzes the change that the products of labor go through when they become commodities, and describes their mystical character (Marx 1976, pp. 163–177). According to Marx, the commodity reflects the image of the social characteristics of labor back to human beings, but in an objectified form. Like a mirror that distorts the figure in its frame, in commodities contingent social relations, which are determined by the capitalist system of production, seem like natural and objective relations (Lefort 1978a, p. 83). "Real" human relations are thus disguised so that humans simply perceive them as relations between things. Commodities therefore become detached from their producers, who, estranged from their own product, become their object. Such a theory depends first and foremost on a naturalistic conception of labor that Lefort finds problematic. In *Capital*, he says (101), Marx exposes the naturalistic substratum of fetishism when he links the determination of value to the expenditure of the functions of the human organism, and when he confuses the particular form of labor with

---

[6] Lefort is probably referring to a passage in the preface to the first edition of *Capital* in which Marx repeatedly advocates the scientific method of his study and the desire to examine, just as a physicist examines natural processes, the economic development of society as a process of natural history. See Marx (1976, pp. 89–93).

its natural form. The reality-alienation dichotomy thus proceeds from this starting point and is translated into the dissociation between the reality of labor and the illusion of capital. On one side is the living, real, particular labor proper to the worker, and on the other the mystification elaborated at the level of the commodity, of the universalization of production, in which the worker is objectified and reduced to a product.

However, Lefort continues, to halt the analysis at this point (as both economistic and Hegelian readings do) is to disregard the originality and critical potentiality of Marxism. It means ignoring the fact that Marx's work contains other interpretations of alienation. In contrast to this, it should be understood that the novelty and distinctiveness of his concepts cannot be grasped through either scientific, Hegelian interpretations, or from the perspective of the reality-fiction or nature-mystification dichotomies. There is instead another way to read Marx, and especially the first section of *Capital*, but doing so first entails reacting to the naturalism and essentialism present in some passages of Marx's texts and teasing out the contradictions in his argumentation. It is necessary to bring Marx's discourse back to the critical conditions that underpin its validity and revolutionary potential. This above all means understanding that Marx "cannot *return to us* unless he is considered in terms of his separation from Hegel" (85–86):

> By grounding the dialectic of alienation in the real, Marx, it is said, would have brought about the complete identification of the rational and the real for which he criticized Hegel. On the contrary, it is precisely at this point that he splits from Hegel, because if alienation is real, the rational cannot be rightfully re-established through a Hegelian sleight of hand; existing social conditions, the form taken by the division of labor are the framework within which all knowledge is developed; science itself develops within alienation: Reason per se no longer exists. (86)

In short, once detached from essentialism the meaning of alienation no longer rests on the dichotomy between the real and the rational but in fact implies the renunciation of any idea of Reason at all. Thus in Marx's thought, Lefort argues, it is precisely the awareness of the reality of alienation that determines the conditions within which both knowledge and action proceed. There is therefore a consciousness both that Marxism is caught in the web of alienation and that there is no history, society, or nature per se that can be known by alienated reasoning. Failing to understand this means falling into the error of bourgeois thought which, precisely because it is alienated without being conscious of being so, turns into ideology: that is, it constructs abstractions to which it ascribes an indisputable reality (111–112).

Lefort's goal during the 1950s is thus to find a theory within Marx's work that rejects any overriding vision and any foundational idea and instead arises from within the reality and social relations it analyzes. The idea of a theory that becomes praxis, that takes shape in the concreteness of practices and human relations (which we have already seen in the "proletarian experience") is obviously based on Marx's work. However, the terms in which Lefort translates it—by rejecting any scientific analysis of the social and any illusion of objectivity—are clearly a legacy of phenomenology and reveal traces of Merleau-Ponty's teachings.

The latter, from the late 1940s, had not shied away from criticizing dialectical materialism, of mechanistic interpretations of Marxism and any kind of *pensée de surplomb*, that is, any knowledge that considered itself objective and external to the reality it analyzed (Merleau-Ponty 2012, 2022a). For the phenomenologist, the relation between theory and society, philosopher and being, should not be the direct one of the spectator watching the spectacle. Rather, it is an oblique relationship, a "clandestine and complicit relationship" in which the two terms are already forever intertwined (Merleau-Ponty 1988, p. 15). As he stated in the *Phenomenology of Perception*, this relationship does not distinguish between a separate object and subject. If perception is a set of jointly implicit relations in which subject and the world emerge together, being is always its own experience and every phenomenon is established in a series of relations from which it is inseparable (Merleau-Ponty 2012, pp. 100–148). Thus for Merleau-Ponty too Marxism is not a science, nor a theory that provides the ability to unveil an objective, material reality beneath alienation, of revealing certain social significances. Marx "does not transfer the dialectic into things; he transforms it into men, understood of course with all their human equipment as being engaged, through work and culture, in an enterprise which transforms nature and social relations" (Merleau-Ponty 1988, p. 52).

From the perspective of phenomenology, Marx's work thus offers Lefort the fertile territory in which to lay out the contours of a theory that rejects all foundations, all illusions of objectivity, and is instead conscious of being involved in the very social reality that it analyzes. Following this path first and foremost means combating all mechanism and "crass materialism", grasping the human dimension of production and praxis, and redefining the social as something beyond the reality-alienation dichotomy that cannot be reduced to the economic structure (Lefort 1979, pp. 33–116).

THE SOCIAL AS CULTURE

This new conception of the social and of the relationship between society and theory, which Lefort attempted to define during his decade of activity with SouB, was stimulated by a series of studies to which he devoted himself from the early 1950s (Lefort 1978a). Between 1950 and 1951, at the library of the Musée de l'Homme, he avidly read the classic works of French sociology (Marcel Mauss, Roger Bastide, Claude Lévi-Strauss), American culturalism (Ralph Linton, Abram Kardiner, Gregory Bateson), and British functionalism (Bronislaw Malinowski, Edward Evans-Pritchard). The view and the language of anthropology offered the Parisian philosopher the tools he needed to define his own idea of praxis, that of an interrelation between material reality and social meanings.[7]

It was this attempt to clarify the Marxist distinction between structure and superstructure and the reality-representation binomial that drove Lefort toward the work of the anthropologist Abram Kardiner, to whom he devoted an early essay in 1951 (Lefort 1978a, pp. 113–130).[8] Kardiner had aimed to demonstrate the relationship between childhood experience in a given culture and its institutions. In *The Individual and His Society*, for instance, the ethnologist considered the population of the Alor Islands, a small archipelago on the fringes of Indonesia, and noted how the organization of labor, which left women responsible for production, directly affected methods of raising children (Kardiner 1939).[9] Since they spent most of their time in the fields, Alor women were unable to care for their children and therefore left them with siblings or other relatives fourteen days after birth. The children thus stopped receiving systematic care and lost any stable parental influence in their lives. According to Kardiner,

---

[7] On the importance of anthropology for Lefort, see Lanza (2021) and Moyn (2013).

[8] For a sometimes different analysis of Lefort's reflection on Kardiner see: B. Flynn (2005, pp. 89–94).

[9] The French translation did not appear until 1969, when it was published under the title *L'individu dans sa société*. Lefort himself edited the introduction. See Lefort (1978a, pp. 131–187).

in such a climate of neglect children accumulated a series of frustrations that affected their personalities. Unable to differentiate the permissible from the forbidden, and rewarded and punished inconsistently, they failed to develop a strong ego. These childhood experiences thus shaped the "basic personality" of the inhabitants of Alor, which was characterized by insecurity, a lack of a stable system of values, an inability to develop emotional relationships, low self-confidence, and a lack of ideals.

Kardiner used this particular example of childhood experience and the personality type that developed from it to explain a number of institutions common to the communities in question. The lack of proper parenting, for example, was reflected in primitive deity worship. Similarly, the development of fragile personalities was the cause of the islanders' particularly crude art, their rudimentary building techniques, and interpersonal relationships characterized by exploitation and little mutual trust.

These studies capture Lefort's attention because they made clear "the social background of individuals' lives", the continuous interplay between individuals and the community (Lefort 1978a, pp. 113–187).[10] Moreover, Kardiner considered culture in its totality and, by examining the relationship between individual experience and institutions, shed light on the interwoven threads that bind the various spheres of social life together. At the same time, however, the Parisian philosopher notes that this position reveals "the mechanistic tendency of the author", given that these connections could be traced back to a causal relationship (118). Indeed, Kardiner classified institutions into primary and secondary ones, and while the former—the organization of the family, the type of nutrition, the method of weaning children, and methods of subsistence—governed childhood development, the others transmitted the resulting behavioral reactions to the social level. Religions, myths, taboos, and thought mechanisms were therefore all in this secondary group. His intention was that this distinction would enable a reciprocal causal relationship between society and the individual, mediated by the basic personality. Secondary institutions, in other words, were the result of transposing the effect that primary institutions had on the basic personality.

---

[10] I am referring here to two articles: "L'idée de 'personnalité de base'", published in 1951, and "Ambiguités de l'anthropologie Culturelle: introduction à l'œuvre d'Abram Kardiner", published in 1969.

However, in Lefort's view, every example given to demonstrate the causal connection between fundamental personality and primary and secondary institutions in fact only serves to reveal the interdependence of all the factors that make up social life. Furthermore, by maintaining that a certain sexual education is responsible for the development of a particular religion we condemn ourselves to failing to see how sex education is already an expression of a particular type of personality that already has a certain sense of religion; that is, we neglect the pre-existing interplay between personality and institution, the symbolic dimension that constitutes society as a whole (118–121):

> This concept [of basic personality] in our view means that society and the individual belong to the order of *phenomena*, not of the in-itself, and that their relationship is one of expression or symbolization, since the one alternately plays the role of signifier and signified towards the other. (130)

The point is not only to highlight that so-called secondary institutions can retroact on the earlier level. Rather, it is to grasp the unattainable anteriority of any interrelation, the *indeterminacy* revealed when one grasps in the individual the transcendence of society and in society the transcendence of the individual: an *antecedence* that is impossible to comprehend through cause and effect.[11]

Marcel Mauss' "The Gift" led Lefort to develop this conception of the social and the relationship between the material basis and social meanings further (Mauss 2002).[12] In his celebrated essay the French anthropologist outlined a theory that interpreted the exchange of gifts as a "total social fact", a phenomenon that, having at once economic, legal, moral, religious, and aesthetic meanings, involves all the institutions of a given community. Above all, gift-giving involves a relationship of trust: the belief on the part of the donor that the gift will be reciprocated despite the fact that there is no contract to guarantee this. At the same time a magical dimension is involved: gifted objects may have special powers or healing abilities. Moreover, gift-giving is connected to particular life

---

[11] Lanza (2021, p. 2) refers to Lefort's socio-anthropological approach as a particular "way of conceptualizing the interrelationship between the individual and the social".

[12] I state this for the sake of clarity. Mauss's theories, as well as those of Durkheim, were somehow present in Lefort's worldview from the very beginning.

events such as marriage, childbirth, initiation rites, illness, death, and military expeditions. In attempting to understand these phenomena, it is also not possible to disregard the moral and political value of gifts: people see the exchange of gifts as the basis for agreement, honor, friendship, and enmity. The giver gains personal prestige, while the one who does not give or who refuses a gift is immediately regarded as an enemy. In short, gifts structure community ties and establish differences between those who are and those who are not part of the community, as well as determining relations between different groups and tribes.

This mechanism is particularly evident in the *potlatch*, a form of gift exchange practiced by the indigenous people of the north-western Pacific seaboard that is dominated by the principle of rivalry. In the *potlatch*, members of the participating communities face off in an authentic contest played out through gifts, with each having the duty and the obligation to give and to receive, in a custom that leads to a usurious spiral of exchange. People give because they are compelled to, to assert their social prestige, to be part of the community, and to be considered its leader. Gifts are thus a vector of recognition, of rights, and of identity construction, and their validity lies at the intersection of personal relationships, politics, morality, magic, and religion. It is therefore not possible to separate the mechanism of gift exchange from its various meanings. Gifts and their ability to structure social relations can only be understood in their totality, as a "total social fact" and in terms of their interrelation with the various institutions and dimensions of the social.

The form of exchange described by Mauss outlined a method of structuring social relations in which everything contributes to a single general meaning. From this point of view, one cannot distinguish a clear separation between economic exchange and magical meaning, between the exchanged object and the interpersonal relationship. There is no causal relationship. No aspect of the social is autonomous and worthy of being elevated to the sole or primary cause of the ways in which men relate to each other. No single element can provide the answer to the question of how the social is possible. The holistic perspective offered by Mauss and the discipline of anthropology thus enables Lefort to provide the best possible explanation for the idea that "society is a totality, and that the economic and the ideological, which we are accustomed to consider separate in *reality*, are only values that knowledge demands" (Lefort 1978a, p. 24). Just as proletarian experience was defined by the connection between individual, historical, and ideological factors, society must also be understood as a totality in which it is impossible to discern material reality and social meaning, cause and effect, and in which myth is not separated from economy, nor production from magic. In other words, to take society as an object of study is to ask how a given community gives itself meaning, how it *represents* its relationship to the world. In this way, the object of inquiry becomes first and foremost what Lefort calls the "shaping" (*mise en forme*) of social relations: a totality and an intertwined mass of institutions, practices, and beliefs that acquire meaning in and through their relationship with each other. The task is therefore to understand the essence of a society, the meaning of its culture or, as we shall see later, its symbolic institution.[13]

A Political Issue at the Bottom of the Social

In the early 1950s Lefort engaged in a critical confrontation with the rationalist philosophies of history, namely the readings of historical progress proposed by Edmund Husserl, Friedrich Hegel and especially Karl Marx (Lefort 1978a, pp. 46–77). Despite their differences, all three philosophers seem to have shared a common illusion, the possibility that objective knowledge of history is conceivable, and encountered similar difficulties. Having conceived a single, coherent, and rational becoming, they failed to account for anything that did not fit into it, that did not harmonize with it, including societies that, by persisting in stagnation, in the absence of change, contradicted the identity between rationality and progressive historical development, in other words the identity on which such rationalist theories are based. For Hegel, for example, the historical process did not coincide with the empirical course of humanity but began only with the advent of the state. Societies that do not conform to this type of development, such as India or China, are ejected from history proper. The Hegelian dialectic thus "does not recover these peoples except by subjecting them to a transcendent purpose, preserving them as foreign bodies because of its inability to integrate them". The same criticality characterized Marx's thinking: although he located the elementary conditions of all social life in primitive societies, he marginalized them

---

[13] This is made explicit by Lefort in a 1952 article entitled "Société 'sans histoire' et historicité" (Lefort 1978a, pp. 46–77). Here we find one of the first uses of the phrase *mise en forme* to refer to society in its totality. Once again the debt to anthropology is clear.

beyond the boundaries of "true" history, which unfolds only through the dialectic of class struggle. Even Husserl, while recognizing a kinship between all spiritual forms of humanity, did not refrain from identifying Europe's destiny with the destiny of reason, thus relegating all non-European humanity to irrationality. On the one hand, there were societies "without history", living in perpetual stagnation and in the absence of change, and on the other "historical societies" open to becoming, to transformation and progress. Communities that remained the same over the centuries were thus an obvious problem for rationalist philosophies, which were able to integrate them into their conceptions of becoming only to reject them immediately as an aporia of the system (46–50).

To break out of this impasse, Lefort argues, it is necessary to abandon the rationalist perspective in order to recognize the phenomenon of stagnant societies beneath their supposed immobility. The anthropological method, by looking beyond the surface of the explicit and implicit rules that make community possible, once again makes a new depiction of stagnant societies possible. Below the level of the *mise en forme*, the discipline reaches out to grasp the complete meaning of a culture:

> Generally speaking, what ethnologists seek to understand and interpret, in contact with so-called primitive societies, is a *culture*, a complex of institutions, practices, and beliefs, which do not make sense except through the mutual relationship they maintain, and which constitute a possible mode of human coexistence. This shift in perspective is remarkable in that it prevents one from holding to a static view of the social, and forces one to attend to a *becoming*, however indeterminate this may be. (51)

The ethnologist is able to overcome apparent immobility to reveal how it is made possible by a "culturing culture", in other words by "the constantly repeated operation through which a society refers to itself and thereby confirms its teleology" (55). Thus beneath the surface of stagnation one can distinguish society's incessant self-reference. Once the supposed lack of history is abandoned, it becomes possible to consider the implicit becoming of society, at which point a series of "choices", even unintentional, or perhaps unconscious, emerge. Choices which have been made, which continue to be made and which make society what it is, creating what we might call, again resorting to Lefort's own terminology, its *mise en sens*. These are the contingent and continuous solutions that presuppose a mode of relationship between humans and the past and future, and which project a "need for the future".[14] What therefore appears to emerge is a link between a given kind of historicity and a given sociality.[15]

The work of Gregory Bateson provided Lefort with the tools to better clarify this point. The British anthropologist's studies examined the society of Bali, which seemed to order itself on the basis of a fundamental imperative: to maintain stability (Bateson and Mead 1942; Bateson 1949). In pursuit of this end, Balinese society banned all forms of competition and opposition: disputes were resolved by penalties that the disputants agreed to pay should they ever speak again, and wars were dealt with by ceasing all relations between rival groups. Each faction surrounded itself with the necessary fortifications not to prevent others' attacks, but in order to make any fighting, indeed all forms of interaction, impossible. Bateson also noted how this attitude affected all aspects of social life—from music to dance, from rigid hierarchical divisions to the raising of children—and that a particular conception of time and space had developed that corresponds to this disposition toward social immobility and stability. Time was articulated in a particularly complicated way that enabled all events to be fixed in relation to multiple systems of reference, and this way of looking forward bred a general inability to imagine an indeterminate future. The relationship with space exhibited the same characteristics, with the Balinese apparently able to think of themselves only as strictly situated and rooted in a given natural environment and social context. Just as they could not conceive of abstract time, they were also unable to contemplate situations in which they were not present.

In this context the rejection of conflict appeared to be the extreme consequence of a particular representation of the world and its social relations. For Balinese communities, opening themselves up to conflict represented an enormous risk, the possibility of calling into question the firm attachment to the environment, the facts, and the certain reference points that gave meaning to their relationships and to space and time. It was in order to avoid this threat of a disruption to an entrenched worldview that conflict was denied.

---

[14] Merleau-Ponty (2010) uses the term "exigence d'un avenir" to describe the institution of the social and its relationship to time and history.

[15] Lefort's references are the studies of Robert Lowie (1949) and Malville J. Herskovitz (1940), Gregory Bateson and Margaret Mead and (1942).

The case of Bali thus encourages Lefort to connect a particular historicity with a corresponding type of sociality; it urges not to define social stagnation as the product of a natural or material condition, but as the outcome of a culture or *mise en sens* on which a particular conception of time and space depends (Lefort 1978a, p. 73). Stagnation is the consequence of an organization that does not allow for the conceptualization of otherness, which blocks internal division within society and, with it, all forms of change. In short, there is a political question underlying a given society's relationship with history and its own organization, a question that lies beneath every society from which different "forms of history" follow (49–51).[16]

It would be on this theoretical basis that, years later, Lefort would approach the studies of Pierre Clastres.[17] Beginning in the 1960s, the French anthropologist spent several periods living among indigenous tribes in Paraguay, Brazil, and Venezuela. His attention was attracted particularly to the phenomenon of chiefdom, a form of non-coercive power common to such tribes. Clastres's studies describe how such communities denied all coercive power to anyone who acquired a position of authority. The communities' chiefs, he explained, were obliged to accept the will of the whole society and to lead the common effort to assert autonomy, specificity, and independence, but they had no power of their own: they had no authority to coerce, did not hold any form of command over other members of the community, and could not make decisions in the name of others. They were akin to functionaries, charged primarily with representing the voice of the community to the outside world. For Clastres, the case of the chiefdom was paradigmatic in that it highlights what he believed to be the defining characteristic of primitive societies, namely that they order themselves in such a way as to prevent power from autonomizing, separating itself and turning into coercion. The "depowered" form of power of the chiefdom thus responded to

---

[16] Lefort's ideas on this subject, along with the work of Marshall Sahlins, are at the root of François Hartog's concept of "regimes of historicity". See Hartog (2016) and Sahlins (1985).

[17] Born in 1934 in Paris, Pierre Clastres was a celebrated anthropologist and a close friend of Lefort. Among his works see at least Clastres (1987, 1998). Lefort discusses Clastres in Lefort (2000, pp. 207–235; 2007, pp. 383–387). Clastres had a certain influence in the French culture of the period (Moyn 2004) and, in addition to Lefort, on the thought of authors such as Miguel Abensour or Marcel Gauchet. On the relation between Lefort's theory and Clastres' work see Lanza (2021) and Moyn (2013).

the need to maintain social unity and prevent all divisions, even those relating to differences in space and in future times. The maintenance of power within the social body revealed a desire for unity, for non-division. Command, exercised collectively, remained within the body of the community.

Because of this method of organization, Clastres (1987) defined primitive societies as societies that do not have and are opposed to the state. Not only do they not establish separate organs of power, but they organize themselves so as to ensure that such separation does not happen, that an external power capable of coercion does not arise, that the state does not arise.[18] Their *mise en form* and *mise en sens* responds to this need. The anthropologist used this definition to argue against any progressive view of history that, conceiving primitive societies as incomplete and frozen in an embryonic stage of evolution, sees the state as a necessary stage of historical development.[19] Like Lefort, Clastres considered such a conception of becoming as incapable of explaining the forms of primitive societies which, when not expelled from the actual historical process, were relegated to a primordial stage of development. In opposition to this theoretical approach he pointed out how the study of primitive societies does not reveal their supposed incompleteness but rather highlights their particular organization. Their stagnation is not the result of an inability but of a "will" to avoid division, and of the separation of power. These societies do not stand at the beginning of a linear course of History, but organize themselves to fight that History, to oppose the emergence of the state, of separation, of otherness.

---

[18] Clastres uses the term "state" generically, to refer to a form of power that is not internal to the social and is capable of imposing coercive force. This is a deliberately vague definition capable of encompassing various forms of organization of power and different degrees of oppression. In this regard, Lefort expresses his reservations specifically on the legitimacy of such a definition. Not only, he says, is it reductive to limit the definition of the state to the categories of coercion and oppression, but the division of forms of society according to an alleged degree of oppression is also unjustified. See Clastres (2016). On Clastres's idea of state see Viveiros de Castro (2019).

[19] Clastres (1980, pp. 157–170) also contested the Marxist view of history, which he accused of evolutionism. Lefort himself (2000, pp. 207–235) indicates how Clastres's work was of use in countering both rationalist and evolutionist and structuralist readings of history, which he says are equally flawed.

Beyond the differences, even important ones, that divide Clastres and Lefort,[20] what unites the two scholars and is interesting to highlight at this point is precisely the discovery of a political question at the heart of societies. For both writers, the case of stagnant societies highlights how every society orders itself in a peculiar way, as a totality, by means of a political "choice" about its meaning that involves a specific relationship with time, space, internal division and the meaning and role of power.[21]

The Social Is the Real, or Marx's Mistake

The 1955 essay "L'aliénation comme concept sociologique" is a milestone in the development of Lefort's conception of the social (Lefort 1978a, pp. 78–112). The issue at the heart of the text, that of alienation, remains distinctly Marxist, while the references he turns to are once again those of anthropology. However, the essay introduces an unusual case study, namely the investigation of the Nuer of East Africa carried out by the British anthropologist Edward Evans-Pritchard (1968). Living mainly from raising livestock, the Nuer have a particularly close bond with their cows. In addition to being the main source of wealth, these animals are the currency governing the structures of social relations: ownership of cattle offers rank and status within the community and establishes social roles and bonds. Prestige, for example, is directly related both to the number of animals owned and to their beauty, which is defined through a series of precise criteria. Marriage and kinship relationships are determined by the gifting and receiving of cows, while conflicts and divisions, whether internal or with neighboring groups, are also mediated by cattle.

---

[20] See Lefort (2000, pp. 207–235). Lefort criticizes Clastres' idea of a radical opposition between primitive, egalitarian, free and anti-state societies and all other societies that presuppose one. He also thinks that Clastres does not capture the image of the body and otherness of law in the rituals of primitive societies. Finally, he criticizes his definition of the state. Referring to Clastres's reading of rituals and the unity of "societies against the state" Lefort writes: "Not only would such an interpretation fail to recognize the singularity of primitive practices and beliefs (which can't be reduced to the separation of the invisible from the visible), and not only would it identify the essence of religious belief with that of the primitives and make of the great historical religions transitory by-products of the building up of the State, but—and this is the point that to us seems decisive—it would take away all signification from the very notion of the *other*" (p. 227).

[21] On this topic see also Lefort and Gauchet (1971, pp. 20–33), in which the authors discuss "Decision". However, the term is problematic and was not taken up again by Lefort.

Even military valor is associated with the ability to defend livestock or obtain them by violent raids on herds belonging to other tribes. In short, according to Evans-Pritchard's studies, the whole of Nuer society is structured through an objectification in which relationships and obligations are perceived in relation to cattle.

Lefort uses the example of the Nuer to thematize the question of alienation. His aim is to pose the question, from a Marxist point of view, of whether it makes sense to call this society alienated; whether an alienation of the Nuer is recognizable which, by making the cattle their reality, deprives members of that society of the consciousness of their own existence. From the picture drawn by Evans-Pritchard there clearly emerges a form of objectification of social relations, which are perceived and justified through the mediation of cattle. Lefort, however, asserts that only the gaze of the foreigner situated outside Nuer society, that is, a comprehensive and absolute gaze, could distinguish between a "real" and an "imaginary" dimension and define the interest in cattle as an obsession. Instead, the very factors that such a gaze would relegate to the sphere of the imagination from an internal perspective appear to be the most real, as they provide the people with a "permanent frame of reference" (Lefort 1978a, p. 98). Lefort in fact argues that there is no basis for claiming that the mediating role of the Nuer's animals hides or distorts prior human relations, simply because, from an endogenous perspective, there are no relations that prescind or predate this mediation.[22] In other words, the meaning of cattle in Nuer society can only be grasped by understanding how these animals represent what we have called a "total social fact". The cow calls into question the background of meaning within which society understands itself and to which all socializing activities refer. Social relations are therefore not hidden by the objectification of this animal but rather are simultaneously expressed by it and constructed with it. They are the same thing. Nuer society, Lefort concludes, is exactly what it appears to be: its appearance is its reality. Cattle, exactly like commodities in Marxist theory, are the form and medium through which social relations acquire form and meaning. In this sense, cows are just as socializing

---

[22] It may be interesting to point out how Castoriadis (2019, pp. 133–140) criticizes Lefort's text, accusing him of cultural relativism.

as living labor and are part of the unique web that constitutes society (97–98). Within this framework there is no room for any fetishism.[23]

> There is no justification for considering our present-day social existence as a single image detached from the background of a possible human society. In other words, all activities are socializing, part of a single drama, and they produce or reproduce to varying degrees the overall composition: that is why the social *is* the real. (97)

This passage is important. In the texts analyzed in the previous section, Lefort (1978a, pp. 46–77) had presented the idea that the social must be understood as a totality, and that the material base (production) and social representations act on each other in a mutual implication that excludes the simple causal relationship. The 1955 essay takes a further step in this direction. In it the philosopher asserts not only that social representations and meanings can retroact on the material basis but he goes much further, declaring that there is nothing to reveal beneath social meanings. He asserts that the social is a totality of meaning, that it is representation or continuous self-representation, in other words that it is what emerges and continues to emerge from that political "choice" around its meaning, as had also come out in Bateson's studies of stagnant societies.

In 1955, however, Lefort's reflection is still completely internal to Marxism, and his interest is still in finding in Marx a theory that affirms itself in praxis and is conscious of its own presuppositions and critical of absolute knowledge. After analyzing Nuer society and excluding any reality beyond social meanings, the philosopher thus returns to the passages of *Capital* devoted to the theory of alienation, in which Marx asserts that men feel dominated by social relations which, in their eyes,

---

[23] The most accurate interpretation of Lefort's use of the example of Nuer society seems to me to lie precisely in the desire to capture the indissoluble interweaving of the real and the imaginary. I therefore disagree with the reading proposed by Bernard Flynn, for whom Nuer society was an example of a pre-modern society that does not embrace history and does not recognize the difference between the symbolic and the real. See Flynn (2005, pp. 87–89 and 125). It is certainly true that, as we shall see later, a characteristic of modern society is the possibility of the distinction between the symbolic and the imaginary, which would not occur to the Nuer. However, what Lefort is asserting in these pages is quite different: he does not state that only a modern society (such as the capitalist society described by Marx) can discern the difference between reality and representation, but rather that this difference is impossible. And this is precisely the case for a modern observer like Lefort.

take the form of relations between objects. Such a statement, Lefort argues, involves no alienation or fetishism. It merely informs us of the way that men recognize themselves through the mediation of commodities. There is no mystification and no mask: the abstraction of commodities, as well as the abstract form of labor, reproduces a social relation that has equal status as a form of reality. Commodities are simply the result and the expression of relations of production, of their mediation and the mode through which social relations are structured (98–112). There is no reality beneath the capitalist system, and indeed even in Marx's work capitalism is the "real" form through which the "reality" of human relations is structured. Alienation is to be found elsewhere, namely in the clash between universal social meanings and the particular experience of the proletariat and its consequent failure to socialize—that is, in being integrated into capitalist society:

> From this perspective, one cannot speak of a society alienated in technology, money or something else, or of an alienated man, as if it were possible for the essence of man or society to become other than what it is. Alienation is not a state: it is the process in which activities fragment into so many independent spheres, just as they all subordinate themselves to the same productive scheme. (108)

However, following his abandonment of SouB and of Marxism, Lefort felt free to make the terms of his theory more explicit and to move further away from Marx, despite the fact that the latter, far from being abandoned, continued to be his main interlocutor. Two articles devoted to the question of ideology, "La naissance de l'idéologie et l'humanisme", published in 1973 (Lefort 1978a, pp. 401–477), and "Esquisse d'une *genèse de l'idéologie* dans les sociétés modernes", published the following year (Lefort 1986, pp. 181–236), offer an interesting vantage point for assessing the progression of Lefort's theory. These texts are in fact a kind of summary of the Parisian philosopher's long relationship with Marx, centered on the reality-illusion dichotomy. They make explicit certain themes and critical points that, while already present in the 1950s, Lefort made more consistent with the Marxist theoretical framework.

The starting point is once again the *Critique of Hegel's Philosophy of Right* (Marx 1970), the very work in which Marx, seeking to dismantle the "madness" of the Hegelian philosophical system, becomes aware of the phenomenon of ideology. Marx's critique is well known: he accuses the Hegelian system of turning contingent historical phenomena into universal truths. Hegel, by seeking to account for reality through the development of Spirit, turns reality upside down. He disguises the origins of his thought through the illusion of transforming historical institutions into stages in the unfolding of Spirit. As he did in the 1950s, in the two essays of the early 1970s Lefort reiterates the importance of the *Critique* to his own denunciation of any knowledge that, by closing in on itself, conceals its own origin behind praxis. The French philosopher then argues that this work sets out a principle of interpretation that is maintained throughout Marx's work all the way up to *Capital*, namely that of identifying the mechanism of representation, which is initially restricted to the limits of philosophical, political, and religious discourse, in the corresponding institutional level. Marx discovers a mechanism of concealment at the heart of the state: bourgeois institutions that support an illusion that can be used to conceal the division of society and the contingency of power. Political discourse, like philosophical discourse, presents itself as universal and rational, thus masking the conditions of its own origin. Ideology is thus defined as a threefold denial: of the opposition between classes, of temporal contingency, and of the separation between knowledge and practice. Lefort thus discerns in Marx's analysis the rejection of all overhanging thinking. Through his critique of Hegel, Marx binds theory to praxis, to its contingency, and affirms the illusory nature of any attempt to overcome the division between thought and being, of any conquest of totality. In this way, as he had done nearly two decades earlier, the Parisian philosopher emphasizes the possibility of reading into Marx's texts an awareness of the mutual co-implication between thought and the real (Lefort 1978a, pp. 433–446).

However, the difficulties of this perspective, which remained in the background in the interventions of the 1950s, in the work of the 1970s are discussed openly. The difficulty of Marx's reasoning, Lefort now admits, emerges precisely in relation to the definition of the real: his positivist conception of reality stands in the way of a phenomenological reading:

> If this is the path that Marx seems to open up, there can be no doubt that he also closes it off. Indeed, he could not follow this path while claiming, at the same time, to determine the nature of the social by means of the positive sciences, thus succumbing to the fiction of an intrinsic development accessible to the observer, and while reasoning in terms of

a crude opposition between *production* and *representation*. (Lefort 1986, pp. 192–193)

The author of *Capital* impedes the path he opened by choosing to invest in the positive sciences with the certainty of which he had deprived Hegelian philosophy. Henceforth, his reasoning can be constructed only by insisting on the distinction between production and representation, and the productive structure thus becomes the basis from which every other order of the social can be deduced. Likewise, he reduces the language through which social practice is articulated to the effects of the division between capital and labor. The network of meanings that structures society is for him nothing more than the direct consequence of economic relations. Ideology merely becomes a means to conceal objective economic and material reality. The extension of the definition of production, which Marx uses to state that man produces both the means of production and social relations, the same definition to which Lefort himself had "clung on" in the 1950s, does not solve the problem. In fact, Marx continues to think of production as the mute background of reality, linked to the dimension of representation by a cause-and-effect relationship.

The French philosopher identifies several points in Marx's voluminous work that he believes make clear this approach. The best example can be found in *The German Ideology*, where sexual division is placed at the foundation of the division of labor (194). The same approach emerges in *Capital*, where the origins of industrial capitalism are traced back to the widespread adoption of trade and the progressive establishment of the market. According to Lefort, these examples demonstrate how Marx failed to understand that production is always embedded in a pre-existing network of meanings that allows it to exist in the eyes of society and therefore cannot be considered the cause of any particular social form. The naked violence of the powerful that Marx finds at the origin of capitalist accumulation and which he calls the "original sin" of capitalism,

> was also the original sin of his theory, for the violence which "gave birth" to the new mode of production was not silent. It was sustained by a representation of cause and effect, whose articulation was meaningless in other social conditions; it was inscribed in a discourse which could find the criterion of its coherence within its own limits, and which could become the basis for an articulation of the law and the real. (186)

The positivist method led Marx to underestimate the ideological dimension of the social. His thought is constructed on the basis of the production-representation dichotomy, in parallel to the reality-illusion dichotomy. The economic structure and division of labor are the only dimensions of social life to which he confers the status of reality. Anything beyond these, including religion, beliefs, customs, theory, and politics, is merely an incidental derivation or else an illusion. In short, Marx went in search of the reality underneath society and failed to understand how the social is already the real, that there is no reality to be reached beyond social meanings. In other words, he did not understand what Lefort was eventually "freely" able to call the *symbolic dimension of the social*.[24]

> At this point, what seems to me to define the limits of Marx's thought is the fact that he treats the process of representation as if it were produced by the activities of co-operation and division, as if this reality were determined at the natural level of labour. Thus he could not avoid the risk of confusing the order of the ideological with the order of the symbolic, of reducing mythological, religious, political, legal and other discourses to the projection of 'real' conflicts into the imaginary, of demoting the indices of law and power to the empirical level, thereby transforming them into social "products". (195)[25]

This is not all. Through the distinction between production and representation, the positivist method used by Marx betrays the critical axioms of his thought and succumbs to the temptation of absolute knowledge, of the *pensée de surplomb*. By deciding to describe production in its materiality, he hides the fact that his description cannot immediately correspond to the reality of production. That is, he conceals the separation between "reality" and the discourse that names it, as well as the fact that the two dimensions are already inexorably intertwined (Lefort 1978a, pp. 429–435).

The point that, in the 1950s, Lefort had considered one of the most interesting elements of Marx's discourse and of the idea of praxis—a theory conscious of its own presuppositions, of being in alienation—now

---

[24] It is not possible here to analyze therelationship between Lefort's and Castoriadis's works. It is sufficient to highlight how Lefort's critique of Marxism has remarkable similarities with that proposed by Castoriadis in SouB years and later in his major work (Castoriadis 1987).

[25] See also pp. 185–186 and Lefort (1978a, pp. 235–236).

comes under challenge. Marx's positivism develops an idea that claims to reach down to the essence, placing itself outside of all alienation, all representation. It is a thought that believes it has seen the social "as it really is", in its fullness, and thus deludes itself into thinking that it is a discourse in which the social analyzes itself, without outside mediation.

Lefort then compares the positivism of Marx and of Marxism to the lessons he learned from phenomenology and anthropology, from Merleau-Ponty and Mauss, and from Kardiner, Bateson, and Evans-Pritchard. As Mauss and Kardiner had shown, the division between production and representation, and their subsequent connection through causation, disguises the continuous co-implication of the various elements of the social within its totality of meaning. Social relations, Lefort argues, are structured on the basis of conditions that it is impossible to ascribe to objectivity since the real opens itself to humans only through the attribution of meanings, through representation. That is, society is structured purely from a discourse about itself that immediately separates it from nature and from any direct relationship with a supposed reality. Any economic or environmental condition is already filtered through an interpretation. Any social practice becomes real, "take[s] hold",[26] only within a discourse that refers and opposes it to others, within the framework of a universal meaning. There is no indisputable foundation, no solid ground on which society is built and by which it can be judged. At the basis of any society there is only a question of meaning, a political question.

At this point it is easy to understand why, in Lefort's scheme, one cannot reduce politics to an ideological superstructure, to a mere tool used by the ruling class to hide the real relations of production. On the contrary, the political dimension is unearthed at the core of the social. It is constitutive of the social as self-representation. The political relationship

---

[26] Lefort (1986, p. 186) states: "It is impossible, in my view, to deduce the order of law, of power or of knowledge from the relations of production; it is also impossible to reduce the language in which social practice is articulated to the effects of the labour-capital division. These relations are organized, and these effects develop, only as a function of *conditions* that we cannot situate at the level of the real; on the contrary, such conditions become accessible to us, are organized and become intelligible, only when the reference points of a new experience of law, power and knowledge are established, only when a mode of discourse is developed in which certain oppositions and certain practices actually *take hold* – that is, relate to one another and potentially contain a universal sense, in allowing for a regulated exchange between action and thought". In the original French, however, it is clear that the subjects of Lefort's sentence are not the conditions but what we call real.

par excellence, that of the social with itself, is not an illusory dimension but the shape of the institution of the social.

The Symbolic and the Political

During the 1950s and 1960s Lefort's theoretical work is an interlacing combination of Marxism, ethnology, and phenomenology from which emerges the peculiar vision of the social presented in the preceding pages. At its core one can find the notion of the symbolic, which, although already used in these years, would gradually become more explicit and important. While his critique of Marxism in the 1960s centered on this notion, his later analyses of modernity, democracy, and totalitarianism would also be built on it (Lefort 1979, pp. 7–28). It is therefore a pivotal notion in the work of the French philosopher, but one which it is nevertheless by no means easy to define and which he himself never made explicit.[27]

However, if we wish to clarify this concept—leaving aside for the moment references to the work of Jacques Lacan—the first step is once again to turn to anthropology.[28] Indeed, as I have shown, through his reading of Marcel Mauss Lefort understood that society is a totality, a sum of several elements all in pursuit of the same end. This means first of all that it is not possible to ascribe a single cause to the social, that there is no fundamental dimension underlying all others. Everything cooperates in a general sense in which the various dimensions—the political, the economic, the religious, the artistic, the legal, and so on—participate. Relations between individuals and other societies and institutions, and even the relationship with history, change, conflict, and time are considered as a totality. There is no silent dimension, no foundation, whether natural, historical, or economic, in which the cause of social meanings can be found because every dimension is always included in this totality from the beginning. It is already related to meanings and can never be drawn

---

[27] On Lefort's use of the symbolic see: Lanza (2021). Several interpreters, such as Poltier (1998) or Breckman (2013), agree on the indefiniteness of Lefort's concept of the symbolic.

[28] It is not possible here to outline a history, however brief, of the symbolic in anthropological studies. One thinks of structuralism, Lévi-Strauss, but also Clifford Geerz and Victor Turner. For a further discussion see Tarot (1999). Breckman (2013) proposes the idea of a "symbolic" turn that would characterize French theory in the second half of the twentieth century.

3 THE SYMBOLIC DIMENSION OF THE SOCIAL   75

upon in itself. As Lefort wrote in 1955, "the social is the real", in other words there is no other reality underneath social relations and meanings on which to draw. Lefort thus uses the term "symbolic" first and foremost to identify this totality of elements that imply one another, this network of meanings that structure the social sphere and which in the 1952 text he had called "culturing culture" (Lefort 1978a, p. 55).

In later years he deepened this reflection by finding precisely this same general sense underpinning any given ordering of the social. By reading first Bateson and then Clastres, Lefort came to understand how the symbolic dimension determines the conception of conflict, of institutions, of change. There is thus a kind of "choice" at the "origin" of the ways in which a given society relates to history, internal division, and power.[29] This "political question", that is, the overall symbolic dimension, thus acquires the features of a self-representation of society that is continually repeated in all the spheres that constitute it and through which it is structured, including ideologies, personal relationships, institutions, conflicts, and religion.

This symbolic background is therefore the key to understanding the meaning of a society, of reaching, in a phenomenological sense, its essence. This is why, according to Lefort, one should not analyze societies by means of the positive sciences and by considering them simply as regimes. One should understand them as "forms": particular *mise en sense*, *mise en forme* and *mise en scene* of a symbolic dimension (Lefort 1988, pp. 11–12).[30] They are the structuring of a meaning.

It is therefore here that we find the reason for the distinction between politics (*la politique*) and the political (*le politique*) that Lefort explicitly proposed in the 1970s.[31] Politics is the specific activity exercised on a daily basis within institutions, by parties, in parliaments but also outside of them by specific individuals who are more or less formally in charge.

---

[29] These terms, choice and origin, are clearly problematic. Indeed, in Lefort's thought, in this instance choice or origin is nothing more than interpretations or representations of real choice or origin.

[30] The use of the formulas *mise en forme*, *mise en sens*, and *mise en scène*, which make up the triad of the "construction" of the social, owes a debt to Piera Aulagnier, a Lacanian psychoanalyst and Castoriadis' wife from 1968 to 1984.

[31] See Lefort and Gauchet (1971). This distinction has been widely accepted and has been taken up by many scholars. See, for example: Rosanvallon (2003) or Marchart (2007).

The political (*le politique*), on the other hand, is the name for the question of meaning, the choice, the symbolic dimension that lies at the bottom of a given configuration of the social. More specifically, as I will show more clearly below, *le politique* is the name of a symbolic dimension. It is the term by which Lefort indicates the fact that society, in order to *establish itself*, must relate to otherness, to a division.[32]

To claim that society is constructed through self-representation, however, does not mean reversing the causal relationship between structure and superstructure. It would be a mistake to interpret the Lefortian symbolic in terms of an autonomous cultural or discursive dimension that retroacts on the material level. Nor can this be grasped in terms of a formal a priori, of a level separate from materiality that proceeds through its own laws and that can therefore be studied and understood, and its development predicted. For Lefort, in fact, the social cannot be reduced to the discursive. It is not akin to the politics thought of by Hannah Arendt. It is "flesh", a dense and chiasmatic fabric in which there are no autonomous spheres. It is "praxis", a dimension that mutually binds every sphere of the social, that connects consciousness and history, action and theory, and in which discourse is also embedded. For the same reason, the symbolic is not a separate dimension but is the thing that shapes the social, the matrix of its self-representation that always depends on the "experience" of the social itself. In other words, the symbolic is not an attempt to award the superstructural plane some kind of precedence, but is the tool with which to overcome the dichotomy between structure and superstructure, between the subjective and the objective, between production and representation (Lefort and Gauchet 1971, p. 13).

As I will show in the sixth chapter, here then lies the meaning of the critique that Lefort directed toward structuralism on several occasions. Structuralism considers symbolic order as a universal, objective, mathematizable, content-independent structure that has its laws, and as something to which the order of lived experience conforms (Lefort 2007,

---

[32] Lefort (1988, p. 11) states: "The political is thus revealed, not in what we call political activity, but in the double movement whereby the mode of institution of society appears and is obscured. It appears in the sense that the process whereby society is ordered and unified across its divisions becomes visible. It is obscured in the sense that the locus of politics (the locus in which parties compete and in which a general agency of power takes shape and is reproduced) becomes defined as particular, while the principle which generates the overall configuration is concealed".

pp. 275–300; Lévi-Strauss 1969).[33] Lefort's symbolic is an alternative to this analysis, one which rejects objective knowledge and the possibility of grasping the pure logic of a structure regardless of its content. In such a framework, the symbolic is merely the name of the social whole, of the inextricable interweaving of praxis and meanings that eludes the agents themselves but, at the same time, is not autonomous from them. The autonomy of the symbolic sphere is beyond question: it encompasses all elements of the social and is dependent on them. The symbolic is therefore not a fixed and universal structure to which relationships, institutions, and the various dimensions of which a society is constituted adhere. It does not respond to objective laws; it cannot be analyzed through the cause-effect nexus. There is always a chiasmatic relationship between the social and its symbolic representation that makes any causal relationship, any objective knowledge, illusory. It is an unattainable dimension which, while depending directly on the experience and actions of men and being modified by them, is never completely in their hands. It is neither a transcendental and fixed structure that governs human vicissitudes, nor a completely immanent one that men can shape as they wish. The symbolic, we might say, is quasi-transcendent. This is what Lefort himself means when, in one of the rare attempts to define this term during a debate with François Roustang at a conference held in Paris at the Collège de Psychanalystes on October 3, 1982, he states:

> When we speak of symbolic organization, of symbolic constitution, we seek to look beyond practices, beyond relations, beyond the institutions that appear to be established facts, natural or historical, beyond a set of articulations which cannot be inferred from nature or history, but which command the attention of what presents itself as real. While classical philosophy operated by distinguishing between ideas and the perceptible world, and while modern philosophy distinguished between the transcendental conditions of the experience and the phenomenal reality, we try to see them as a layering of organizing schemes that are not beyond time, that do not point towards a pure a priori [...], and which also do not exist within time [...]. (Lefort and Roustang 1983, p. 42)

Beyond ethnology we glimpse here the phenomenological method of Lefort's reasoning and once more the shadow of Maurice Merleau-Ponty

---

[33] On the relationship between Lefort and structuralism see Chapter 6.

in particular. The latter, after all, through the works of Mauss, Lévi-Strauss and even Saussure's theory of language, had taken an interest in the concept of the symbolic on several occasions, to the point of making it part of his own work. He had used this term to overcome the dichotomy between the objective and the subjective in the analysis of history and society, to define a sense that "is neither thing nor an idea" (Merleau-Ponty 1988, p. 56), the inextricable interplay of logic and contingency, of sense and consciousness. Indeed, in his inaugural lecture delivered at the Collège de France in January 1953, he argued that historical forms and processes, classes and epochs, relations and institutions, culture and ideas exist "in a social, cultural or symbolic space which is no less real than physical space" (56). He continues:

> For meaning lies latent not only in language, in political and religious institutions, but in modes of kinship, in machines, in the landscape, in production, and, in general, in all the modes of human commerce. An interconnection among all these phenomena is possible, since they are all symbolisms, and perhaps even the translation of one symbolism into another is possible. (56)

With a certain analogy to the path taken by Lefort that I have presented thus far, the reasoning that leads Merleau-Ponty to make these statements is laid out a few pages earlier when he attempts to clarify the meaning of Marx's praxis and to distance Marx from mechanistic and positivistic interpretations. Thus Merleau-Ponty also uses the term "symbolic" to define society as a structure of meanings that, following Saussure's teachings on language and discourse, is comprehensible only in its totality and in the interweaving of all its constituent elements. The symbolic is what holds sense and consciousness, history and change together in an oblique relationship that we have defined as one of quasi-transcendence. A little further on, specifically to offer a better definition of this particular relationship, Merleau-Ponty uses a term that will prove central to Lefort's thought: "institution" (55–56).

The Symbolic Institution of the Social

"Institution" is the term that Merleau-Ponty uses to translate the word *Stiftung*, which was originally used by Edmund Husserl in *Cartesian Meditations* and *Krisis* (Husserl 1960, 1970). Husserl employed variations of this concept in different contexts, but without providing a precise and unambiguous definition of it. With the word *Urstiftung*, which can be translated as "primal establishment", he first of all indicated the operation through which intentional consciousness first establishes a certain objective sense that later becomes a stable acquisition and persists in the course of experience.[34] In this context he used the term in order to highlight the essential conditions for the genesis of subjective experience, or consciousness. However, the "subject" which Husserl concerns himself with in his analysis is not a static pole corresponding to its acts but a continuous sedimentation of meanings that retroact on the original assumptions and become new stable properties. Consequently, the acquisition of fixed, enduring categories through which the self interprets the world simultaneously modifies the self. In this context, the *Urstiftung*, while remaining a permanent unit, is continuously transformed and corrected by the intervention of successive dimensions of meaning.

This first example allows us to begin to delineate the meaning of *Stiftung*. This is located in the relationship through which any given meaning is referred back to a primal establishment (*Urstiftung*), the results of which settle into a reestablishment (*Nachstiftung*). This, in turn, reactivates and revives the meaning of the primal establishment within a final establishment (*Endstiftung*), which is a teleological point toward which all formations of meaning are oriented. The *Stiftung* thus refers to an enduring dimension that is at the same time a horizon of possible modifications that arose from an original establishment continuously repeated and modified.

This concept is investigated in greater depth in *The Crisis of the European Sciences*. In this text the "genetic program" is extended beyond the limits of the experience of intentional consciousness into the overall horizon of experiential life and especially into history. The *Stiftung* can

---

[34] The term *Stiftung* has been translated in different ways. Merleau-Ponty (1964a) himself initially uses the words *fondation* or *établissement*, as does Derrida (1982).

then be referred to "all spiritual structures which are to be unconditionally and generally capable of being handed down" (Husserl 1970, p. 377). Husserl's intent remains that of understanding how a meaning can be established and then maintained in the face of change, as subjectivities and time themselves change. Particularly relevant is the work's third appendix (353–378). This is devoted to the origin of geometry, or specifically to the way that geometry first appeared in history, its "original meaning" and "beginnings", or in other words the understanding of the enduring meaning of geometry beyond its significance in specific times and isolated consciousnesses, beyond the spiritual acts of individual mathematicians (354–355). In these pages, the *Stiftung* increasingly comes to identify a "tradition", or the correlation between a contingent event (*Urstiftung*) and the enduring dimension disclosed by it, the horizon of meaning that delimits and determines possible subsequent modifications (354 or 370–374). Birth and duration thus emerge as two extremes whose mutual tension establishes the concept's horizon of meaning.

The dense pages of the third appendix of *Krisis* captured Merleau-Ponty's attention, beginning in the early 1950s. While the 1952 essay "Le langage indirect et les voix du silence" (Merleau-Ponty 1964a, pp. 39–83) already demonstrates the philosopher's attention to Husserl's concept of *Stiftung*, he addressed the topic explicitly in particular in a course he taught at the Collège de France between 1954 and 1955, which was also when he translated the term with the word *institution*. The French phenomenologist states that the term refers to

> those events in an experience which endow the experience with durable dimensions, in relation to which a whole series of other experiences will make sense, will form a thinkable sequel or a history—or again the events which deposit a sense in me, not just as something surviving or as a residue, but as the call to follow, the demand of a future. (Merleau-Ponty 2010, p. 77)

Through this definition Merleau-Ponty interprets Husserl's concept by extending its use to the entire field of experience: to the functioning of the physical organism, to man's animality, to his psychic life, and even to the cultural and historical spheres. The hermeneutic circle composed of the continuous cross-references between *Urstiftung*, *Nachtstiftune*, and *Endstiftung* is recovered by the French phenomenologist, for whom every redefinition of meaning is at the same time a reinstitution of the origin, a deviation from the origin, a new institution and a continuation in a direction teleologically established by the institution itself.

As with Husserl, for Merleau-Ponty this concept is of decisive use in accounting for the intertwining of change and permanence, or in other words historical becoming. Against all relativism and rationalism, the institution indicates that it is possible to conceive of a common time beyond the differences between various forms of human coexistence and beyond changes between historical eras.[35] It is a terrain that cannot be reduced to its individual manifestations but which at the same time does not exist except in individual elements, in the historical events that reproduce and determine its contours.

Merleau-Ponty's debt to the father of phenomenology is clear, but his interpretation is evidently also slightly different, as he uses precisely the concept of institution to overcome some of the difficulties inherent in the philosophy of consciousness proposed by Husserl. In particular, he wants to heal the division that separates both objects and consciousness, and consciousness from other forms of consciousness. Thus while for Husserl the search for the enduring dimension of meaning remained linked to individual consciousness and its spiritual acts, for Merleau-Ponty the concept of *institution* refers to a pre-subjective and supra-individual event. It is the establishment of a sense that is anterior to and irreducible to the operations of consciousness, and one that is therefore rather fruitful.[36] The dynamic of the institution unites sense and consciousness, logic and contingency: although it is continually nourished by the experiences of individual consciousnesses, it cannot be reduced to them. The affinity between this and the reflection on the symbolic is clear. It is no coincidence that Merleau-Ponty is able to speak of the institution in

---

[35] Merleau-Ponty's polemical target, beyond the rationalism of philosophical theories, is in this case the excessive relativism of Claude Lévi-Strauss's structuralism. The latter's thought, precisely through its radical relativism and a scientific conception that equates truth with a physical law, stood in the illusory position of the absolute observer who thinks himself outside of society itself. See Merleau-Ponty (2010, pp. 61–75) and Lefort's foreword (pp. IX–XXXI) now also in Lefort (2021, pp. 343–368).

[36] Here there is the meaning of the opposition between institution and constitution. Merleau-Ponty (2010, p. 8) states: "constitute in this sense is nearly the opposite of to institute: the instituted makes sense without me, the constituted makes sense only for me and for the 'me' of this instant. Constitution [means] continuous institution, i.e., never done. The instituted straddles its future, has its future, its temporality, the constituted depends entirely on the 'me' who constitutes (the body, the clock)".

terms of a symbolic matrix that cannot be traced to any individual act and which makes possible the opening of a course, of a future according to common references. Or, put another way, as a "symbolic system that the subject takes over and incorporates as a style of functioning, as a global configuration, without having any need it at all" (Merleau-Ponty 1988, p. 56).

As a contingency that establishes a horizon of meaning, an event that unveils a new dimension beyond itself, the institution connects the transcendental and the empirical in a "chiasma" that does not permit any clear separations or pure elements. *Stiftung*, we might therefore assert, is for Merleau-Ponty the name of a certain mode in which the interweaving of being acquires an enduring meaning. The *résumé* of the course given at the Collège therefore concludes in the direction of

> a revision of Hegelianism, which is the discovery of phenomenology, of the living, real, and original relation between the elements of the world. But Hegelianism situates this relation in the past in order to subordinate it to the systematic vision of the philosopher. Either phenomenology is only an introduction to true knowledge, which remains estranged from the adventures of experience, or phenomenology dwells entirely within philosophy. Phenomenology cannot conclude with the pre-dialectical formula that "Being is," and it has to take into account the mediation of being. It is this development of phenomenology into the metaphysics of history that we wished to prepare here. (Merleau-Ponty 2010, p. 79)

These words make clear the close relationship between Merleau-Ponty's reasoning on the *Stiftung* and the broader framework of his phenomenology. The concept of institution integrates with the attempt—already set out in *Phenomenology of Perception* (Merleau-Ponty 2012)—to overcome the objective-subjective, sense-consciousness bipolarity through situated thinking, and with the ontology elaborated in his later writings, which considers being in terms of an interweaving of all dimensions of the real, of sense, of experience, of the visible and the invisible. Just as occurs with the institution, which exists only in events and yet is not reducible to them, being can be recognized only in the experience of being and, at the same time, cannot be identified within the limits of experience itself. The ontology proposed by Merleau-Ponty is thus a description of a circular movement that remains imperfect. Being is not given immediately but comes only through an experience that involves a gap, the experience of an unattainable otherness: the non-coincidence between being and the experience of being, between the visible and the invisible. It is an indirect ontology (Merleau-Ponty 1969).[37]

As I will show in the following pages, Lefort's conception of the social adheres remarkably closely to Merleau-Ponty's ontology. Moreover, the two philosophers' reflections always proceeded along parallel and repeatedly tangential paths, with the concept of institution being one of the points in which this close relationship can be observed most clearly. Again, Lefort does not openly begin to use the term *institution* to describe the symbolic structure of the social until after his abandonment of SouB and Marxism in the 1970s, and he also never makes the reference to Merleau-Ponty explicit. However, the use of the term fits coherently into a reflection whose trajectory can be observed as early as the 1950s and which appears decidedly in keeping with the work Merleau-Ponty was doing in the same period. I refer in particular to the symbolic dimension that I presented in the previous section.[38]

When, for example, in 1952 Lefort describes "culturing culture" as "the constantly repeated operation through which a society refers to itself and thereby confirms its teleology" (Lefort 1978a, p. 55), it is easy to glimpse the reference to the *Stiftung* circle and the *institution* presented the following year by Merleau-Ponty. Then again, for both authors, the social is experience. It is a dynamic symbolic dimension that crosses over and links subjects and meaning, the contingent and the necessary. The *culture culturante* to which Lefort refers is in fact a description of the dynamic of continuous self-representation or reiteration of the original sense—of the political question at its origin—and the continual renewal of this same sense that establishes the social. In short, in phenomenological terms for Lefort the social is the reiteration of the *Urstiftung* through contingent events that recover and rework its meaning within a teleology. If he uses the term "symbolic institution of the social", it is therefore—in a direct reference to Merleau-Ponty— to attempt to describe how society is structured as a totality through a

---

[37] On Merleau-Ponty's ontology see Morris (2018), Morris and Maclaren (2015), de Saint Aubert (2006), Barbaras (2004), and Dillon (1988).

[38] On the relationship between Lefort and Merleau-Ponty see Poirier (2020), Di Pierro (2019, 2020), Dodeman (2019), Gerçek (2017), Mazzocchi (2013), Flynn (2008), and Labelle (2003). Lefort writes about Merleau-Ponty on several occasions, including in a number of forewords to the latter's works. See Lefort (1978b, 1990) and the works by Merleau-Ponty that he edited, Merleau-Ponty (1964b, 1968, 1969, 1973, 1980, 2010, 2022b).

symbolic dynamic of self-representation that, while contingent and linked to the events and experience of subjectivities and social actors, is at the same time a pre-subjective and supra-individual dimension. It is the continuous representation of an original political question that eludes the political actors themselves. It is a dynamic that cannot be reduced to the events that compose it and does not belong totally to the subjects who experience it. In this sense, it is the openness toward an excess of being, which is the work of society but by which work is at the same time defined. Here is why Lefort asserts that humanity, "opens on to itself by being held in an opening it does not create" (Lefort 1988, p. 223). The social, in short, always experiences itself indirectly, obliquely, by the mediation of alterity.

There is therefore a conspicuous enigma at the origin of the social:

> To say that it [the social] is doomed to the enigma of its institution [...] makes a lot of sense even if here we encounter a limit of the intelligible. It is full of meaning to the extent that we cannot understand any social formations other than our own, nor our own social formation, without grasping this enigma, because it is always this enigma that underlies the arrangement, the choice, provided that we remove from this term all that might be conscious in its determination, or let us say the fundamental decision or disposition of a society to organize itself. (Lefort 1975–1976, pp. 9–10)

References

Barbaras, Renaud. 2004. *The Being of the Phenomenon: Merleau-Ponty's Ontology*. Indianapolis: Indiana University Press.

Bateson, Gregory. 1949. The Value System of a Steady State: Ethos and Schismogenesis. In *Social Structure Studies Presented to A.R. Radcliffe-Brown*, ed. M. Fortes, 35–53. London: Oxford University Press.

Bateson, Gregory, and Mead, Margaret. 1942. *Balinese Character: A Photographic Analysis*. New York: Academy of Sciences.

Bigo, Pierre. 1954. *Marxisme et humanisme. Introduction à l'œuvre économique de Karl Marx*. Paris: Puf.

Breckman, Warren. 2012. Lefort and the Symbolic Dimension. *Constellations* 19/1: 30–36.

Breckman, Warren. 2013. *The Adventures of the Symbolic. Post-Marxism and Radical Democracy*. New York: Columbia University Press.

Castoriadis, Cornelius. 1987. *The imaginary institution of the society*. Cambridge: Polity Press.
Castoriadis, Cornelius. 2019. *Histoire et création. Textes philosophiques inédits (1945–1967)*. Paris: Seuil.
Chollet, Antoine. 2019. Claude Lefort, un intrus à Socialisme ou Barbarie? *Rue Descartes* 96: 41–53.
Clastres, Pierre. 1980. *Recherches d'anthropologie politique*. Paris: Seuil.
Clastres, Pierre. 1987. *Society Against the State: Essays in Political Anthropology*. New York: Zone Books.
Clastres, Pierre. 1998. *Chronicle of the Guayaki Indians*. New York: Zone Books.
Clastres, Pierre. 2016. *The Question of Power. An Interview with Pierre Clastres*. Los Angeles: Semiotex(e).
Derrida, Jacques. 1982. *Edmund Husserl's Origin of Geometry: An Introduction*. Lincoln: University of Nebraska Press.
de Saint Aubert, Emmanuel. 2006. *Vers une ontologie indirecte. Sources et enjeux critiques de l'appel à l'ontologie chez Merleau-Ponty*. Paris: Vrin.
Dillon, Martin. 1988. *Merleau-Ponty's Ontology*. Evanston: Northwestern University Press.
Di Pierro, Mattia. 2019. Il concetto di istituzione in Claude Lefort. *Discipline filosofiche* 19/2: 99–120.
Di Pierro, Mattia. 2020. *L'esperienza del mondo. Claude Lefort e la fenomenologia del politico*. Pisa: ETS.
Dodeman, Claire. 2019. Claude Lefort, Reader of Merleau-Ponty: From "the Proletarian Experience" to the "Flesh of the Social". *Journal of the CIPH* 96/2: 108–116.
Dosse, François. 1998. *History of Structuralism*. 2 vol. Minneapolis: Minnesota University Press.
Dosse, François. 2014. *Castoriadis: une vie*. Paris: La Découverte.
Dosse, François. 2018. *La saga des intellectuels français 1944–1989. I. À L'Epreuve de l'histoire 1944–1968*. Paris: Gallimard.
Evans-Pritchard, Edward E. 1968. *The Nuer: A Description of the Modes of Livelihood and Political Institutions of a Nilotic People*. Oxford: Clarendon.
Flynn, Bernard. 2005. *The Philosophy of Claude Lefort: Interpreting the Political*. Evanston: Northwestern University Press.
Flynn, Bernard. 2008. Lefort in the Wake of Merleau-Ponty. *Chiasmi International* 10: 251–262.
Gerçek, Salih Emre. 2017. From Body to Flesh: Lefort, Merleau-Ponty and Democratic Indeterminacy. *European Journal of Political Theory* 19/4: 1–22.
Geroulanos, Stefanos. 2017. *Transparency in Postwar France: A Critical History of the Present*. Redwood City: Stanford University Press.
Hartog, François. 2016. *Regimes of Historicity: Presentism and Experiences of Time*. New York: Columbia University Press.

Herskovitz, Melville J. 1940. *The Economic Life of Primitive People*. New York: Knopf.
Husserl, Edmund. 1960. *Cartesian Meditations: An Introduction to Phenomenology*. The Hague: Martinus Nijhof.
Husserl, Edmund. 1970. *The Crisis of European Sciences and Transcendental Phenomenology*. Evanston: Northwestern University Press.
Hyppolite, Jean. 1955. *Études sur Marx et Hegel*. Paris: Rivière.
Hyppolite, Jean. 1979. *Genesis and Structure of Hegel's "Phenomenology of Spirit"*. Evanston: Northwestern University Press.
Jay, Martin. 1986. *Marxism and Totality: The Adventures of a Concept from Lukács to Habermas*. Berkeley: University of California Press.
Kardiner, Abram. 1939. *The Individual and His Society*. New York: Columbia University Press.
Labelle, Gilles. 2003. Maurice Merleau-Ponty et la genèse de la philosophie politique de Claude Lefort. *Politique et Sociétés* 22/3: 9–44.
Labelle, Gilles. 2015. Parcours de Claude Lefort: de l'«expérience prolétarienne» de l'«aliénation» à la critique du marxisme. *Politique et Sociétés* 34/1: 17–36.
Landshut, and Mayer. 1935. Introduction. In *Œuvres philosophiques*, ed. K. Marx. vol. IV. Paris: Costes.
Lanza, Andrea. 2021. Looking for a Sociology Worthy of Its Name: Claude Lefort and His Conception of Social Division. *Thesis Eleven* 166/1: 70–87.
Lefort, Claude. 1975–1976. La genèse de l'État moderne et l'institution du social. Cours 1975–1976. In *Archives Claude Lefort*, EHESS-CESPRA, CL. 8, boîte 3: 9–10.
Lefort, Claude. 1978a. *Les formes de l'histoire. Essais d'anthropologie politique*. Paris: Gallimard.
Lefort, Claude. 1978b. *Sur une colonne absente. Écrits autour de Merleau-Ponty*. Paris: Gallimard.
Lefort, Claude. 1979. *Éléments d'une critique de la bureaucratie*. 2nd edition. Paris: Gallimard.
Lefort, Claude. 1986. *The Political Forms of Modern Society: Bureaucracy, Democracy, Totalitarianism*. Cambridge: MIT Press.
Lefort, Claude. 1988. *Democracy and Political Theory*. Cambridge: Polity Press.
Lefort, Claude. 1990. Flesh and Otherness. In *Ontology and Alterity in Merleau-Ponty*, ed. G.A. Johnson and M.B. Smith, 3–13. Evanston: Northwestern University Press.
Lefort, Claude. 2000. *Writing: The Political Test*. Durham and London: Duke University Press.
Lefort, Claude. 2007. *Le temps présent. Écrits 1945-2005*. Paris: Belin.
Lefort, Claude. 2021. *Lectures politiques. De Dante à Soljenitsyne*. Paris: Puf.
Lefort, Claude, and Gauchet, Marcel. 1971. Sur la démocratie: le politique et l'institution du social. *Textures* 2/3: 7–78.

Lefort, Claude, and Roustang, François. 1983. Le mythe de l'Un dans le fantasme et dans la réalité politique. *Psychanalystes* 9: 3–70.
Lévi-Strauss, Claude. 1969. *The Elementary Structures of Kinship*. Boston: Beacon.
Lichteim, George. 1966. *Marxism in Modern France*. New York: Columbia University Press.
Lowie, Robert. 1949. *Social Organisation*. New York: Rinehart and Co.
Marchart, Oliver. 2007. *Post-Foundational Political Thought: Political Difference in Nancy, Lefort, Badiou and Laclau*. Edinburgh: Edinburgh University Press.
Marx, Karl. 1923. Nationalökonomie und Philosophie. Über den Zusammenhang der Nationalökonomie mit Staat, Recht, Moral, und bürgerlichem Leben (1844). In *Der historische Materialismus*, ed. K. Marx, 283–375. Leipzig: Die Frühschriften, Kröner.
Marx, Karl. 1970. *Critique of Hegel's Philosophy of Right*. Cambridge: Cambridge University Press.
Marx, Karl. 1976. *Capital: A Critique of Political Economy*. London: Penguin.
Mauss, Marcel. 2002. *The Gift: The Form and Reason for Exchange in Archaic Societies*. London: Routledge.
Mazzocchi, Paul. 2013. Fleshing Out the Political: Merleau-Ponty, Lefort and the Problem of Alterity. *Critical Horizons* 14/1: 22–43.
Merleau-Ponty, Maurice. 1964a. *Signs*. Evanston: Northwestern University Press.
Merleau-Ponty, Maurice. 1964b. *L'Œil et l'Esprit*. Paris: Gallimard.
Merleau-Ponty, Maurice. 1968. *Résumés de cours. Collège de France, 1952–1960*. Paris: Gallimard.
Merleau-Ponty, Maurice. 1969. *The Visible and the Invisible*. Evanston: Northwestern University Press.
Merleau-Ponty, Maurice. 1973. *The Prose of the World*. Evanston: Northwestern University Press.
Merleau-Ponty, Maurice. 1980. *Humanisme et terreur. Essai sur le problème communiste*. Paris: Gallimard.
Merleau-Ponty, Maurice. 1988. *In Praise of Philosophy and Other Essays*. Evanston: Northwestern University Press.
Merleau-Ponty, Maurice. 2010. *Institution and Passivity: Course Notes from the Collège de France (1954–1955)*. Evanston: Northwestern University Press.
Merleau-Ponty, Maurice. 2012. *Phenomenology of Perception*. London: Routledge.
Merleau-Ponty, Maurice. 2022a. *Humanism and Terror*. London: Routledge.
Merleau-Ponty, Maurice. 2022b. *The Possibility of Philosophy: Course Notes from the Collège de France, 1959-1961*. Evanston: Northwestern University Press.
Morris, David. 2018. *Merleau-Ponty's Developmental Ontology*. Evanston: Northwestern University Press.
Morris, David and Maclaren, Kym (ed.). 2015. *Time, Memory, Institution: Merleau-Ponty's New Ontology of Self*. Athens: Ohio University Press.

Moyn, Samuel. 2004. Of Savagery and Civil Society: Pierre Clastres and the Transformation of French Political Thought. *Modern Intellectual History* 1/1: 55–80.

Moyn, Samuel. 2013. Claude Lefort, Political Anthropology, and Symbolic Division. In *Claude Lefort: Thinker of the Political*, ed. M. Plot, 51–70. New York: Palgrave Macmillan.

Poirier, Nicolas. 2020. *Introduction à Claude Lefort*. Paris: La Découverte.

Poltier, Hugues. 1998. *Passion du politique. La pensée de Claude Lefort*. Genève: Labor et Fides.

Pompeo Faracovi, Ornella. 1972. *Il marxismo francese contemporaneo fra dialettica e struttura*. Milano: Feltrinelli.

Rosanvallon, Pierre. 2003. *Pour une histoire conceptuelle du politique*. Paris: Seuil.

Sahlins, Marshall. 1985. *Island of History*. Chicago: University of Chicago Press.

Tarot, Camille. 1999. *De Durkheim à Mauss, l'invention du symbolique*. Paris: La Découverte/MAUSS.

Viveiros de Castro, Eduardo. 2019. *Politique des multiplicités. Pierre Clastres face à l'État*. Bellevaux: Éditions Dehors.

CHAPTER 4

A Sociology of a Divided Society: Alienation, Ideology and a Project for a Study of Democracy

Alienation, or a Sociology of the Division of the Social

According to Lefort, the inevitable starting point of all thought, and of all political inquiry and struggle, is the need to "face society as it is" (Lefort 1979, p. 320). This formula, in addition to renouncing all forms of utopianism in favor of an analysis that starts from the "fact" of the social, from the idea that "the social is the real", also implies a rejection of any total knowledge supposedly capable of distinguishing between the reality and the appearance of social relations. It also repudiates any normative ideal. In other words, "dealing with society as it is" is a prescription for realism without reality, for a way of thinking that is conscious of the mutual relationship between the observer and the observed and of the impossibility of any absolute foundation. It is an approach that sums up the awareness that the contradictions of society are not problems requiring solutions but the means through which the social itself is constituted.

But once we recognize the symbolic dimension of the social, once we learn that the social *is* the real, is critique still possible? Once thought, which is embedded in the very contradictions of the real, rejects all normative dimensions, what space is left for any idea of emancipation? For Lefort, the answer is clear: a critical theory based on the image of a community liberated from its contradictions does not imply the passive acceptance of the status quo. Assuming that it is necessary to confront society as it really is does not necessarily mean that

> one must accept the economic and social system in which we live or the institutions as they are, or give our allegiance to existing forms of power. It only means that one must accept that what happens in history fundamentally affects our destiny. It means agreeing to see the present as something other than an evil, deciding to decipher it to understand the meaning of our undertakings and thus find the conditions of our thought and action, and, while becoming sensitive to the existence of exploitation and the need to denounce it, remaining conscious that we are still speaking from within the present society and that we must extrapolate the truth from within it, rather than escaping into the myth of the good past [...] or into that of a future socialism. (320–321)

In short, instead of dreaming up new possible worlds, the task of radical thought is that of doggedly engaging in a critique of power relations. Having abandoned the dream of a united and pacified society, Lefort's focus shifts to contestations of the legitimacy of power and the established order. These reveal the "creativity of men" and their "fundamental need" to understand the meaning of their actions (321). They also involve identifying the forms of resistance to which men spontaneously resort, in industry or in any other social sphere, in order to undermine the plans of those in power. Such a critique, while effectively abandoning the notion of revolution as a general overthrow, in Lefort's eyes remains revolutionary since it

> reveals the real antagonisms that conservatives and reformists constantly attempt to conceal, explains in terms of the concrete relations established between men the operating rules of the organizations that disguise these antagonisms, and thus illuminates and sustains the social struggle. (322)

According to Lefort, the tools needed to pursue this goal can be provided by a sociological analysis able to unveil the structure of alienation and denounce the functioning of ideology in capitalist society. The sociological method he refers to, however, is not that of the social sciences, of which he had always been deeply critical, but is a term which as early as the 1950s he had used to refer to a way of observing social life from an internal perspective purged of any lingering metaphysical content.[1]

Once again Marx is the point of reference, the instrument for the investigation. After expunging from his texts any essence or founding reality from which alienation can be deduced, the Parisian philosopher returns to the analysis of industrial capitalism in which Marx appeared to have laid out a totally different perspective than the one that characterized his work on commodities and fetishism. The third volume of *Capital* in particular describes industrial capitalism as something profoundly different from any previous mode of production, and as something that subordinates all individual activities by integrating them into a total process responding to a common logic. Unlike manufacturing production, which was structured around the isolation of individual work processes, big industry creates a unitary process made up of the sum of all productive actions, in which all activities are interdependent. However, this very act of creating a totality, a universal society, contradicts itself due to the multiplicity and compartmentalization of the tasks that comprise it. The split between capital and labor means that productive activity manifests its universality at the same time as it is deprived of it. This contradiction is made evident in the very constitution of abstract labor, in which the specificity of the parcellation of individual labor is brought into communication with the logic of generalized equivalence.

The proletarian experience once again offers the best perspective from which to view this opposition: it is possible to understand from it the contrast experienced and suffered by those who sell their labor power for employment on the assembly lines of major industries (Lefort 1978, pp. 78–112).[2] Producers in fact experience two opposing imperatives. On the one hand, by selling their labor they become part of the universal exchange value, and in this context their work is, in the abstract and when placed in relation to the global logic of capital, revealed as a collective, socialized form of labor. On the other hand, their exclusion from the management of production expels them from that logic, pushing them back into a direct relationship with the specificity of their task. On this

---

[1] On Lefort's critique of the social sciences, see Lanza (2021) and Caillé (1993).

[2] I refer to the article "L'alienation comme concept sociologique", published in 1955 in the journal *Cahiers internationaux de sociologie*, which I will analyze in the next few pages. Gilles Labelle (2015) best captures the meaning of capitalist alienation and its connection to abstract labor and the proletarian experience.

level, however, the abstract nature of labor, its ability to fit into the logic of general equivalence, tips over into homogenization, parcellation, and interchangeability: characteristics that do not allow producers any form of identity. This therefore leaves producers simultaneously bound to the total production process and isolated within the repetitiveness of their work, unable to recognize themselves in any of the dimensions that strike them, socialize them, and de-socialize them. The individual experience is self-contradicted by giving itself away as a deprivation of the universal, and the experience of the universal degenerates into a fragmentation that extinguishes all forms of the particular. It is in this internal self-contradiction that Lefort locates the sense of alienation in capitalist society (108–109, Labelle 2015, p. 27).

Conceived in this way, alienation is independent of any essence or foundation: it does not refer to the concealment of human relations behind the veil of relationships between commodities, but to the contradiction between the dimensions of totality and particularity that make up society. Alienation, in other words, is a specific "social condition" formed in a given society, and one that contradicts itself at different levels (Lefort 1978, p. 108). This inconsistency emerges most acutely in relation to the proletariat, for whom alienation becomes a failure to socialize. Indeed, the clash between the domain of capital and that of labor leaves workers with no space to develop any form of stable social identity. They are expelled from the universal and unable to recognize themselves in the particular.

However, Lefort continues, this process is not confined only to one aspect of the social, nor is it limited to a specific subject: neither the factory nor the workers have a monopoly on alienation. Science, for example, by establishing a split between intellectual and manual activities, emerges from Marx's own descriptions as the most powerful agent of alienation (108–109). As a result, alienation does not reside in any particular location, but "it is the phenomenon par excellence that exposes the ruptured structure of society and is found at all levels and in all sectors of reality" (109). While it may be manifested most clearly in the proletarian experience, there is no social sphere that is not permeated by the dialectic of alienation. Every form of action and thought—production and science, intellectual and manual labor—develops through a continuous shift from the particular to the universal, which in turn cannot be comprehended except as a particularity. In this context, the capitalist form of production is not so much the cause of alienation as an expression of a much broader dialectic that encompasses it. The meaning of alienation, like that of any social phenomenon, can therefore not be contained within the dimension of production but can only be located in the totality of social dynamics and outside of any notion of cause and effect.

The dynamic between the particular and the universal that determines alienation thus increasingly appears to be the means through which the social is constituted. Moreover, this is already made clear in the last part of the 1955 article "L'alienation comme concept sociologique" that we considered when explaining Lefort's analysis of alienation. In it the author refers to the pages of *The German Ideology* in which Marx attempts to identify a dissociation between the real and its imaginary expressions (Marx and Engels 1998). For the Parisian philosopher, Marx actually ends up "revealing the contradictory structure of the real" (Lefort 1978, p. 109). By highlighting the duality of ideology, which is both the inversion of reality and the language of the real, Marx's analysis shows that the inversion of reality is an inherent aspect of the social process and thus highlights the contradictory structure of the real:

> Society, as we have seen, is not unreality but a process of self-unification and self-parcellation; it exists at the same time as plurality and as unity, and this produces within it a constant dissociation between the unreal and the real or ensures that the problem of truth arises in it. (112)

To fully understand this thesis, it is necessary to return to the anthropological studies we discussed in the previous chapter, and in particular to the 1951 article devoted to the work of Marcel Mauss (21–45). In this text, Lefort had already argued that the social is founded precisely out of an initial separation between material and natural reality: a fundamental division that opens up the possibility for both individuality and the collective dimension (44–45). This differentiation from the materiality of the thing gives rise to the experience of the subject in its relationship with the other and with the total sense of its community. Subjective experience, then, is itself a separation, a split. Placed back in this framework, the dialectic of alienation is no longer a concealment of natural reality but rather can be read in terms of a distorted revival of the dynamic that establishes the social. The merit of Marx's work and his analysis of industrial production therefore resides first and foremost in its ability to hide this dynamic and criticize its effects, namely the workers' failure to socialize and the unequal distribution of power and wealth. Not only that, but

Marx's achievement was also to have placed critical thinking itself within the dialectic of alienation.

Through this modification of Marx's theory of alienation, Lefort thus shows us how it is impossible to break out of the divisions that characterize and constitute the social, that there is no way to establish a foundation on which to construct both social life and thought. He does so not by postulating any naturally divided human or social essence, but by defining an epistemological limitation: the impossibility for thought to escape from history and from the contingency in which it takes shape, and thus to embrace the totality of Being. Building on Merleau-Ponty's lesson, he rejects any overarching perspective that believes it can overcome the differentiations and contrasts through which the social is constituted, and instead favors the realization that:

> there is no deception on the part of consciousness: if error, misrepresentation, and falsehood are possible, it is first of all because reality itself is torn and therefore no expression of reality can be adequate. (109)

Ideology

The definition of ideology as the set of representations fashioned by the ruling class to make the ruled believe in the legitimacy of its authority and to conceal its contingency is, according to Lefort, both the most widespread and the most misleading in Marxist theory. He argues instead that the same analysis of commodities set out in *Capital* actually points in a different and far more productive direction, and it is at this point that he brings to light how reality is not hidden by the bourgeoisie but by the division of labor and the modes of production. The ideological dynamic conveyed by commodities is clear: products separate themselves from their producers by masking the conditions of their production; the division of labor, in turn, is shown to coincide with a movement that takes place directly in things. Commodity exchange, in other words, passes itself off as the principle of the real while in fact this is determined by the method of production, in all its historicity and contingency. The distinction between capital and labor reflects this dynamic: the capitalist division of labor produces a contradiction between the universality of commodities and the fragmentation of labor (Lefort 1978, pp. 435–441).[3] The dynamic of concealment characteristic of ideology thus seems to encompass the very structure of capital:

> If anything, the movement of *ideology* is confused with that of Capital. The schism between the world of ideas and the real world is one of mere appearance. The real split is the one between Capital and Labor that emerges in social practice, and which makes capital both a term of division and the thing that makes this division invisible, representing the principle of economic reality. (440)

The ruling class itself, rather than possessing ideology as its own tool, also appears to be caught within this larger dynamic. This is particularly evident in the pages of *The Eighteenth Brumaire of Louis Bonaparte*, where the denial of temporal difference—the disavowal of the present and its disguise as the Roman past—is described as being a contributing factor in the formation of the bourgeoisie as a class and also as a necessary tool for its own revolutionary action. The point of view of class domination and that of representation thus do not seem to harmonize. Marx's works, Lefort therefore argues, invite us to understand ideology on the basis of its deepest origin, social division (195–204).[4] That is, they show how the capitalist system of production masks the mutual dependence of social actors with the separation of their activities, creating a universalistic discourse that at the same time conceals the division between classes and establishes it in a supposed reality. It is only in this process that ideology inserts itself, in an attempt to offer a depiction of the universal from the perspective of the dominant class. As such, the ideological debate seems to be of secondary importance, running in parallel to a broader mechanism and always involving the point of view of the powerful. Bourgeois ideology constitutes only one instance and form of this mechanism.

If, then, Lefort continues, ideological discourse is a phenomenon that tends to disguise the conditions of its own institution by depicting itself

---

[3] I analyze here the article "La naissance de l'idéologie et l'humanisme" published in the journal *Textures* in 1973 and now in Lefort (1978, pp. 401–477), and "Esquisse d'une genèse de l'idéologie dans les sociétés modernes", originally published in the same journal in 1974, then in Lefort (1978, pp. 478–569), and now in Lefort (1986, pp. 181–236).

[4] Lefort again works with and against Marx. He follows some of the paths outlined by him but emphasizes the limitations of his thought that we analyzed in the previous chapter.

as universally valid, and if, in agreement with Marx, such a mechanism can be located in the division between commodities and labor enacted by capitalism, it is then possible to trace this type of discourse back to a specific type of society—the modern capitalist society—and to a specific symbolic dimension to which it is consubstantial. The particularity and novelty of ideological discourses are most clearly revealed when they relate to different societies in which, for example, religion possesses a symbolic structuring role, a role that is contested under capitalism. Indeed, as we shall see more clearly in the next chapter, in "religious" or pre-capitalist social formations, the distinction between the reality of social relations and the transcendent or imaginary dimension that makes ideology conceivable is not possible. In such societies, social relations and hierarchies are governed with reference to an origin or to an Other, an imaginary place beyond the reach of man that justifies them and shelters them from any dispute, from any possible distinction from a sphere of "reality". In contrast, capitalism establishes its typical phantasmagoria in a completely self-referential society in which no form of transcendence is required to justify power, knowledge, or law. The existing state of affairs is justified through the very movement of things turned in commodities.

> One is thus able to assess what differentiates ideology from all types of representation established before the birth of capitalism; for the latter it is essential to dispense signs of the rationality of the real and produce knowledge discourses *about* the real that seem to be implied within it. (440–441)

In short, in a society in which the dominant discourse draws legitimacy from a transcendent order, the distinction between the imaginary and the real, the masking of the contingent origin of the social appear impossible. Only when power is brought back into the hands of men, when it loses all stable justification, does the possibility of this distinction and, with it, of masking it emerge, in the form of ideology. This situation can be traced back to the now possible separation between political power and law, to the split between institutions and the social discourses that underlie and justify them. In other words, capitalist society, in which all transcendent justification has been lost and in which the distinction between the imaginary and the real has become conceivable, resorts to the "ideology of material reality" to justify its *mise en forme*.

Once ideology is connected to the symbolic dimension of the social characteristics of modern capitalist societies, one can redefine Marx's concept of ideology. This can be interpreted as a product of the symbolic dimension of a particular form of society, as a second-degree discourse that follows the contours of the institution of the social but which

> is organized by a principle of occultation which does not derive from its activity: it marks a folding over of social discourse on to itself, thereby suppressing all the signs which could destroy the sense of certainty concerning the nature of the social: signs of historical creativity, of that which has no name, of what is hidden from the action of power, of what breaks apart through the dispersed effects of socialization—signs of what makes a society, or humanity as such, alien to itself. (Lefort 1986, pp. 202–203)

Again, ideology can be more precisely defined as the set of concatenations whose aim is "to reduce the indetermination of the social to its own determination" (189). This is a conservative discourse that seeks to conceal the revolution evident at the level of production. Ideology, in short, is any conscious concealment carried out by any knowledge or power that disguises its own contingency and indeterminacy, that creates fictitious principles designed to justify itself.[5]

Lefort thus salvages Marx's definition of ideology as a threefold negation, but strips it of any reference to the real or to any foundation. While it is unacceptable to define ideology in reference to an alleged reality, it is nevertheless possible to attempt to clarify how the dominant discourse is structured to disguise the process of social division. Of course, one must be aware that this very discourse is integral to the division and part of the representation, but this does not make critiquing it impossible. This is because a discourse that is the bearer of knowledge whose principle it does not possess is one thing, but a discourse arranged to dissimulate the traces of social division is quite another. It is this second type of discourse that it is possible to criticize as ideological. The ideology of capitalist societies, Lefort therefore asserts, is not the misrecognition of a phantom reality of social relations, as Marx also believes. Rather, it is the

---

[5] Lefort's use of imaginary and symbolic is different from that proposed by Castoriadis (1987). On the distinction between ideology, the symbolic and the imaginary for Lefort and Castoriadis, see Thompson (1982).

mechanism for masking social division, consubstantial with reference to a reality in itself, whether this takes the form of the commodity or of the real.

Capitalist ideological discourse, which, as we shall see, might be better referred to as "modern" discourse, thus appears to be profoundly linked to the search for immanence, to the illusory reference to an objective, empirical reality that motivates and justifies the contingent arrangement of the social. In this sense, even Marx's positivism is part of the same ideological mechanism, as are all those reflections which, referring to a radical immanence, fail to recognize something that is always evasive and beyond reach: the division of the social.

The best explanation of the critical potential of this can be found in the final pages of the article "Esquisse d'une genèse de l'idéologie dans les sociétés modernes" (Lefort 1986, pp. 181–236), which are devoted to outlining the characteristics of an invisible ideology that characterizes contemporary Western democracies (224–236). Lefort describes a logic of dissimulation that masks the distance between representation and the real and, at the same time, renounces the total fulfillment of representation. Contemporary discourse, he asserts, does not speak from above, it simulates immanence, its consubstantiality to the plane of civil society. The dimension of communication, in particular, has taken on the function of an imaginary universality that, through the fictitious elimination of distances, conceals social division.[6]

---

[6] Lefort (1986, p. 227) states: "In no other period has so much been said: the discourse on the social, facilitated by modern means of transmission, natters on; it is overcome by a dizzying infatuation with itself. Nothing escapes the agenda of conferences, interviews and televised discussions, from the generation gap to traffic flow, from sexuality to modern music, from space exploration to education. This narcissism is not that of bourgeois ideology, since the new discourse is not spoken from above. It does without capital letters; it pretends to propagate information, pretends even to question and to probe. It does not hold the other at a distance, but includes its 'representative' in itself; it presents itself as an incessant dialogue and thus takes hold of the gap between the *self* and the *other* in order to make room for them both within itself. In this way, the subject finds himself (almost) lodged in the system of representation, in an altogether different way than in totalitarian ideology, since he is now invited to incorporate the terms of every opposition. And at the same time, he is lodged in the group—an imaginary group in the sense that individuals are deprived of the power to grasp the actual movement of the institution by taking part in it, by confronting the fact of their differentiated relation to one another". On this theme see Breckman (2019).

In conclusion, we can state that the reflection on ideology clearly demonstrates how, at least until the 1970s, Lefort continued his close confrontation with the works of Marx, who he reproached for his positivism and for his failure to recognize the true nature of the dimension of the real. On the other hand, ever faithful to the lessons of phenomenology and anthropology, the Parisian philosopher approaches the social as a totality that cannot be analyzed according to the laws of cause and effect. His perspective remains inside a phenomenological approach that, while aware of being inscribed in the reality it describes, questions its own foundations and finds itself unable to understand the totality. This hermeneutic perspective is reflected in the conception of the social: just as thought must be conscious of the impossibility of coinciding with the real, in the same way the social, as a "political discourse" about itself, as a symbolic dimension, is always different from itself. Ideology, consequently, consists in the attempt to bridge this continuous difference, this "indeterminacy".

From the Proletariat to the People

If the end of his time with SouB also represented Lefort's initial departure from Marxism and the revolutionary perspective, by the 1970s this detachment has become explicit and theoretically grounded. In the afterword to the first edition of the *Éléments d'une critique de la bureaucratie* in 1971, reflecting on his own theoretical and political journey, he clearly argues that Marx's work is inadequate for attempts to understand and criticize a reality that has been transformed on the basis of a different logic from the one described in *Capital*:

> Now it seems to us that we have lacked boldness, in fear of admitting that the transformation of the social mode of domination involved a profound modification of the antagonistic terms described by Marx and, consequently, required a revision of the model through which some claimed the ultimate reality of society was defined. When considering the framework of the economy we should already have begun by questioning the changes affecting the nature of social labor. (Lefort 1979, pp. 354–365)[7]

---

[7] The article, included, with the title "Le nouveau et l'attrait de la repetition", in the second edition of *Éléments d'une critique de la bureaucratie*, originally appeared as an afterword to the 1971 first edition cited above (Lefort 1971, pp. 351–362).

A new phase of capitalism has emerged, accompanied by an unprecedented configuration of antagonistic subjects that elude the categories of Marx's analysis and that the majority of the SouB, led by Castoriadis, have not taken sufficiently into account. In parallel with the process of bureaucratization already described in the 1950s in the *Socialisme ou Barbarie* journal, the development of capitalism follows a trend toward the standardization of patterns of social action and relation. Norms that were once in place only within large-scale industry, and were thus connected to blue-collar labor, have now extended beyond the factory walls and invaded other parts of society, including the state administration, science, tertiary services, healthcare, even legal and educational institutions. This spread of the productive model into the social fabric has been followed by a change in the labor relationship, which has moved to the center of a network of obligations that exceed those analyzed by Marx and tend to take over a considerable part of life outside of working hours. Finally, one should not underestimate the profound change brought about by technology, which has come to affect the relationship between skilled and unskilled labor. In short, although exploitation has continued, it no longer operates by excluding a social class from socialization. On the contrary, the proletariat appears to have been absorbed into the capitalist process, which results at the same time in power relations and alienation previously characteristic of the production relation expanding into all social spheres (365).

In a nutshell, Lefort argues that the proletarianization of society has expanded by following a different pattern and direction than those envisaged by Marx and Marxism. The contemporary masses, though exploited by production whose means they did not possess, no longer resemble those described in *Capital* or the *Manifesto*. Indeed, the proletariat that arose out of the spread of the logic of production has developed a considerable and unprecedented internal heterogeneity. Exploitation, alienation, deprivation, dispossession and the frustration of creative capacities no longer apply to a specific social stratum, but appear to be scattered throughout the whole of society (366). This crumbling of the proletarian subject makes it difficult for struggles to converge toward a single revolutionary goal.[8] Given this situation, it is difficult to argue that capitalism or

---

[8] The pattern outlined by Lefort reflects the difficulty, widespread in the Marxist intelligentsia during 1970s, of understanding the new class composition. Indeed, in this period unprecedented modes of production and speculation brought a new appearance to world capitalism. Many, faced with these changes, felt the need to grasp the new physiognomy

bureaucracy is moving toward their inevitable contradiction and epilogue: differentiation and heterogeneity stand as obstacles to any possible spontaneous communist vocation. In other words, what becomes clear is the lack of a natural disposition on the part of the proletariat to fight against exploitation and adhere to the revolutionary ideal.

This observation does not lead Lefort to abandon any prospect of struggle, nor to declare a new, complete, and peaceful form of social homogeneity. Instead, it leads him to the realization that contemporary struggles can no longer be sustained by an outdated revolutionary ideal. The faith in revolution, the Parisian philosopher argues, was rooted in a total worldview that, precisely because of the differences between those involved in the struggle and the prospects for change, no longer appears valid (366–368). The abandonment of a shared revolutionary perspective is also the result of the maturation of the working class, which has become more sensitive to the complexity of the social problem (318).[9] However, this does not imply a total cessation of the struggle. On the contrary, bureaucratization and the expansion of exploitation lead to protests in all sectors of social and cultural life. In addition to the oppositions imposed in the labor process, what seems to be emerging in this period is an unprecedented resistance to rules that aspire to assert comprehensive control over behaviors in order to subject them to the logic of the market. A shared and widespread dissent that is in turn expressed in different methods of resistance, which, however, do not come together in a unified revolutionary purpose.

One mode of contestation, for example, arises from within the bureaucratic system, from its inability to meet the needs raised by the multiplication of organizational systems. Other forms of contestation, on the other hand, channel the desire for the collective management of resources. Finally, some sectors of the population, the youth in particular, express their dissent in terms of a total rejection of the dominant social order and of a desire to destroy its symbolic reference points (366–367). It is

---

of social classes. In this context, it is interesting to note the convergence of some of the boldest theoretical work. Lefort, like Mario Tronti, Antonio Negri, or Hans Jürgen Krahl, locates the characteristics of the new form of capital in the diffusion of the productive logic into the social logic. Like the others, the French philosopher deduces from this new framework the possibility of generalized opposition. See Tronti (2019), Krahl (2008) and Negri (2005).

[9] I am referring to the 1963 article "La dégradation idéologique du marxisme" (Lefort 1979, pp. 308–322).

precisely the variety of contestations that makes the inadequacy of Marx's model clear to Lefort. Whereas for Marx revolutionary potential arises from a class of producers, the proletariat who have been ousted from the model of production, in contemporary society contestation arises not only from producers but from anyone who rejects the norms and models of industrial society. The profusion of different conflicts, therefore, cannot be reduced into a formation that pits producers against the owners of the means of production. The Parisian philosopher's accusation is thus that Marxism has failed to adapt to this new phase of capitalism. Intellectuals and politicians have been unable to amend the theory, to adapt their analyses to the unprecedented configuration of subjects and social ties, and to the maturation of the proletariat. The disconnect between a theoretical apparatus faithful to outdated categories and a profoundly changed reality has increasingly led Marxism to resemble an ideology.[10] Unable to reflect on real issues, it has turned into a rationalistic utopia that denounces the contradictions and conflicts of society on the basis of a total vision of the social that is as rational as it is illusory.

Lefort thus denies the possibility of uncovering in a single subject the meaning of emancipation and the direction of history. The investigation of the capitalist phase reveals the inconsistency of the proletariat, its shattering and its unwillingness to engage in revolutionary action, and this is corroborated by philosophical reflection. Lefort finds that even Marx's works contain the key elements of a society in which there is no center of alienation. He uncovers in *Grundrisse* and *The German Ideology* traces of an essential division of the social, elements that fundamentally call into question any possibility of conceiving of a single and absolute driving force of the future, of any subject capable of unifying the social, of any totality and any foundation. After all, if the dialectic is widespread, if alienation and ideology structure the social, then a pure subjectivity capable of being the sole engine of dialectics and the truth of history is unthinkable.

---

[10] For Lefort this "ideological degradation of Marxism" also conceals the reformist attitude of those who champion it. Scientific reformism, moralizing reformism, and revolutionary reformism are hidden behind the mask of revolution. In the eyes of the Parisian philosopher, this happens because the proletariat lacks a disposition toward revolution. In other words, the encounter between the maturity of the proletariat, which abandons its faith in revolution, and a Marxist theory incapable of evolving and adapting to reality, creates reformisms disguised by ideology (Lefort 1979, p. 318).

This theoretical and political position shares a clear connection with the ideas that mark the final phase of Merleau-Ponty's life and work. Beginning in the late 1950s, Merleau-Ponty had engaged in a re-evaluation of his relationship with Marxism and with the work of Marx himself, and come to question the relationship between his reflection and the communist sphere. The publication of *Humanism and Terror* in 1947 and then *Adventures of the Dialectic* in 1955 makes this path clear (Merleau-Ponty 1973, 2022).[11] According to the phenomenologist, Marxism's main error was to attribute the universal sense of history to the actions of the proletariat, as if it were possible to identify a single place where the dialectic is developed, thought through, and resolved. Like a commodity that discovers itself to be a commodity and must deny this fact to itself, in Marxism the proletariat becomes a "totality in intention", the advent of truth (Merleau-Ponty 1973, p. 45).[12] However, for Merleau-Ponty this truth is inscrutable, pervaded by error, and by other possibilities, and certainly cannot be ascribed to a single, real historical, and economic subject.

> Is it then the conclusion of these adventures that the dialectic was a myth? The illusion was only to precipitate into a historical fact—the proletariat's birth and growth—history's total meaning, to believe that history itself organized its own recovery, that the proletariat's power would be its own suppression, the negation of the negation. It was to believe that the proletariat was in itself the dialectic, and that the attempt to put the proletariat in power, temporarily exempted from any dialectical judgment, could put the dialectic in power. It was to play the double game of truth and authoritarian practice in which the will ultimately loses consciousness of its revolutionary task and truth ceases to control its realization. Today, as a hundred years ago and as thirty-eight years ago, it remains true that no one by himself is subject nor is he free, that freedoms interfere with and require

---

[11] In *Humanism and Terror*, published in 1947, Merleau-Ponty considers the Marxist conception of history and finds the theory of the proletariat at its center. In *Adventures of the Dialectic* his position shifts toward a more decisive a-communism that clashes with the theses of Jean-Paul Sartre. For an in-depth study of his theoretical and political journey from the positions of *Humanism and Terror* and his work of the early 1950s to his final reflections of a liberal bent, see first of all the studies by Howard (2019, pp. 171–200), Cooper (1979), Brena (1977), and Dodeman (2023).

[12] The expression "totality in intention" is taken from Georg Lukács's essay "History and Class Consciousness" (Lukács 1971).

one another, that history is the history of their dispute, which is inscribed and visible in institutions, in civilizations, and in the wake of important historical actions, and that there is a way to understand and situate them, if not in a system with an exact and definitive hierarchy and in the perspective of a true, homogeneous, ultimate society, at least as different episodes of a single life, where each one is an experience of that life and can pass into those who follow. (Merleau-Ponty 1973, pp. 205–206)

Like Merleau-Ponty, Lefort's analysis of society also demands that the theory of the proletariat be subject to critique. Multiplication, contradiction, and indeterminacy replace totality, opposition, and solution, the assumptions underpinning the Marxist view of history and society. The struggle of the proletariat, a group which in fact does not exist, is replaced by multiple, dispersed, different and sometimes irreconcilable conflicts that arise in the contemporary organization of capital.[13] The teleological vision of the future, founded on the promise of eventually overcoming class division and finding a solution to social conflict, must be replaced by a contingent analysis of real struggles and of the conditions that promote the resistance to exploitation. These conditions are not determined once and for all in the society of the past but instead are endlessly transformed and created anew:

> Those who pay attention to the social struggle in fact discover something other than the problems of irrational organization—flaws that could be remedied by good planning or a better integration of individuals into institutions. They discover a demand concerning the legitimacy of power which man claims for himself at the expense of others. (Lefort 1979, p. 321)

The proletariat's status as the subject of autonomy and of direct opposition is therefore taken over by the "people", a disparate and differentiated set of competing needs, individuals, and interests that forms a community and opposes power but that at the same time is fully involved in the contradictions of reality. The autonomy of the proletariat defended

---

[13] There are internal tensions within Lefort's own work in relation to the notion of conflict. While this term is at the heart of his work on Machiavelli, it is interesting to note that in "La dégradation iéologique du marxisme", a publication drawn from a 1963 lecture, Lefort rejects the term "conflict", perhaps considering it too strong, and prefers "contestation", which indicates a struggle concerning the legitimacy of power. (Lefort 1979, p. 321).

in the articles published in *Socialisme ou Barbarie* groans under the weight of co-involvement, of widespread alienation, and of the realization that every moment, every subject has always been a response to a pre-existing situation.

In Lefort's eyes, the new forms of struggle and the events of 1968 in particular confirmed the divided, differentiated, and conflictual physiognomy of the social and the new antagonistic subjectivities (Morin et al. 1968, pp. 35–62).[14] Workers and students stage a "new disorder": a broad-based opposition without a center that is not based on any class definition and does not involve hierarchies. They revolt against the contemporary form of power without, however, adhering to the illusion of a good society liberated from contradictions. They create new spaces and places, and they oppose institutions in spontaneous and unpredictable ways, beyond any bureaucratic and party logic. The demonstrations and clashes that take place in the streets, universities, and factories between workers, technicians, and students are the manifestation of widespread, contingent, centerless contradictions, which can nevertheless be bound together on the basis of their symbolic effectiveness (47–60).[15]

If the people are still credited with a dose of spontaneity, this now leads to a totally contingent opposition, one that is not embedded in any teleology and is outside of any revolutionary perspective. The new forms of contestation have freed themselves from responsibility for human destiny; they do not set themselves the task of eliminating all divisions, but rather aim to disrupt current ones in order to give rise to new, possibly

---

[14] Jean-Marc Coudray is a pseudonym for Castoriadis. Lefort's essay in the book is entitled "Le désordre nouveau" (*A New Disorder*). Twenty years later the same authors returned to these themes by publishing a new version of the book (Morin 2008). Antoine Chollet (2015) highlights the similarities and differences between the positions of Castoriadis and Lefort. Both agree about the innovative and unpredictable nature of the May events, and both recognize that at the heart of the struggles is a questioning of all hierarchy and the desire for self-management. The two are divided, however, in their judgment on the relationship between the protests and power, and on whether or not they were revolutionary. While for Castoriadis the year of conflict represents the failure of a revolution that was unable to seize power, for Lefort it was the realization of a new disorder based on a contestation of power and not on the desire for a revolution.

[15] In his text Lefort (Morin, Lefort, Castoriadis 2008, pp. 43–44) devotes a few lines to an interesting theory of the symbolic effectiveness of forms of contestation that seems very close to what Ernesto Laclau would elaborate years later. It is interesting to note, however briefly, this point of connection. Laclau, after all, was familiar with Lefort's work. See Laclau (2005) and Marchart (2007).

more acceptable ones. Each contestation addresses power and its image, and demands its legitimacy.

> I will translate it in my own way: Power, wherever it claims to reign, will find opponents who are not, however, inclined to install a better one. Such opponents will always be willing to disrupt the plans of a society that seeks to enclose itself in illusion and trap men in its hierarchies. They will take advantage of every opportunity to stimulate collective initiatives, break down barriers, circulate things, ideas, and men, and command everyone to confront conflicts rather that concealing them. If I am not mistaken, this language does not sustain itself on the illusion of a *good society* freed from contradictions. It may inspire new kinds of action in the years to come. If groups were to heed it in greater numbers than before, it would get a taste for the possible without losing a sense of the real; one would then have to agree that the revolution has matured. (62)

The investigation of alienation, ideology, the proletariat, and social conflict leaves Lefort with a picture of a very different society than the one described by official Marxism. The contemporary and capitalist society does not seem to be driven by a fundamental antagonism destined to be resolved by the victory of the proletariat, the center and driving force of history. Rather, it seems to be divided and struck by scattered, unfocused criticisms, like those that emerged in May 1968.

According to Lefort, the task is then to understand this social form in symbolic and political terms, that is, by studying its self-representation or the narrative it creates for itself. In short, if the social is the real, if every society is built on a self-representation, one must begin to understand why contemporary societies—Western, capitalist societies and French society in particular—define themselves as democracies. What does this term mean? Which "essence" of the social does it introduce? Lefort, of course, recognizes that "the concept of democracy is so old, applied to so many different regimes, and nowadays so commonly appropriated in support of diverse, even antagonistic, policies, that it often discourages any thought somewhat concerned with rigor" (Lefort 1979, p. 323). Nevertheless, he believes that forgoing the analysis by declaring the concept to be mere ideology

> would mean making another kind of mistake; it would be to exclude from reality, in the name of absolute knowledge, the representation that

mankind makes of it, and to forget that this representation is itself constitutive of reality. That there is, for example, a confused image of ancient democracy, a tradition which is continued in complacent ignorance of its origins, a vain restlessness around present and future democracy that does not excuse the need to investigate why the notion resists the passing of time, and which memory, which practice, and which desire it feeds on. (Ibid.)

As early as 1963, when he writes these lines, Lefort therefore already has a long research program about democratic society in mind. His first aim is to understand what the institutions of bourgeois democracy have to say about a broader democratic political and symbolic model. He then extends his inquiry to the economic level, to the level of information, and even to the level of the personality of individuals participating in a given culture, going so far as to ask whether it makes sense to speak of a democratic personality (333–343).

In short, understanding democracy as a form of society opens up an enormous field of inquiry that Lefort believes should be the basis of his future work. In his conclusions to the 1963 article from which I have taken the preceding sentences, he therefore sets out to define the field through certain key concepts and enigmatic elements that require clarification in order to unravel the meaning of democracy. First, he believes it is necessary to define the democratic community and the role that the people play in it. The question to ask is, "what is the meaning of this call to the people? What is the identity of this constantly invoked but always uncertain subject?" (344). After equality (in a clear reference to Tocqueville), autonomy, participation, and mobility, the fifth concept mentioned is that of openness (*ouverture*). Lefort uses this term first and foremost to refer to the absence of concealment, that is the idea that in a democratic society every sector should by right be open to others, should be visible and open to their judgment, and available to public debate (347). However, this *ouverture*, understood as non-occultation, as publicity, must immediately be distinguished from the fiction of a society that is transparent to itself and in which immediate communication occurs between all its members and elements. Here then, in the last sentences, comparing democracy and totalitarianism, he introduces the last concept by asking:

> Can we not say that democracy is characterized, on the contrary, by its intention to confront the heterogeneity of values, behaviors and desires, and to make conflicts an engine of growth? (348)

The blueprint for several years' work is contained in this quotation. Of course, not everything is clear at this point. To some extent these research intentions would be disregarded and some concepts introduced as key elements for understanding democracy would be abandoned. Others would be looked at in greater depth and take on a new and specific meaning. However, even in these early years Lefort is gathering together the scattered elements of the SouB period, especially those relating to history and modernity, and is clearly preparing for the long search for the meaning of democratic society to which he would dedicate himself until the final days of his life.

References

Breckman, Warren. 2019. Retour sur «l'idéologie invisible» selon Lefort. *Raison Publique* 23: 37–54.

Brena, Gian Luigi. 1977. *Alla ricerca del marxismo. M. Merleau-Ponty*. Torino: Dedalo.

Caillé, Alain. 1993. Les sciences sociales et la philosophie politique. In *La démocratie à l'œuvre. Autour de Claude Lefort*, ed. C. Habib, C. Mouchard, 51–76. Paris: Éditions Esprit.

Castoriadis, Cornelius. 1987. *The imaginary institution of the society*. Cambridge: Polity Press.

Chollet, Antoine. 2015. Claude Lefort et Cornelius Castoriadis: regards croisés sur Mai 68. *Politique et Sociétés* 34/1: 37–60.

Cooper, Barry. 1979. *Merleau-Ponty and Marxism: From Terror to Reform*. Toronto: University of Toronto Press.

Dodeman, Claire. 2023. *La philosophie militante de Merleau-Ponty*. Paris: Vrin.

Howard, Dick. 2019. *The Marxian Legacy. The Search for the New Left*. London: Palgrave Mcmillan.

Krahl, Hans-Jürgen. 2008. *Konstitution und Klassenkampf. Zur historischen Dialektik von bürgerlichen Emanzipation und proletarischer Revolution*. Frankfurt A. M.: Neue Kritik.

Labelle, Gilles. 2015. Parcours de Claude Lefort: de l'«expérience prolétarienne» de l'«aliénation» à la critique du marxisme. *Politique et Sociétés* 34/1: 17–36.

Laclau, Ernesto. 2005. *On Populist Reason*. London/New York: Verso.

Lanza, Andrea. 2021. Looking for a Sociology Worthy of Its Name: Claude Lefort and His Conception of Social Division. *Thesis Eleven* 166/1: 70–87.

Lefort, Claude. 1971. *Éléments d'une critique de la bureaucratie*. Paris: Droz.
Lefort, Claude. 1978. *Les formes de l'histoire. Essais d'anthropologie politique*. Paris: Gallimard.
Lefort, Claude. 1979. *Éléments d'une critique de la bureaucratie*. Paris: Gallimard.
Lukács, Georg. 1971. *History and Class Consciousness*. Cambridge: MIT Press.
Lefort, Claude. 1986. *The political forms of modern society: Bureaucracy, democracy, totalitarianism*. Cambridge: MIT Press.
Marchart, Oliver. 2007. *Post-Foundational Political Thought: Political Difference in Nancy, Lefort, Badiou and Laclau*. Edinburgh: Edinburg University Press.
Marx, Karl and Engels, Friedrich. 1998. *The German Ideology*. Lanham: Prometheus.
Merleau-Ponty, Maurice. 1973. *Adventures of the Dialectic*. Evanston: Northwestern University Press.
Merleau-Ponty, Maurice. 2022. *Humanism and Terror*. London: Routledge.
Morin, Edgar, Lefort, Claude, and Coudray, Jean-Marc. 1968. *Mai 68: la brèche. Premières réflexions sur les événements*. Paris: Fayard.
Morin, Edgar, Lefort, Claude, and Castoriadis, Cornelius. 2008. *Mai 68: la brèche. Suivi de Vingt ans après*. Paris: Fayard.
Negri, Antonio. 2005. *Books for Burning. Between Civil War and Democracy in 1970s Italy*. London-New York: Verso.
Thompson, John B. 1982. Ideology and the Social Imaginary: An Appraisal of Castoriadis and Lefort. *Theory and Society* 11/5: 659–681.
Tronti, Mario. 2019. *Workers and Capital*. London-New York: Verso.

CHAPTER 5

The Modern Symbolic Change

THE IMAGE OF THE BODY AND HETERONOMY

Understanding historical development became one of Lefort's core concerns in the early 1950s. The challenge he set himself was to bring reason to discontinuities both in the progressive sphere (the fractures in becoming) and the synchronic sphere (the coexistence of different forms of historicity). During his militancy with SouB, he had bitterly contested the mechanistic and teleological conceptions propagandized by "crass Marxism". These turned history into an anonymous and progressive process driven entirely by the silent forces of economics. Similarly, Lefort criticized the rationalist views—of Husserl, Hegel, and Marx himself—that interpreted becoming as something linear, unique, and rational (Lefort 1978, pp. 46–77). In opposition to them, he proposed an understanding of the relationship between the "form of history" and the "form of society": the idea that a given society's relationship to becoming is a political matter that rests on its symbolic foundations. The 1960s, once the symbolic dimension of the social was fully understood and made explicit, thus brought the opportunity for a whole raft of new investigations, as the history of capitalism and modernity (mostly European modernity) was opened to interpretations no longer confined to the narrow terms of economics, but open to an attempt to understand changes in the form and institution of the social. In embarking on this, Lefort once again turned to Marx.

The question which ends Lefort's 1952 article, namely that of what the historicity of a given society depends on, represented the starting point of a course that he taught at the Sorbonne in 1965.[1] The lectures aimed to highlight the coexistence of two contrasting visions of history within Marx's work. The first is the one enunciated in the opening of the *Manifesto*, according to which "the history of all hitherto existing society is the history of class struggles" (Marx and Engels 2002, p. 219). This is a linear conception of historical becoming, whose driving force is the conflict between classes and whose subject is a single, undivided humanity. Not only that, but in this formulation Marx and Engels explicitly affirm the disjunction between the contemporary or capitalist era and all the eras that preceded it. The simplification of social antagonisms goes hand in hand with the extension of the capitalist mode of production, clearly pointing to the imminent end of the class struggle (220). This simplification also involves the acceleration of history, as the voracity of capitalism replaces the slow pace of ancient conflicts, destroys the past, and does not allow the present to stabilize itself (223). The relentless upheaval of the mode of production proceeds in parallel with the dissolution of the beliefs and myths that underpinned earlier societies and kept men from perceiving the true nature of their relationships. With capitalism, egoism erases representations of the sacred and naked self-interest manifests itself. The dissolution of tradition makes it possible for society to understand itself for the first time. The direction of travel described by the two authors is unambiguous and total: history as a whole moves through different stages that capitalism appears to simplify and take to extremes (225–227).

According to Lefort, these theories could not be explained away as the product of contingent political texts and thus expunged from Marx's overall theory, since the same model of history presented in the *Manifesto* is also implicit in some of his other works.[2] However, this does

---

[1] Lefort based on this course the article that is the main point of reference for the analysis that follows in the next few pages: "Marx: d'une vision de l'histoire à l'autre" (Lefort 1986, pp. 139–180).

[2] In the *Grundrisse*, Marx attempts to explain change in society, labor relations, and history as the result of the development of a new form of production. He then locates the first signs of this as early as the Middle Ages, and traces its evolution over the centuries

not mean that this conception of historical becoming represents the full extent of his theory. Indeed, it is possible to discern the presence of another discourse, a different conception of history, within the same texts. A tension can already be found in the preface of *A Contribution to the Critique of Political Economy*, in which the evolutionist schema is simultaneously reintroduced and rejected (Marx 2010, pp. 91–94). However, the example that best supports this thesis is found in the *Grundrisse*, whose passages devoted to pre-capitalist modes of production do not highlight the linearity of the historical process, but focus instead on its radical discontinuity (Marx 2005). Pre-capitalist structures, which do not correspond simply to those preceding capitalism chronologically, demonstrate a temporal and theoretical inconsistency. They constitute a whole that, standing in contrast to capitalism, allows its specificity to be seen in the light of day. They highlight a caesura in historical development, a "mutation of humanity", a transformation that cannot be equated to the linear course envisaged in the *Manifesto* and Marx's other works.

Lefort's analysis begins with Marx's definition of the worker. Marx describes the pre-capitalist proto-worker as owning the objective conditions of his labor, which are not external to him.[3] Capitalism, on the other hand, brings about the separation between labor and its objective conditions that creates the worker. In other words, if the worker is disconnected from the means and material of labor, the proto-worker, being inextricably linked to the land as his material, location, and source of tools, is not separated from his activity and from the environment in which he carries it out. According to Lefort, the description of pre-capitalism first and foremost highlights the fact that labor is not at the origin of property, but that in fact property is at the origin of labor.[4] Only with capitalism

---

through the expansion and changing nature of trade, the emergence of manufacturing, and the earliest forms of industry, which contribute to a noticeable acceleration of the process. In addition to the passages of the *Grundrisse* concerning the forms preceding capitalist production, it is useful to refer to the section devoted to original accumulation. An obligatory reference is also the first book of *Capital*, specifically the parts relating to the industrial revolution and, especially, the chapters devoted to original accumulation. See Marx (1976 and 2005).

[3] Lefort's main reference point here is Marx 2005.

[4] Marx, when analyzing tribal collectives, defines community as the "presupposition of appropriation" and communal land use. Lefort's interpretation also refers to the pages in which Marx directly links the concept of property with that of community. In pre-capitalist forms, he states, property "means membership of a tribe", a relationship to the

does labor acquire an anterior position and cease to depend on property and land. In the context of pre-capitalist forms, on the other hand, the concepts of the individual, land, and property turn out to be intimately linked to that of community (Lefort 1986, pp. 141–142).

A specific inclusive relationship between the individual, labor, and community thus appears to be the unique feature of the pre-capitalist forms of production described in the *Grundrisse* (Marx 2005, pp. 471–472). And although Marx defines this relationship as something belonging to tribal societies, it can be extended to other pre-capitalist forms, since they all respond to the same basic characteristics. For example, formations of the despotic or Asiatic type, organized around an idealized tribal system *embodied* in the despot, are only one variant of the primitive model. The form of generalized slavery established in these societies means that everyone is deprived of property and is a possession of the ruler, and thus the ownership pattern connected to the communal form is preserved. Even more remarkable appears the communitarian connection in the second mode of production analyzed by Marx, that of the ancient Greeks and Romans. In these societies, the relationship of the individual to the land is here mediated by his relationship to the city, and the independence acquired by the individual "derives from an original state of dependence which he has not produced but which attests to the power of a transcendent entity" (Lefort 1986, p. 146). Again, the changes, while perceptible, do not alter the basic structure: property continues to derive from the membership of a community that is prior to and external to the individuals that comprise it. The analysis is also not contradicted by the third pre-capitalist form considered, that of the Germanic or feudal mode of production. Although Marx emphasizes the weakening and shattering of community among the Germans, he does not call into question the persistence of the communal form and the relationship to the land associated with it. Indeed, in these societies individual property continues to make sense only if one considers how members of the community come together and unite in pursuit of shared interests (147).

In short, all pre-capitalist forms appear to share a community that mediates relations between individuals and between them and their

---

land mediated by the community in which the individual is embedded and through which he alone can be the owner. See Marx (2005, pp. 471–489).

labor.[5] The property owner is such only in reference to the community and the land to which he or she belongs. Individuals, land, and community are bound together in an interplay of mutual inclusions that result in a monolithic and organic representation of society.

In this regard, the Asian mode of production is particularly significant (152–155). Marx portrays India as a country in which men are completely dependent on the community and positioned in a quasi-corporal social relationship.[6] There is no division of labor and no distinction between manufacturing and agriculture. Individuals cannot lose the connection that binds them to the community, while autarky shelters them from the disruptive effects of trade. Any differentiation that might generate social division is eliminated, and Indian society thus behaves as a single organism. The relationship between the various components of the community is not even affected by the formation of the despotic state. In this case, the nucleus of property is simply transferred to the state or to the person who embodies it. The figure of the body survives and the underlying organization of society remains unchanged.

In this way, through Marx Lefort glimpses within the heart of pre-capitalist, stagnant, or "history-less" societies the "image of the body" (*image du corps*): an organic and monolithic representation of the community that counteracts all structural modifications, resists all change and nullifies the disturbing effects of the dimension of otherness.[7] In

---

[5] In the *Grundrisse* (Marx 2005, p. 479) Marx states: "In the first form of this landed property, an initial, naturally arisen spontaneous [*naturwuchsiges*] community appears as first presupposition. Family, and the family extended as a clan [*Stamm*], or through intermarriage between families, or combination of clans. Since we may assume that pastoralism, or more generally a migratory form of life, was the first form of the mode of existence, not that the clan settles in a specific site, but that it grazes off what it finds—humankind is not settlement-prone by nature (except possibly in a natural environment so especially fertile that they sit like monkeys on a tree; else roaming like the animals)—then the clan community, the natural community, appears not as a result of, but as a presupposition for the communal appropriation (temporary) and utilization of the land".

[6] For Marx's analysis of Indian society see: Marx (2005, pp. 490–491). Lefort refers specifically to the fourteenth chapter of the fourth section of the first book of *Capital*, entitled "The Division of Labour and Manufacture" (Marx 1976, pp. 455–491). The study of Karl A. Wittfogel (1957) is a central reference in his analysis.

[7] Lefort deduced the idea of the inclusion of the individual into the communal "body" from certain passages in the *Grundrisse* where the series of mutual inclusions between individual, land, and community that characterizes pre-capitalist societies is highlighted. See Marx (2005, pp. 471–473).

these forms of society each element is in its proper place, like the organs in a body, and questioning the established structure is not permitted. The community therefore presents itself in the form of a transcendent, anterior power of which men are not the authors. A heteronomous structure that is always antecedent—justified by tradition, religion, history, and nature—determines the social structure and remains beyond discussion, just as the functioning of an organism cannot be disputed:

> In sum, what Marx is calling attention to, with his emphasis on the constancy of what he calls the communal character, is an *image of the body* which eliminates the dimension of externality. [...] And this image seems so resistant to all structural modifications that the enigma of history comes to be concentrated in the moment of its decomposition. (151–152)

The image of the body is thus the most obvious symptom of a peculiar symbolic institution and a particular form of history that has characterized different societies for centuries before the advent of the contemporary, capitalist form of society. This is the meaning underlying these societies, the political "choice" around self-representation on which the relationship to change and to internal division depends. Pre-capitalist societies use the image of the body to eliminate the effects of otherness by rejecting it as heteronomy and setting themselves against internal change or evolution. They thus maintain themselves in a state of unity and stagnation that contradicts the linear and progressive development envisaged in the *Manifesto*.[8] They take no part in this advance, but like the societies "without history" described in the previous chapter, they instead represent another form of history.

It is therefore no coincidence, Lefort notes, that in the *Grundrisse* Marx does not place pre-capitalist forms on an evolutionary pathway: they do not follow one another, and they do not represent successive solutions to the contradictions of earlier forms (145–152). They are merely different modes of society organized to preserve a different mode of coexistence. Pre-capitalism thus establishes the guiding lines of a repetitive history that cannot be understood within the framework of a universal,

---

[8] Marx himself states that the purpose of such communities is conservation. However, his comments on this conclude by further hinting that this reproduction of conditions is necessarily also a new form of production, and thus involves the destruction of an old form. This element, which also injects dynamism into stagnant societies, does not seem to be one that Lefort considers. See Marx (2005).

progressive history. This is a stagnant, heteronomous, and monolithic form that cannot be compared to the capitalist one characterized by the "actuated" self-transformation of class struggles. The question at this point is how this symbolic institution failed and what replaced it. How did European society abandon repetition and stagnation? Or, in other words, how was modern capitalist society made possible?

Indeed, once more following Marx, we can see how in the capitalist form of society the worker first becomes separated from the land, and how labor becomes disassociated from the tools that it requires.[9] It has become possible to be a worker without being part of a community, without owning land and the means of production. This reveals a revolutionary mode of production and a society that, in contrast to the social form that preceded it, is open to continuous change. Capitalist society thus challenges the image of the body that structures pre-capitalist forms, becoming a new symbolic institution of the social: it represents a deconstruction of the body, a "disincorporation" (*désincorporation*) which is connected the possibility of an evolutionary history, of change, of division, of the adoption of otherness.[10]

Marx, therefore, understood how things were. He was able to describe the link between the form of society and the form of history, although he failed to put a name to it. He perceived the separation between pre-capitalist forms and capitalist society. Or rather, beyond any form of economism, he detected the caesura between modernity—of which capitalism is only one element—and pre-modern societies. He grasped the disincorporation. However, by failing to recognize the symbolic dimension of the social, he failed to analyze this transition adequately, and it was therefore necessary to supplement his work. The change that disrupted European societies by ending their traditions and hierarchies had to be understood in its full symbolic meaning: through the image of the body and the loss of any transcendental foundation.

---

[9] In the wake of Marx Lefort states that land itself becomes an independent power, one included in the capitalist mode of production and of use in exploiting the labor force. It thus ceases to be a pivotal element of social life. It is transformed from Earth-Mother to Earth-Death.

[10] As I will show, Lefort will use the term "disincorporation" only later. Nevertheless, it seems to me that the same idea is already present here and that the term itself merely provides a more precise definition.

Ancien Régime Societies and the Theological-Political

Lefort delved further into his venture to interpret modernity symbolically in a series of courses that he taught at the École des hautes études en sciences sociales (EHESS) in the first half of the 1970s.[11] In these lectures, his analysis is rather less influenced by Marx's lexicon, instead focusing more specifically on the difference between the societies of the *ancien régime* and modern, democratic society. The image of the body was a category helpful to understanding a symbolic element common to all pre-modern societies, whether the medieval monarchies ruled by divine right or the absolutist states of the sixteenth and seventeenth centuries. These societies did indeed present themselves as organisms, or as a set or organisms, that depended on a heteronomous foundation. The law and the structure of society were therefore imposed from the outside, while within them each individual was treated as a member and had a place and a role that could not be questioned. Everything was where it should be and as it should be, and each organ performed a specific function. The possibility of change was minimized as social division, though present, was unable to generate any movement (Lefort 2007, p. 464).

Lefort notes that this representation of community corresponds to a specific image of power and, in the case of pre-modern European societies, to a specific conception of the monarch. As the summit of the bodies of communities—their head—monarchs are the point of contact between all elements of society, including the cities, guilds, nobility, fiefdoms, and the Church. They are the representation of the whole, of the unity of the communities they embody, yet at the same time also the link and mediating power with the transcendent dimension in which the communities themselves are founded. In such societies, divine and human power coalesce in the monarchs, who represent the unquestionable otherness that shapes society, and the rules regulating the body. They personify the law, knowledge, and power, with a body split between mortality and immortality, and they serve as God's instrument, as the

---

[11] Lefort joined EHESS in 1976 where he stayed until his retirement in 1989. Some of these course as *Florence à la fin du Trecento et au début du Quattrocento* (Lefort 1975a–1976a), *Formation de l'État moderne, pouvoir, corps politique* (Lefort 1976–1977) or *La genèse de l'État moderne et l'institution du social* (Lefort 1975b–1976b) have not been published and are kept in the Lefort Archives at EHESS.

earthly representation of the divine knowledge to which only they have access.

This link with the transcendental is particularly evident in the religious justification of power characteristic of the monarchies of the *ancien régime* from the Middle Ages to the eve of modernity. Yet it is even more evident in the analogy between the monarch and Christ typical of the medieval monarchies.

> The image of the body that informed monarchical society was underpinned by that of Christ. It was invested with the idea of the division between the visible and the invisible, the idea of the splitting of the mortal and the immortal, the idea of mediation, the idea of a production which both effaced and re-established the difference between the producer and that produced, the idea of the unity of the body and the distinction between the head and the limbs. The prince condensed in his person the principle of power, the principle of law and the principle of knowledge, but he was *supposed* to obey a superior power; he declared himself to be both above the law and subjected to the law, to be both the father and the son of justice; he possessed wisdom but he was subjected to reason. (Lefort 1986, pp. 305–306)

Behind these words is a clear reference to the research conducted by Ernst Kantorowicz, published in 1957 under the title *The Two Bodies of the King* (Kantorowicz 2016).[12] In this celebrated study, the German historian traces the evolution of the two-bodies theory of the king and its translation into legal terms from the year 1000 to the sixteenth century. The theory, in a nutshell, is that the body of the sovereign is both mystical and mortal, encompassing the limited life of an individual person and, at

---

[12] Lefort's discussion of medieval monarchy and its sacred character also does not seem to discount the ideas presented by Marc Bloch (2015). Finally, it is important to note that although articles concerning Kantorowicz's work appear only in the early 1980s, it is possible to say that Lefort was already studying him in the previous decade. Indeed, Kantorowicz is cited in the course given by the French philosopher at EHESS between 1975 and 1976, "Florence à la fin du Trecento et au début du Quatrocento" (Archives Lefort EHESS-CESPRA, CL 8 envelope 3, p. 24). On Kantorowicz, see Schöttler (2014) and Boureau (2001). To understand the further parallels and differences between Lefort and Marcel Gauchet, it may be interesting to note that Gauchet himself also makes use of Kantorowicz's theory of disenchantment. On this topic see Breckman (2013, pp. 139–182), Comensoli Antonin (2013) and Doyle (2003).

the same time, the political body of a community, the imperishable transcendence of the divine. While in the early Middle Ages, this idea provided the justification of the monarch's divine lineage, in the sixteenth century it became the means by which to represent the political unity of the nascent nation-states. Not coincidentally, the starting point of Kantorowicz's research is the English political thought of the Elizabethan and early Stuart eras, a period in which the doctrine of the two bodies of the king takes the form of a legal fiction used first and foremost to justify the superiority and autonomy of the body politic over the natural body of the individual in power. Precisely in an attempt to find the origin of this pattern of thought, Kantorowicz traces the continuous interactions between politics and theology, between the juridical and the sacred, that shape the development of both jurisprudence and the conception of European kingship. He locates an early forerunner of the theory in the idea of *persona mixta* that appears in around 1100, when the conception of a royal "superbody" mysteriously joined to the individual body of the king is already in circulation. For Kantorowicz, however, the reality most credited as the kernel of the theory can be found in the idea of the *duplex corpus Christi* that emerges in around 1200, when some theologians begin to distinguish between the Lord's natural, personal and individual body and his "supra-personal" and collective mystical body.

> The kings of the New Covenant no longer would appear as the "foreshadowers" of Christ, but rather as the "shadows", the imitators of Christ. The Christian ruler became the *christomimétés*, literally the "actor", the "impersonator" of Christ, who on the earthly stage presented the living image of the two-natured God, even with regard to the two unconfused natures. The divine prototype and his visible vicar were taken to display great similarity, as they were supposed to reflect each other. (47)

Through the connection to Christianity, the king becomes, *in officium*, the symbol and image of the Anointed in heaven and therefore the image of God (48). He personifies the community body, mediates a transcendent power beyond the reach of subjects and human laws, and embodies the realm, the political community, and the nation.

It is certainly true, as Kantorowicz himself argues, that this image of the monarch as a divine incarnation did not survive for long. Yet in spite of this, and in spite of the changes that redefined the idea of kingship over the centuries, the historian repeatedly emphasizes how this continued to be rooted in theology, in the sacredness of the crown and the connection to the figure of Christ. As Lefort states, "the changes that occurred did not entirely eliminate the notion of the kingdom as a unity which was both organic and mystical, of which the monarch was at the same time the body and the head" (Lefort 1986, p. 302). The king's body, or its transcendent and mystical part, continues for centuries to reflect the image of the community and the *Res publica*. Even when theology is translated into the language of law, and the ruler's *corpus mysticum* begins to denote the public sphere or the finances of the kingdom, the idea of community continues to be structured by the image of the body.[13] Even as the secular state begins to strive toward its own glorification, the king's body continues to be a crucial reference point, to the extent that, as Kantorowicz states toward the end of the volume, the doctrine of the two bodies lies at the foundation of the English Parliament and its constitutional theory. This representation is still present and operating in the eighteenth century, although by this point it has been deeply undermined. The link between community and body, between politics and religion, has not been dissolved (Kantorowicz 2016, pp. 496–506).

According to Lefort (1986, pp. 292–306), this representation of power, which spans centuries of European history, highlights a symbolic dimension that cannot be relegated to a mere fiction. Moreover, from his point of view, just as "the social is the real", the social meaning of power is its own reality. As a result, the task is not, or at least not only, to untangle how medieval rulers sought to justify their role by claiming a direct link to the divine Word. Rather it is necessary to understand how such a view of power is connected to the representation of the community, that is, how it is a reflection and the most visible aspect of a given symbolic institution, a conception of knowledge, law, and power. On the other hand, in order for the figure of the sacred king to be effective, for sovereignty to legitimize itself through the theory of the two bodies of the king, it is necessary for this discourse to be reflected in the structure of the social, and for it to actually respond to the questions of legitimacy that are addressed to power. From this perspective, in addition to establishing a mechanism with which to legitimize constituted power, the inventions of the jurists described by Kantorowicz highlight the theological-political

---

[13] We refer here, in particular, to the pages devoted by Kantorowicz to *Christus-fiscus*, in which he demonstrates the new application of the theological lexicon to the secular sphere, such as in matters of taxation and public property. See Kantorowicz (2016, pp. 164–192).

core of that social form. Their ideas and their sleights of hand are effective precisely because they are consistently situated within the theological-political institution of the social, which is revealed in the image of power. The latter can then be described in terms of a symbolic point of convergence where a given form of society is represented most clearly, or where society recognizes itself as it tries to make sense of itself.

For Lefort, the religious conception of power and the representation of the body related to it survived at least until the eighteenth century, and its traces can even be found in the events of the French Revolution.[14] The work of Jules Michelet attests to this. In his *History of the French Revolution* (Michelet 1989; Lefort 1988, pp. 213–255), the historian is acutely aware of the symbolic dimension of power and repeatedly emphasizes how kingship is inscribed in the matrix of the Christian religion. He points to a link between political and religious law in the *ancien régime* and recognizes that Christianity was at the root of the French monarchy and the set of institutions that sustained it. The people's love of the monarch and the legends that grew up around the priest-king, Good King Henry IV, and the God King Louis XIV provide further evidence of the religious spirit that animated the French monarchy. Michelet finds within this an image of a ruler whose body conveys some aspects of Christ and his infinite justice and exposes a link to pre-revolutionary French society, which is established in direct relation to this body and whose institutions are organized in line with organic principles.

The analysis of the trial of Louis XVI is a particularly clear reflection of the historian's sensitivity to the theme of the embodiment of the monarchy. In his book, Michelet presents this event as a judgment on the French monarchy as a whole, an opportunity to condemn the institution for all eternity. The trial made it possible to bring "into the light that ridiculous mystery which a barbarian humanity had for so long turned into a religion: *the mystery of monarchical incarnation*, the bizarre fiction that the wisdom of a people concentrated in an imbecile" (Lefort 1988, p. 245). The deep understanding of the religious dimension of kingship

---

[14] Lefort does not distinguish adequately between "corporal" and "organic". The two adjectives actually refer to two entirely different imaginaries or ontologies. While "corporal" refers to the analogical systems that link together, for example, Christ, the Church, the community, and thus the king, "organic" refers to the emergence of a science of life and the conception of society as an evolving and self-balancing system. This view imposes itself precisely in the period that Lefort defines, through disincorporation. I thank Andrea Lanza for sharing his views on this point.

once again leads the historian to argue for the monarch's imprisonment rather than his beheading, on the basis of an understanding that kingship outlives the physical body of the king, that his mystical body survives the death of the individual.

According to Lefort, Michelet's work thus makes it clear that eighteenth-century European society was still imbued with a religious core and organic representation. On the eve of the Revolution, the mystical body of the king still represents Christ and embodies the community, his image continuing to enable a mediation with transcendental law and knowledge. Michelet's own language continuously interweaves politics and religion. Unable to renounce definitively the depiction of the community as an organism, he merely transforms the theological-political images that characterize the monarchy into representations—such as the people or the nation—that, however novel, still betray their religious roots. The religious allusion, Lefort concludes, continues to be present even in revolutionary ideals (Lefort 2000, pp. 159–171).[15]

Underlying the history of Europe in the *ancien régime* is a dynamic that reflects that same complex interplay of chiasms highlighted by Kantorowicz: a continuous interplay not between the theological and the political but between an already politicized theology and an already theologized politics (Lefort 1988, pp. 249–250).[16] The divine monarchy provides only one element—the symbolic focal point—of a much larger symbolic structure involving the development of the city-state, city organizations, and trades over centuries of European history. From this

---

[15] The article "La révolution comme religion nouvelle" originates from a talk given by Lefort in September 1988 at the conference "La révolution française et la culture politique moderne". In the article, the author argues that both Michelet and Edgar Quinet successfully grasp the essence of revolution in religion. This belief differentiates them from Tocqueville.

[16] In this text, Lefort identifies an error in the interpretation of Michelet, who is guilty of separating the theological and political dimensions, and then capturing the ways in which the latter was subordinated to the former in the *ancien régime*. In this way the historian describes an essence of Christianity independent of any relation to political fact, although this, however, is illusory, nonexistent and erroneous. These two dimensions, Lefort instead argues, always exist alongside each other. He states: "We will also discover a dynamic schema imprinted upon the complex play of chiasmata which Ernst Kantorowicz analyzes with such subtlety; these are not, I repeat, chiasmata between the theological and the political, as his formulations sometimes suggest, but, if I may be forgiven the barbarism, between the already politicized theological and the already theologized political".

perspective, it is possible to grasp how the dimension of the body remained unaltered within the long process of secularization of monarchical power, even through the various transliterations of religious language into legal and political language outlined so well, albeit in different ways, by Kantorowicz and Michelet. In short, there was a theological-political core within *ancien régime* societies, a heteronomous justification of the social that presided over an organic self-representation.

Thus a break in this path occurs when the idea of the body falls apart when transcendence abandons power. It is this discontinuity, already identified by Marx, that profoundly transforms communities and fractures the forms of history. This is the hiatus that clears the stage for a new society, a new representation of power, a new form of production, the possibility of internal division, and the progressive development of history. It is the symbolic upheaval that opens the way toward the modern form of society (Lefort 1986, pp. 292–306; 1988, pp. 213–255).

THE STATE, DISINCORPORATION, AND THE MODERN FORM OF SOCIETY

What form of society replaced the monarchies of the *ancien régime* "designed" to ensure perpetual stagnation and immobility? How did capitalism, with its insistence on the constant renewal of forms of production, come into being? What happened when the heteronomous and religious foundation of power waned? What is the meaning of a society without such a foundation? What is democracy? These are the questions that drove Lefort to develop a definition of modernity. The object of his research in this area is the social as a form, as a symbolic institution. He is therefore not intent on tracing a cause of symbolic change—the symbolic dimension is after all not altered by cause and effect[17]—but rather on understanding

---

[17] I therefore think that Hugues Poltier is wrong when he questions the difficulty of understanding "what" caused symbolic change. Poltier, in using the category of causality to understand modern symbolic change, runs into the very error that Lefort sought to avoid, which consists in using the symbolic as an empirical datum, distinct from the real. Poltier (1998, p. 217) argues: "Le problème qui se pose est donc le suivant: comment concevoir l'avènement du nouveau? Comment rendre intelligible la transition d'une matrice symbolique à une autre? Même limitée à la question de Lefort […], la difficulté reste redoutable. La raison est qu'on ne peut se contenter de chercher une explication par les circonstances économiques, climatiques, militaires, etc. Nous venons d'évoquer en effet le cas de dispositifs symboliques que les plus grands cataclysmes n'ont

the modern institution of the social in the light of its difference from the forms that it diverged from or which, at least in Europe, preceded it. Exactly as in Marx's reasoning, the utility of pre-capitalist forms of production lies in their ability to bring out the characteristics of capitalist organization, and for Lefort pre-modern societies therefore reveal the originality of the modern institution of the social.

All the questions at the beginning of this section can therefore be translated and synthesized into the two that guided Lefort's research: how did that transcendent, religious power capable of structuring society from the outside crumble, and what are the consequences of this? In other words, Lefort sets himself the task of understanding how the organic representation of the community disintegrated (disincorporation), or how the transcendent foundation lost its power. It is necessary to understand how the structuring role of religion was called into question. Lefort asks whether it is possible to retrace the radical alteration of symbolic references that unlocks the meaning of modernity.[18]

---

pas renversés. De ces cas, il semble légitime de conclure que les circonstances de fait n'exercent aucune influence sur l'ordre du symbolique. [...] [N]ous sommes amenés à faire l'hypothèse que seuls des facteurs internes à la matrice symbolique d'une société peuvent 'expliquer' son aptitude à se transformer au contact des événements et nous faire comprendre las mutations qui affectent cet ordre au cours de la révolution démocratique". Poltier does, however, highlight a difficulty with Lefort's proposed definition of the symbolic that I have already pointed out.

[18] It is worth noting that although, since the early 1970s, Lefort's reflection already defined a clear idea of modernity in terms of the separation of the political and the religious (Lefort 1986, pp. 181–236), only later and thanks to the contribution offered by his consideration of Kantorowicz's essay does the concept of "disincorporation" emerge clearly, although the Parisian philosopher never devotes much analysis to it. See in particular Lefort (2007, pp. 139–146). Lefort (143) states, "I therefore speak of the *disincorporation* of power, whereas the sociologist might prefer to restrict himself to the notion of a limitation of politics. This is because politics is not only the result of a juridico-functional apparatus. In order for it to become institutionalized, for the distinction between political authority and state administration to be precisely defined, and also for the space of civil liberties on which that authority should not encroach to be delimited, it is necessary that the sovereign has ceased to incarnate the community and that he no longer appear above the law". On disincorporation see also Bataillon (2014) and Breckman (2013, pp. 93–96).

Within this context, one element appears particularly significant to Lefort, namely the emergence of the modern state between the fourteenth and fifteenth centuries.[19] The modern state is much more than the mere result of a new economic structure but rather lays bare a new symbolic dimension, an unprecedented relationship between the social and power. State power implies first and foremost the imposition of a legitimate order on a social whole made up of constituents in a particular territory. This territory, in turn, is not only a physical space but is determined by the power operating in it. That is, by the fact that individuals within it recognize themselves as being bound to the same authority. Power therefore splits away from the social and acquires an external point of view: it overwhelms the social and at the same time shapes it. State power, Lefort argues, is "instituting" (*instutuent*), in the sense that the social is recognized precisely in reference to a given political power. It is only through the totalizing gaze of power that the social can recognize itself as a unity, seeing beyond its internal differences. At the same time, however, this power only exerts itself because of its connection to the territory and because of the legitimacy that is conferred on it by the social. The imposition of legitimate order is linked to the social recognition of the legitimacy of power. Political power is thus the "founder of society just as much as it is founded in society" (Lefort 1975a–1976a, p. 13). Its detachment from the social involves the birth, for the first time, of a true social. The two sides have a reciprocal effect on each other. The power of the modern state, then, is something radically new: it is no longer tied to a transcendent dimension but is rooted in society, which, as a symbolic reference point, it also shapes. It is not completely internal to the social, but neither is it completely external.

[19] As Hugues Poltier once again noted in *Passion du politique* (Poltier 1998, pp. 218–220), Lefort's consideration of the role of the state and European monarchies in the emergence of modernity is not developed in depth and in full in the edited writings, nor, I would add, is it entirely coherent. However, his reflections are decidedly more consistent in the typescripts of seminars held in the Archives. During 1975–1976, the philosopher highlights clearly the link between events in the Tuscan city in the late fourteenth century and the early fifteenth century, and the emergence of nation-states in the sixteenth century. In the *résumé* of the Seminar held between 1976 and 1977, which Lefort dedicates to the "Formation de l'État moderne, pouvoir, corps politique, nation", we read: "Le séminaire s'est ouvert par une introduction aux problèmes de l'Etat moderne. Etat qui se dessine dès le milieu du 13ème s., en rupture avec l'autorité de l'Empire et de l'Eglise, se définit peu à peu par la délimitation d'un territoire, l'identité d'une nation, l'unification d'un peuple sous un pouvoir souverain (*rex imperator in suo regno*)" (Lefort 1976–1977, p. 1).

And it is in this sense that the modern state is distinguished from other types of state. Where detached political power is supposed to be founded elsewhere, in a place away from the social whole, a place indicated by mythical or religious discourse, power does not appear to be essentially political. And the society over which it reigns does not, I would say, appear to be essentially social. (Lefort 1975a–1976a, pp. 13–14)[20]

The disintegration of the link with the transcendent dimension leads to a fundamental change in the image of power. No longer being external and inaccessible, this is drawn into the contingency of human reality, into the confines of the city. No longer sustained by an invisible Otherness, it is opened to constant questioning by the individuals who make up the community. Its place can be contested. Its actions can be debated, and their legitimacy requires constant reaffirmation. But what changes is the entire self-representation of the social. Indeed, power, having now entered society, announces that it is self-generated, according to its own rules and laws. The contingent social order thus appears first and foremost as distinct from the necessary natural order. Human reality splits from the transcendent world and acquires a dignity of its own.[21] The gap between the symbolic and the real, which is insubstantial in premodern societies, becomes visible, perceptible, and conceivable (Lefort 2007, pp. 142–144).[22]

The fact that power becomes circumscribed within society does not, however, mean that it becomes purely immanent, nor does it mean that it is constituted as a de facto power without a symbolic dimension. On the other hand, if it were a de facto power only, it could not maintain the coordinates of social identity. Modern power, however, while generated by the community, is not completely internal to it. It is founded by society

---

[20] The original text preserved in the Archives is as follows: "Et c'est en ce sens que l'Etat moderne se distingue des autres types d'état. Là où le pouvoir politique détaché est supposé trouver son fondement dans un lieu autre, lieu à distance de l'ensemble sociale, lieu pointé par le discours mythique ou par le discours religieux, le pouvoir n'apparaît pas essentiellement comme politique. Et la société sur laquelle il règne n'apparaît pas, je dirais, essentiellement sociale".

[21] I think, beyond this reading, one can also clearly detect the influence of Max Weber, whom Lefort was already reading in the early 1950s. See Lefort (1978, pp. 188–214). *The Protestant Ethic and the Spirit of Capitalism* (Weber 1978) is the main point of reference.

[22] This does not mean that it becomes possible to consider reality per se as separate from the symbolic dimension. Rather, it means that the symbolic can now be perceived as a dimension generated by society itself and therefore as something contingent.

but at the same time is its foundation (Lefort 1988, pp. 217–219). It is the symbol of a place of the Other that continues to be present, even when the political validity of the religious dimension is entirely gone.

> Even before we examine it in its empirical determinations, this symbolic pole proves to be power; it manifests society's self-externality, and ensures that society can achieve a quasi-representation of itself. We must of course be careful not to project this externality on to the real; if we did so it would no longer have any meaning for society. It would be more accurate to say that power makes a gesture towards something *outside*, and that it defines itself in terms of that outside. Whatever its form, it always refers to the same enigma: that of an internal-external articulation, of a division which institutes a common space, of a break which establishes relations, of a movement of the externalization of the social which goes hand in hand with its internalization. (225)

The transcendence that structured the monarchies of the *ancien régime* is now replaced by what we might refer to as merely relative autonomy.[23] The symbolic pole of power, in fact, represents both something purely human and the "separation" from that which eludes human determination. It represents humanity's openness to itself and an otherness that always precedes it, the openness to the impossibility of grasping itself as a totality. Power is the reference point that enables the representation of society and defines the distance that helps society to look at itself, to define itself and to return to itself. In the modern form of society, therefore, otherness is not erased but undergoes a change. It continues to refer to the unattainability of origin and foundation, but these origin and foundation are now no longer transcendent and indisputable foundations but are instead contingent and tied to social representation itself. Rather than ushering in the era of autonomy, then, for Lefort modernity is the form of society that "rather than effacing the dimension of Other in the experience of life" unveiled it (Lefort 2007, p. 144).[24]

---

[23] Lefort does not use the term autonomy to describe this type of society. This is instead a term used by Castoriadis or Gauchet. However, I believe that in this case it is descriptive and therefore useful.

[24] In this reading, there certainly emerges a difference or at least a tension with the ideas of Cornelius Castoriadis, who defines modern democratic society precisely in terms of "autonomy". In fact, perhaps referring specifically to Castoriadis, Lefort states: "Are

However, this does not make modern power any less radically unprecedented. On the contrary, its new appearance involves a genuine upheaval of the entire symbolic order: it calls for a revolution. Once it has freed itself from the religious dimension, power can no longer present itself as the repository of absolute and unquestionable law and knowledge, and these consequently become autonomous and gain independence. This opens up the possibility of thinking according to patterns different from those established and permitted by Scripture or tradition. Different ways of exercising power and alternative systems of coexistence can be explored and proposed. Hierarchies and social relations, no longer being ordered by the divine Word or the forces of Nature, appear contingent and require a new, human justification. Every order appears human and therefore contingent and transitory, and no role continues to be beyond question. The same process takes place in the field of law, which is brought back to the confines of the community and therefore requires social ratification to be considered legitimate. It is no longer an expression of God or the unquestionable wisdom of power. It is a human instrument for the management and organization of the community, and it is therefore perfectible and questionable. Moreover, it is now open to challenge (Lefort 1986, pp. 181–236).

This *disintrication*, the split between law, power, and knowledge also enables the emergence of different spheres of knowledge, such as economics, justice, and, above all, politics.[25] The latter can now be thought of as a human activity with its own rules, distinct from the religious dimension and separate from both the idea of absolute knowledge and divine law.[26] Politics arises as a particular knowledge concerned with

we therefore to believe that modern democracy opened the era of autonomy? The disincorporation of power—the fact that those who are entrusted with it depend on popular suffrage and enjoy only a legitimacy granted to them—does not mean that the site of power is limited to the interior of society. If it becomes forbidden to occupy that site, it is always from it that society acquires a representation of itself, as differentiated as that society may be and as manifold the oppositions that shape it" (Lefort 2007, p. 143). For a comparison between the two authors see at least Poirier (2022).

[25] It may be interesting to point out that in the development of this theory of modern symbolic change Lefort is still working in the context of Marx's description of modernity as the autonomization of the economic sphere.

[26] This new image of politics develops, not coincidentally, alongside the evolution of a specific branch of knowledge concerned with it, that of political science. Esteban Molina (2005, p. 200) has written on this theme.

the management of the city, with governance, and with the methods of conservation and expansion.[27] The delimitation of a specific area of political affairs coincides with the appearance of a different field of relations, one that is external to politics and in which the social appears with a substance of its own: civil society (Lefort 1978, pp. 286–332).[28] This, in short, is an unprecedented mode of sociality and is obviously accompanied by an original form of historicity.

At the same time, the loss of the foundation, of the distinction between the human and transcendent worlds, calls into question the rigidity of time as a repetitive, immobile phenomenon in which everything has already been resolved by the generating principle, in which the origin is present.[29] The contingency of institutions and especially of the principles that justify them, and the fact that these can all be questioned, opens up the possibility of change in orders and societies. The ability to question tradition makes it plausible to imagine alternative futures, to critique the present, and to abandon the past. In this way, human time becomes mutable and linear. Past, present, and future are separated and set on a line of development that allows one to envisage change and progress,

---

[27] Lefort outlines an autonomy of the political dimension, that is, its distance and independence from economic and social factors. This distinction between politics and economics is also clearly rooted in the critique of Marxist economism and the distinction between the productive/economic structure and the ideological superstructure. From these perspectives, the French philosopher's analysis could be included in the long-running discussion on the autonomy of politics that involved several scholars in the twentieth century. One thinks first of all of Carl Schmitt and those who built on his work, from Mario Tronti to Chantal Mouffe. See Schmitt (2007) and Mouffe (2005). However, on closer inspection, Lefort's view does not seem completely the same. Due to its instituting nature, Lefort's concept of the political cannot be reduced to a friend-enemy relationship independent of, say, the economic or social level. On this topic see: Wiley (2016) and Marchart (2007).

[28] On the emergence of the sphere of civil society separate from the state, see also: Lefort (1978, pp. 236–332 and 215–237). In these articles Lefort highlights the link between the modern power described by Machiavelli and the emergence of modern civil society. However, it is important to emphasize that Lefort's idea of civil society is not separate from the idea of the political. See Lefort (1988, pp. 218–220).

[29] Here again one can find the lesson of Max Weber. Marcel Gauchet (1997) articulates the idea of world disenchantment with Lefort's (and Castoriadis') theory of the institution of the social. Gauchet also emphasizes the role of the modern state and divine right monarchies in the transition to modernity. See also Gauchet (2014). On Marcel Gauchet's theory of modernity see Doyle and McMorrow (2022).

and human beings become the main actors in this history. The imaginary occupation of a vantage point from where history can be seen in its entirety and in terms of its progress makes the movement of "the institution of the social" perceptible.

For Lefort, the modern form of society is open to constant change, to the acceptance of internal conflict, and to a questioning of institutions, and in it power no longer embodies a transcendent principle and does not contain knowledge and law within itself. Modernity is a time of society and politics.

This is an idea of modernity that is in itself different from the Hobbesian one. In the picture painted by Lefort, the author of *Leviathan*'s idea of the inclusion of subjects in the body of the sovereign, and his justification of community arrangement and covenant through transcendence, mean that he is still firmly tied to pre-modern conceptions.[30] Modernity, on the other hand, is characterized by its disincorporation, by the demise of the theological-political nexus, by its openness to the possibility of a community without foundation, and by an idea of indeterminacy.[31] The authors who might be considered the forerunners of this symbolic shift are therefore not the theorists of contractualism, who sought to find a rational justification for community. Instead, the intellectual current worth focusing on is the one inaugurated, along with the birth of the modern state, by Florentine humanism and developed by republicanism. Coluccio Salutati, Leonardo Bruni, Francesco Guicciardini, and, above all, Niccolò Machiavelli will be the protagonists of "true" modern thought.[32]

---

[30] Lefort does not describe his idea of modernity as an alternative to Hobbes's, but his work is open to this possibility.

[31] Lefort's interpretation obviously fits into a very broad debate on the rise of modernity and secularization. In addition to the aforementioned Weber (1978), one thinks also of Löwith (1949) and Schmitt (1986). On the role of political theology in Lefort's thought and its relation to the debate on secularization, see Flynn (2013) and Labelle (2006). Following the definition of secularization proposed by Hans Blumenberg, Flynn concludes that "Lefort's position cannot be characterized as one of secularization" (Flynn 2013, p. 134).

[32] Several authors have attempted to define an alternative pathway to modernity by taking the work of Niccolò Machiavelli as a starting point and continuing through the theorists of republicanism. See in particular Negri (1999), Esposito (1986 and 2023), and the now classic study by Pocock (2017). Negri argues that Machiavelli, Spinoza, Harrington, and then Marx would delineate a political philosophy characterized by the immanence and emergence of constituent power, as opposed to the Hobbesian hegemonic

Dante, Civic Humanism and the Birth of Modernity

According to Lefort, the symbolic upheaval that opened the door to modernity cannot be defined as a single process with obvious causes and consequences. The forms of history and the social are to some extent incommensurable, and this transformation should not be perceived as a specific event that comes out of nothing (*ex nihilo*). Rather, it is better to understand it in terms of the continuous redefinition of meaning proper to the mechanism of the institution. This is a perspective that a theory of the institution of the social can make explicit.[33] Thus while it is possible to periodize, to distinguish between antiquity, the Middle Ages, and modernity, it is worth doing so not to describe the phases of development and transformation of this meaning, but rather to observe, from within a given symbolic institution, the changes in meaning that have taken place. Within this context, Lefort could attempt to symbolically reinterpret the birth of modernity in terms of the loss of the transcendent foundation.

In this framework, the figure of Dante Alighieri plays a key role, and one of his works in particular, *Monarchia*, attracts Lefort's attention (Dante 1996).[34] The merit of this treatise is that it questions the subordination of temporal power to the spiritual power that characterized

---

philosophy centered on the paradigm of sovereignty, institutions, and the theological-political verticality of the power relation. Roberto Esposito has also attempted, starting with Machiavelli, to trace a line of development of modern political thought that contrasts with that of Hobbes. In his most recent book, he presents Machiavelli as the first theorist of an idea of the institution that, through Spinoza and Hegel, reaches as far as Lefort. Pocock looks at the ideal of the classical republic proposed by Machiavelli and its consequences for modern historical and social thought.

[33] Hugues Poltier (1998, p. 219) points out the fragmentary and excessively disorganized nature of Lefort's reflection on the origins of the modern, especially when we consider only what he published. The tension between modernity as an event and a process is not completely resolved in Lefort's scheme. Another problem is that of the incommensurability of symbolic institutions of the social that nevertheless become part of the same history.

[34] In 1993, Lefort signed an introduction to the French edition of *De Monarchia* for the publishing house Belin titled "Dante's Modernity", now in Lefort (2021 and 2020). As the title indicates, Dante is credited with anticipating some of the key themes of modernity. In this text, Lefort refers to a number of studies when developing his interpretation of Dante, including: Gilson (1985), Nardi (1944), Renaudet (1951), Dragonetti (1961), and Goudet (1969). The most recent ICI edition contains an interesting essay by Judith Revel.

medieval thought and was theorized by Augustine, political Augustinianism, and Thomas Aquinas. Augustine of course described the difference between a *civitas terrena*, in which human passions dominate, and a *civitas Dei* governed by the law of love and sacrifice. However, he did not renounce his belief in the superiority of the Church over Christian states. In Dante's reflection, on the other hand, Lefort notes that the difference between the secular and religious spheres is significantly greater and becomes paradigmatic. For the first time, the city of God and the city of man, the church, and the empire are considered radically independent. The two powers express two parallel purposes toward which human life appears to be directed: the pursuit of happiness on earth, which is attained through philosophical teachings, and the pursuit of happiness in heaven, arrived at through revealed truths and spiritual teachings. Two forms of power correspond to the two aims of human life, namely the secular power of the emperor and the spiritual power of the pontiff, which are autonomous and have equal dignity. The former, no less than the latter, is invested directly by God, without any intermediary, and the two, therefore, owe each other respect and devotion, and there is no justification for imperial power to subordinate itself to the papacy.

Although Dante's reflection remains connected to the medieval "image of the body" and a transcendent justification of power and community, Lefort identifies in it an early sign of the separation of the theological and political, along with some of the pivotal mechanisms on which modern thought would be built. His attention is directed first and foremost to the first book of the *Monarchia*, in which the author uses the term *humanitas* to refer to humankind as a whole and in its broadest sense.[35] Taking a decisive step beyond ancient philosophy, Dante perceives humanity outside the narrow limits of natural sociality or citizenship (Lefort 2020, p. 6). If for Aristotle the ideal city consisted of a restricted community located in a clearly defined space, Dante's *humanitas* instead includes the most diverse populations inhabiting very different climates and adhering to distinct cultures and customs.[36] Humanity becomes the totality of all men and women, whose unity rests on a common submission to a monarch and a shared goal, namely the power of intellectual virtue (13).

---

[35] It should be pointed out that Lefort's interpretation ignores the coeval and earlier use of the term.

[36] Lefort again avoids the limitations of Dante's thought.

This can be attained neither by any individual nor a particular community but only by humanity as a whole, whose complete form emerges from the submission to a single prince (Dante 1996, p. 13). Dante thus introduces a new kind of universality whose dignity does not reside in a transcendent justification. Moreover, the *civitas humanitatis* that he describes is not a pure ideal, but an earthly matter that depends entirely on human will and develops in the course of history. Its occurrence was evident in the time of Augustus, when the goal of a universal empire in which humanity can identify itself as united and live in peace emerged (Lefort 2020, pp. 24–25). Dante is thus the first to describe the autonomous dignity of a human race understood not only as a universal entity but as one with complete historicity.

This novel assessment of human activity and its autonomy is accompanied by an original reflection on history. Abandoning the cyclical conception of time, Dante accepts history as a progressive, uniquely human path affected by time and change (22). The result is a profound alteration in the relationship with classical works. In opposition to the sterile repetition of the lesson of the ancients, Dante proposes a principle of non-repetition. This is how Lefort interprets the opening lines of the first book of the *Monarchia*, which outline a modern idea of the endeavor of thought, one based on the desire to innovate and produce something new. The passage expresses the desire to surrender the legacy of the ancients to posterity, but to do so while developing the talent and original thinking capable of grasping truths that others have not sought (Dante 1996, p. 3).[37]

Lefort also notes that in the same few lines, the work's validity and originality are linked to its usefulness to the community. New truths unearthed by one's own talents must not only bring personal glory but also "bear fruit for the benefit of all" (*ibid.*).[38] Thought must aim to

---

[37] In the first line of *Monarchia*, Dante writes: "For all men whom the Higher Nature has endowed with a love of truth, this above all seems to be a matter of concern, that just as they have been enriched by the efforts of their forebears, so they too may work for future generations, in order that posterity may be enriched by their efforts. For the man who is steeped in the teachings which form our common heritage, yet has no interest in contributing something to the community, is failing in his duty: let him be no doubt of that; for he is not 'a tree planted by the rivers of water, that bringeth forth his fruit in due reason', but rather a destructive whirlpool which forever swallows things down and never gives back it has swallowed".

[38] The opening lines of Dante's work had a great impact on Lefort's interpretation.

impact the administration of the community, and the contemplative life and the active life therefore appear linked, as the principles of philosophy are imprinted on the world order. This is the formulation of an unprecedented relationship between philosophy and politics.

This, in a nutshell, is the legacy that, in Lefort's interpretation, Dante leaves to modern thought. Although his work is still rooted in the medieval world, and his reflection does not renounce the appeal to transcendent legitimacy, the profound theoretical innovations entrusted to the pages of the *Monarchy* do not go unnoticed:

> Whether he inspired praise or refutation, Dante was never forgotten. And forgotten he could not be, for his work contained something other than a theory of Empire. He had opened a new field to thought, given form to humanity, broken the image of cyclical time, bestowed upon life on earth its dignity, and fully rehabilitated the part therein of the *vita activa*, without ceasing to hold the highest opinion of the *vita contemplativa*. Finally, he had conjured up an idea of the oeuvre—of the work of thought governed by the demands of beginnings and unveiling—which was to be essential for all subsequent philosophical writers. (Lefort 2020, p. 43)

It was the exponents of Florentine civic humanism in particular who confronted this legacy in depth. Moreover, by then Dante's work had opened a new and unexplored field of intellectual inquiry, which the humanists could not resist. Writers, poets, and thinkers such as Cino Rinuccini, Gregorio Dati, Buonaccorso da Montemagno, Coluccio Salutati, and Leonardo Bruni (the foremost exponent of political humanism) would continue Dante's lesson by further questioning the theological conception of the world, by reflecting on the peculiar dignity of the human, by tying theory even more tightly to political practice, and by renouncing the transcendent justification of power and the organic view of community.[39] They would, in other words, take a break with theological-political thought prefigured in Dante's work to its extreme consequences.

For Lefort, who follows the lessons of Hans Baron and Eugenio Garin closely, humanism represents a far-reaching phenomenon that could not

---

[39] For example, Coluccio Salutati and Leonardo Bruni, while not adhering to Dante's imperial ideal, would not refrain from referring to his works. Bruni himself in fact composed, probably in around 1436, a *Life of Dante* (see Bruni 2000). As for Salutati, Lefort refers to his treatise on tyranny that appeared in 1400 (Salutati 1942).

be limited to the literary sphere and which disrupts the habits of Western thought by inaugurating an unprecedented relationship with knowledge and social experience (Garin 1965 and Baron 2021).[40] To understand this, it is necessary to refer to developments in Florence between the late fourteenth and fifteenth centuries.[41] In this period, Dante's idea that the world is the only theater of human adventure found further development. Human discourse was found to be self-intelligible and emancipated itself from the limits imposed by an external authority by creating space for a new relationship with knowledge and power. Florence, in other words, was the birthplace of a modern, truly political discourse (Lefort 1975a–1976a, pp. 1–2).[42]

---

[40] In his analysis of humanism Lefort refers mainly to the works of Eugenio Garin and Hans Baron. References in Lefort's speeches and the bibliography compiled by the Parisian himself for the course on Florentine humanism (Lefort 1975a–1976a and 1975b–1976b) delivered between 1975 and 1976, which is preserved in the Archives Claude Lefort at the EHEAA (EHESS-CESPRA, cl 8, boîte 3), confirm this thesis.

[41] During the course, Lefort frequently dwells on Baron's work. See also the notes grouped under the title "Hans Baron" preserved in the same *boîte*. In the same 1975–1976 course cited above, one can read a critique of Baron's ideas, which accuse him of reducing Florentine civil humanism to a special case within the broader phenomenon of European humanism. On the contrary, for Lefort the Tuscan city was at the heart of the humanist phenomenon rather than being home to a variant of it. See Lefort (1975a–1976a, p. 54).

[42] The typescript of the aforementioned "Florence" course contains the following: "Nous traiterons d'un ensemble d'évènements qui ont pour théâtre Florence à la fin du *Trecento* et au début du *Quatrocento* (*sic* !), soit durant un période qui s'étend approximativement de 1390 à 1435. Le début de cette période prétend, est en matière à discussion, je dirais plus tard pourquoi et la fin de cette période en revanche étant tout à fait nette en ce sens qu'elle marque un changement de régime, l'avènement de Cosme de Médicis et on peut dire l'embryon d'un principat, c'est-àdire l'abandon du modèle républicain qui avait été celui de Florence pendant des décennies et même on peut dire depuis qu'elle s'était affranchie de la noblesse et que dans un système que l'on peut qualifier de plus oligarchique que démocratique, elle avait néanmoins mis en place une république, des organes délibératifs et consultatifs entre les mains des citoyens. Mon intention est donc d'aborder ces problèmes parce que ces événements nous font voir à la fois une transformation profonde dans le statut du pouvoir à Florence. En deux mots, ce pouvoir s'affirme comme pouvoir central de la commune aux dépens des foyers de puissance qui contestaient la légitimité jusque-là. D'autre part, la représentation même du pouvoir change c'est-à-dire que naît un discours proprement politique, discours universaliste dans sa prétention tandis que, en même temps, on voit s'imposer pour la première fois l'image de la bourgeoisie comme celle d'une classe dominante, d'une classe rassemblée, d'une classe consciente d'elle-même, je risque ce mot emprunté du vocabulaire marxiste qui mérite toutes les réserves" (Lefort 1975a–1976a, p. 1).

The first result of this was a radical reconsideration of education. Some of the protagonists of civic humanism paid anything but marginal attention to the development of new pedagogical principles defined in open contrast to those of the scholastic tradition (Lefort 1992, pp. 209–226).[43] The latter had formalized a coherent and enduring system of teaching linked to the idea of a transcendent truth of which the church was the sole repository. A series of institutions, programs, and methods connected to a strict division between particularly specialized areas of knowledge—theology, medicine, law—had been the principal offshoots of that educational approach. Within this framework, knowledge was synonymous with notionism and with the transmission of traditional knowledge. The humanists, however, were determined to fundamentally rediscuss this approach, and the result was not only a change in educational programs and institutions but a completely new mindset. Knowledge came to be conceived as something independent of the object of study, as a means unto itself. Education was no longer limited to the acquisition of certain aspects of knowledge but was defined as a more general relationship to learning, with no predetermined limits or definite ends. Teaching and learning were no longer linked to a utilitarian purpose or to specialized disciplines. Their purpose was to develop the spirit and provide a broad-based education.

> It seems to us that this notion implies that there are no longer defined limits or terms assigned to the concrete practice of education. In a sense it welcomes indeterminacy, since the learner is no longer required to master a certain set of knowledge, but to enter into a new *relationship with knowledge*. [...] If education acquires value in itself, reveals itself to be in search of itself, and its practice generates a discourse that sees it as such, it is by virtue of this very indeterminacy, and of the fact that it is no longer reduced to a function that can be articulated from the starting point of extrinsic certainty. (213)

---

[43] The essay I am referring to here, titled "Formation et autorité: l'éducation humaniste", is a transcript of a talk given by Lefort in 1979. Garin's essay *Education in Europe* (Garin 1957) was a constant reference during the drafting of this article. The underestimation of Lefort's study of humanism is amply revealed by the fact that the English translation of Lefort (1992) does not include the two articles on humanism that we can find in the original French edition: see Lefort 2000.

The renewed relationship with knowledge also affects the study of the classics. The restoration of the Latin language and the return to classical sources involves a new relationship with texts, a new conception of time, and thus a new understanding of the authority of the ancient authors.[44] The *return to the authors* that characterizes the *studia humanitatis* is at the same time an attempt to restore them to identity and context. The new philological techniques aim to foster direct knowledge of the classics by dispensing with intermediaries. This criterion of inquiry recognizes at the same time the difference between the author and the reader and the temporalities proper to both. Reading the texts defines a new way of relating to the *sense of history* that involves the discovery of the split between the past and the future. Time separates into parts and is no longer stagnant and indistinct but progressive and linear.

Culture no longer ends in a dialogue with past authors and unchanging knowledge. "[T]he effort to restore the identity of the ancients is the means by which the moderns determine their own identity" (187). Once questioned, the ancient authors come back to life, become part of the sphere of *humanitas*, and gain the ability to communicate with the here and now. Thought and education provide the means to interrogate their own time and critique the institutions of the city and the family. Knowledge, in short, is no longer derived from an external authority or merely a continuation of tradition. It is now part of a relationship that continually involves a connection with the city and channels a new ethic of the life of the individual in the world and of his civic engagement. The active life is now seen as a means of acquiring knowledge rather than engaging in pure contemplation. Reflection becomes civil: it abandons metaphysical subtleties to engage with the rough and tumble of earthly matters, of politics. The humanists identify first and foremost as citizens of Florence, and it is from this perspective that they cross-examine the texts and solicit the authors of the past. Taken together, these elements make up a revolutionary frame of reference, a new relationship with the world that would be impossible to trace back to the effects of expanding trade or the dissemination of the classics.[45]

---

[44] The new relationship with time is a key element in understanding humanism and the novelty of its new way of interrogating ancient texts. Garin (1965) himself had repeatedly emphasized how humanism was characterized by a new way of reading texts linked to an unprecedented relationship with history.

[45] Lefort refers here to the study by R.R. Bolgar (2010).

There is a clear connection between the new idea of the author and the reader, of antiquity and modernity, and the new idea of fatherhood and childhood. Moreover, there is not only symmetry between the idea of language and the idea of the family, or the city; what gives authority to the city, or the family, is culture [...]. The city and the family represent themselves through culture. The discourse on the "idea" of the city or the "idea" of the family is part of their existence. *The institution "says" itself, holds a discourse about itself, and sustains itself because of that discourse, which passes through its members.* (191)

According to Lefort, humanist thought thus provides an escape from the theological-political core that structures and will continue to structure *ancien régime* societies for centuries. It establishes knowledge as something fully human and connected to the city, to civic experience, and to politics. This is a radical symbolic shift that affects the very categories that preside over the determination of the real (Lefort 1978, pp. 405–407). Through an unprecedented relationship with history, with knowledge, and with power, humanism calls into question the theological conception of the world and paves the way for thought capable of confronting indeterminacy: modern thought. The split between knowledge and the theological dimension develops in parallel with the city institutions' new autonomy from religion. Authority is shown as completely contingent, open to being criticized and questioned by members of the community. A new understanding of power thus takes shape, and the symbolic dimension of the social is completely restructured.

Lefort identifies this symbolic upheaval in the reinterpretation of Florence's Roman origins by the humanists, which challenged the narrative that had been prevailing since the thirteenth century. Caesar's legionaries are replaced as the mythical founders of the city by Sulla's veterans. Emphasis is placed on the republic over the empire, and Florentines can be said to be the descendants of free Roman citizens. Civic virtue and political responsibility are preferred to the valor of the emperor. The condemnation of Caesar is accompanied by the rehabilitation of Brutus, who sought to defend the freedom of Rome (Lefort 2012, p. 499). Through a series of daring historical expedients, Florence is thus established as the heir to republican ideals, the free Etruscan cities, and the Athenian democratic tradition.[46] The outbreak of conflict with the Duchy of Milan brings the political utility of this self-representation into the open: against Gian Galeazzo Visconti's despotic project, the Tuscan city proclaims itself the interpreter of the universal values of Dante's *humanitas*, equality, and civil liberty (Lefort 1975a–1976a, p. 55).

> The new idea is that men are recognized in Florence as having equal rights to win public honor, that they are spurred on to a noble competition for the advancement of their standing, and that their energies are greatly enhanced by their aspirations—as a result of which the entire social body is strengthened by their enterprises and their equality. (Lefort 2012, p. 498)

None of this equates to the birth of democracy, nor to any unveiling of "real" social relations concealed by previous religious models. These ideal references are obviously not unrelated to a new and complex ideological narrative in service of the citizen oligarchy. They represent a propagandistic narrative whose importance is based not so much on the novelty of the ideals upheld but on the original relationship between knowledge and politics (Lefort 1986, pp. 181–236).

Coluccio Salutati, chancellor of Florence from 1375 to 1406, is the person most obviously responsible for this clear innovation. During a thirty-year-period, as an important political figure, he never took off his academic robes, continuing to research and comment on new manuscripts and to enlarge what would become the city's greatest humanist library. In his public role, in speeches and missives celebrating the Florentine Republic and its ideals, Salutati employs dialectic, culture, classical texts, and the legacy of Rome in the service of the interests of the state. He thus makes clear the originality of a way of thinking in which knowledge and politics are no longer separated, and of a discourse that consistently legitimizes power and is engaged in a struggle for it.[47] However, the

---

[46] Lefort refers in particular to the oration delivered by Bruni in 1428, which contains frequent references to Pericles's speech honoring the victims of the Peloponnesian War and which was a celebration of Athenian democracy. See Lefort (2012, p. 498).

[47] During 1975–1976 Lefort refers in particular to the *Invective against Antonio Loschi*, written by Salutati during the conflict with Milan. In 1397 Loschi, then secretary to the duke of the Lombard city, had written an *Invectiva in Florentinos* in which he denounced the falsity of Florentine republican ideology. Salutati's response came in 1403, with the *Invectiva contra Antonium Luschum*, in which republican ideals were reiterated and defended. See Lefort (1975a–1976a, pp. 54–59).

ideological nature of this discourse does not take anything away from the importance of the radical novelty to which it points. What Salutati highlights is a discourse that is for the first time "political": it is intent on representing conflict, and grounded in an attempt to legitimize power that no longer has a natural or divine justification. This discourse is no longer internal to the power it speaks of but is in a relationship with it. For the first time, it is an element at the root of the power it seeks to legitimize. This discourse of power, in short, also marks the advent of the power of discourse (Lefort 1975a–1976a, p. 81). "To know that this discourse is a discourse of truth that is concerned with truth, and that somehow it is the discourse of no-one" (83)[48] and is profoundly universalistic. It is a discourse of a specific city but also of the city in general, of *civitas*, of the city as an instrument of defense of *libertas* against any political order that imposes subjection to a *maitre* (82–83).

Although Coluccio Salutati and Leonardo Bruni's speeches are not democratic in nature, according to Lefort it is in Florentine civil humanism that one must trace the nucleus of the republican tradition that will nurture modern democratic thought (Lefort 1978, p. 403). Figures such as Salutati or Bruni are therefore the first exponents of this, and their proclamations enable their work to find space to critique aristocratic values and tyranny, providing a universalist and rationalist conception of politics and a defense of the equality of citizens before the law. They advocate the division of power between those entitled to it, the idea that labor is the only legitimate source of distinction between men, and the principle that the proper use of reason and acquired knowledge is the only source of authority. These themes will run in the background through centuries of Western history before bursting forth in the eighteenth-century revolutions.[49]

It was therefore not Hobbes, Locke, and the contract theorists who helped trace the route to modernity, as the origin of modern political

---

[48] Lefort writes the following in the original typescript preserved in the archives: "A savoir que ce discours est un discours de vérité qui e place sous le signe de la vérité, et que d'une certaine façon il est le discours de personne".

[49] Further analyses of the relationship between politics and humanism are conducted by the philosopher in courses taught at the EHESS and available at Archives Claude Lefort (see especially Lefort 1975b–1976b).

thought was instead to be found in the theory of republicanism.[50] It was republican ideas that spread among the French intellectual elite of the sixteenth century and inspired Montesquieu, La Boétie, and Rousseau.[51] The same ideas proliferated in English colleges, universities, and law schools during the seventeenth century and inspired a rising *gentry* determined to exercise its public responsibilities. These ideas were also the trigger for the revolution of 1640–1650.

And along this path, in this interpretation of political modernity, one figure is especially important: Niccolò Machiavelli.

References

Baron, Hans. 2021. *The Crisis of the Early Italian Renaissance: Civic Humanism and Republican Liberty in an Age of Classicism and Tyranny*. Princeton: Princeton University Press.

Bataillon. Gilles. 2014. Claude Lefort, pratique et pensée de la désincorporation. *Raison politiques* 56/4: 69–85.

Bloch, March. 2015. *The Royal Touch: Sacred Monarchy and Scrofula in England and France*. London: Routledge.

Bolgar, Robert Ralph. 2010. *The Classical Heritage and its Beneficiaries*. Cambridge: Cambridge University Press.

Boureau, Alain. 2001. *Kantorowicz: Stories of a Historian*. Baltimore: Johns Hopkins University Press.

Breckman, Warren. 2013. *Adventures of the Symbolic: Post-marxism and Radical Democracy*. New York: Columbia University Press.

Bruni, Leonardo. 2000. The Lives of Dante and Petrarch. In *Images of Quattrocento Florence*, ed. Jeffery Rowthorn and Russell Schulz-Widmar, 125–138. New Haven: Yale University Press.

---

[50] In an article that has not been translated into English, *Foyers du Républicanisme* (Lefort 1992, pp. 181–208), Lefort discusses the links connecting humanism; fourteenth- and fifteenth-century Italian republicanism; the ideas of James Harrington, Jean-Jacques Rousseau and Etienne de La Boétie; and modern democracy. Not only does he highlight a continuity of thought, but he places republicanism at the foundation of the modern concept of democracy. For a history of this concept, its major interpretations and an overview of the debate see Pocock (2017), Skinner (2012), and Pettit (1997). In Marco Geuna's essay (Geuna 1998) about the history of republicanism, Lefort, together with Sheldon Wolin, is taken as an example of the attempt to consider together, through an idea of the republic understood as an alternative form of political community to the state, republicanism and radical democracy.

[51] Lefort criticizes the thesis, also taken up by Claude Nicolet (1982), which claims there was an absence of republican thinking in France before the Revolution.

Comensoli Antonin, Lorenzo. 2013. Gauchet lettore di Kantorowicz. Apporti alla teoria del disincanto. *Filosofia politica* 2: 271–294.
Dante. 1996. *Monarchy*. Cambridge: Cambridge University Press.
Doyle, Natalie. 2003. Democracy as Socio-cultural Project of Individual and Collective Sovereignty. Claude Lefort, Marcel Gauchet and the French Debate on Modern. *Thesis Eleven* 75: 69–95.
Doyle, Natalie and McMorrow, Sean. 2022. *Marcel Gauchet and the Crisis of Democratic Politics*. New York: Routledge.
Dragonetti, Roger. 1961. *Aux frontieres du langage poetique : études sur Dante, Mallarme, Valery*. Gent: Romanica Gandensia.
Esposito, Roberto. 1986. *Ordine e conflitto. Machiavelli e la letteratura politica del Rinascimento italiano*. Naples: Liguori.
Esposito, Roberto. 2023. *Vitam instituere. Genealogia dell'istituzione*. Torino: Einaudi.
Flynn, Bernard. 2013. Political Theology in the Thought of Lefort. *Social Research. An International Quarterly* 80/1: 129–142.
Garin, Eugenio. 1957. *L'educazione in Europa 1400–1600*. Bari: Laterza.
Garin, Eugenio. 1965. *Italian Humanism: Philosophy and Civic Life in the Renaissance*. New York: Harper and Row.
Gauchet, Marcel. 1997. *The Disenchantment of the World: A Political History of Religion*. Princeton: Princeton University Press.
Gauchet, Marcel. 2014. *La révolution moderne. L'avènement de la démocratie I*. Paris: Gallimard.
Geuna, Marco. 1998. The Republican Tradition and its Interpreters: Theoretical Families and Conceptual Discontinuities. *Filosofia politica* 12/1: 102–132.
Gilson, Étienne. 1985. *Dante et la philosophie*. Paris: Vrin.
Goudet, Jacques. 1969. *Dante et la politique*. Paris: Aubier-Montaigne.
Kantorowicz, Ernst. 2016. *The King's Two Bodies: A Study in Medieval Political Theology*. Princeton: Princeton University Press.
Labelle, Gilles. 2006. Can the Problem of the Theologico-Political be Resolved? Leo Strauss and Claude Lefort. *Thesis Eleven* 87/1: 63–81.
Lefort, Claude. 1975a–1976a. *Florence à la fin du Trecento et au début du Quatrocento*. Archives Claude Lefort, EHESS-CESPRA, CL. 8, envelope 3.
Lefort, Claude. 1975b–1976b. *La genèse de l'État moderne et l'institution du social. Cours 1975b–1976*. Archives Claude Lefort, EHESS-CESPRA, CL. 8, envelope 3.
Lefort, Claude. 1976–1977. *Résumé du Séminaire 1976–1977*. Archives Claude Lefort, EHESS-CESPRA, CL 9, envelope 4.
Lefort, Claude. 1978. *Les formes de l'histoire. Essais d'anthropologie politique*. Paris: Gallimard.
Lefort, Claude. 1986. *The Political Forms of Modern Society: Bureaucracy, Democracy, Totalitarianism*. Cambridge: MIT Press.

Lefort, Claude. 1988. *Democracy and Political Theory*. Cambridge: Polity Press.
Lefort, Claude. 1992. *Écrire. A l'épreuve du politique*. Paris: Calmann-Lévy.
Lefort, Claude. 2000. *Writing: The Political Test*. Durham: Duke University Press.
Lefort, Claude. 2007. *Complications: Communism and the Dilemma of Democracy*. New York: Columbia University Press.
Lefort, Claude. 2012. *Machiavelli in the Making*. Evanston: Northwestern University Press.
Lefort, Claude. 2020. *Dante's Modernity. An Introduction to the Monarchia*. Berlin: ICI Berlin Press.
Lefort, Claude. 2021. *Lectures politiques. De Dante à Soljenitsyne*. Paris: Puf.
Löwith, Karl. 1949. *The Meaning in History: The Theological Implications of the Philosophy of History*. Chicago: University of Chicago Press.
Marchart, Oliver. 2007. *Post-Foundational Political Thought: Political Difference in Nancy, Lefort, Badiou and Laclau*. Edinburgh: Edinburgh University Press.
Marx, Karl. 1976. *Capital: A Critique of Political Economy—Volume One*. London: Penguin.
Marx, Karl. 2005. *Grundrisse: Foundations of the Critique of Political Economy*. London: Penguin.
Marx, Karl. 2010. A Contribution to the Critique of Political Economy. In: Sitton, J.F. (eds) *Marx Today Selected Works and Recent Debates*. New York: Palgrave Macmillan.
Marx, Karl and Engels Friedrich. 2002. *The Communist Manifesto*. London: Penguin.
Michelet, Jules. 1989. *History of the French Revolution*. Chicago: University of Chicago Press.
Molina, Esteban. 2005. *Le défi du politique. Totalitarisme et démocratie chez Claude Lefort*. Paris: L'Harmattan.
Mouffe, Chantal. 2005. *On the Political*. Routledge.
Nardi, Bruno. 1944. *Nel mondo di Dante*. Roma: Edizioni di Storia e Letteratura.
Negri, Antonio. 1999. *Insurgencies: Constituent power and the modern state*. Minneapolis: University of Minnesota Press
Nicolet, Claude. 1982. *L'idée républicaine en France (1789–1924)*. Paris: Gallimard.
Pettit, Philip. 1997. *Republicanism: A Theory of Freedom and Government*. Clarendon: Oxford University Press.
Pocock, John Greville Agard. 2017. *The Machiavellian Moment: Florentine Political Thought and the Atlantic Republican Tradition*. Princeton: Princeton University Press.
Poirier, Nicolas. 2022. Wild Being, between Ontology and Politics: Merleau-Ponty, Lefort, Castoriadis. *International Journal of Social Imaginaries* 1: 84–106.

Poltier, Hugues. 1998. *Passion du politique. La pensée de Claude Lefort*. Genève: Labor et Fides.
Renaudet, Augustin. 1951. *Dante humaniste*. Paris: Les belles lettres.
Salutati, Coluccio. 1942. *Trattato «De Tyranno» e lettere scelte*. Bologna: Zanichelli.
Schmitt, Carl. 1986. *Political Theology: Four Chapters on the Concept of Sovereignty*. London-Cambridge: MIT Press.
Schmitt, Carl. 2007. *The Concept of the Political*. Chicago: University of Chicago Press.
Schöttler, Peter. 2014. Ernst Kantorowicz en France. *Éthique, politique, religions* 2/5: 159–182.
Skinner, Quentin. 2012 [1978]. The *Foundations of Modern Political Thought*. Cambridge: Cambridge University Press.
Weber, Max. 1978. *The Protestant ethic and the Spirit of Capitalism*. Los Angeles: University of California Press.
Wiley, James. 2016. *Politics and the Concept of the Political*. London: Routledge.
Wittfogel, Karl A. 1957. *Oriental Despotism: A Comparative Study of Total Power*. New Haven: Yale University Press.

Niccolò Machiavelli

The Critique of Tradition, or the Loss of Foundation

In 1972, Lefort published his most important work, *Le travail de l'œuvre, Machiavel* (Lefort 1972 and 2012). The volume analyzes the major texts of the Florentine Secretary and is the result of more than a decade of research.[1] It can be considered a first staging post on the path we have followed up to this point, an initial "systematization" of the ideas Lefort had been developing since his years in SouB. In it, he settles some issues with Marxism and presents the results of his lengthy reasoning on history, modernity, and democracy. As explained in the previous chapter, the subject is not accidental: for Lefort Machiavelli was the key author for understanding modern symbolic change, in other words, the loss of foundation that opened the way to the contemporary form of society and democracy.

According to the French philosopher, understanding the relationship between the Florentine Secretary's thought and modernity first of all means paying attention to the temporal dimension of his texts, the caesura

---

[1] Lefort wrote his first essays on Machiavelli as early as 1960. See Lefort (1978, pp. 215–237, 259–285, and 286–332). These articles are dated 1974, 1971, and 1960. His interest in Machiavelli thus begins well before and continues after the 1972 essay.

represented in them and the innovative elements they identify. It involves appropriating the historical horizon of Machiavelli's work and attempting to assume the position of a reader contemporary to him.[2] This opens up the possibility of a particular experience of history, one that can be discovered in the text but at the same time flows beyond it, and can therefore enable us to understand Machiavelli's works along with the meaning they contain beyond their own time, in the broader context of the symbolic change of modernity, right up to contemporary democracy.[3] In short, Lefort's intention is to search for the author's word in his world, in the actuality of a discourse located in a particular place and time, and, at the same time, to accommodate the overhanging meaning of his thought. Although the institutions and political mores of sixteenth-century Italy are now in the past, and while it would be wrong to locate the features of contemporary experience in the crisis of the Florentine Republic, the ability of Machiavelli's thought to speak to our time, to enable us to understand the signs of symbolic change that might help us understand our contemporaneity, has not been extinguished (3–60).

It is on the basis of this method of analysis that Lefort undertakes to read the works of the Florentine Secretary, with *The Prince* as the starting point of this interpretive journey. His first objective is to grasp the book's meaning through the eyes of the person to whom it is addressed and through the book's relationship to the political and social situation of Florence and Italy in its own period. First, Lefort is convinced that the

[2] On Lefort's way of interpreting the works of Machiavelli see Di Pierro (2018, 2020), Ménissier (2017), Marcotte-Chénard (2015), Janvier and Mancuso (2013), Trindade (2013), Audier (2005), Molina (2000), and Manent (1993), in addition, of course, to Flynn (2005) and Poltier (1998). The thesis set forth in my 2020 text essentially follows, albeit with different references, the one I present in this chapter. Sfez (2007) analyzes the twentieth-century French debate on the interpretation of Machiavelli and considers readings by Raymond Aron, Jacques Maritain, Louis Althusser, Michel Foucault, Maurice Merleau-Ponty, and Lefort.

[3] Lefort repeatedly rails against interpreters who intended to find a way to study Machiavelli's work based exclusively on the terrain of historical facts. One of the targets of this criticism is the work of the historian Augustin Renaudet, to whom is devoted a chapter of *Le travail de l'œuvre* (Lefort 1972, pp. 178–190). Renaudet, Lefort asserts, believes he is merely reviewing objective facts and ideas, and that he can analyze Machiavelli's work as if it were an empirical fact, but in so doing only conceals the intentions that guide his interpretation and draws a veil over the radical weakness of his discourse (186). Moreover, it is not far-fetched to think that Lefort's critique could also be directed toward the interpretation of Federico Chabod (1964), who the philosopher knew well and who he mentions several times in the 1972 text.

work was not written merely to respond to a specific moment, something that he deduces from an examination of the possible date in which it was completed, which Machiavelli's letter to his friend Francesco Vettori and certain reports written during his time in the Chancery indicate would have been within a few months after the summer of 1513.[4] Lefort's conclusion is clear: although composed in only a few months, *The Prince* is clearly the outcome of a much greater effort, of reflections already developed during the years when Machiavelli was involved in the Florentine political scene and was already an *homme de plume*, a recognized and esteemed theorist (81–89). The treatise therefore represented the first moment of the author's theoretical-political reflection, into which he poured the "long experience in modern affairs and a continuous study of antiquity" (Machiavelli 2005, p. 5).[5] It was thus an intellectual product of long-running, mature research, the originality of which the author must have been fully aware.

In fact, Lefort argues that only a superficial reading could interpret Machiavelli's treatise as a simple reflection on government or an account of its author's desire to help Giuliano de' Medici. The first eleven chapters of the work, which deal with themes typical of certain literary genres prevalent at the time, do in fact appear to lead in this direction, offering portrayals of the various types of principality and examining the ways of acquiring, maintaining, and defending dominion over a territory. A closer look, however, casts doubt on this first impression. First of all, the elements typical of scholastic treatises of the same genre, the *specula principis* (mirrors for princes), or of ancient works of a similar type, are absent. In addition, Machiavelli does not place the relationship between the prince and his subjects in the more general framework of man's relationship with Nature or God, as would have been typical. The argument

---

[4] Lefort is well acquainted with the studies of this period and sides with Federico Chabod in supporting the thesis that *The Prince* was written in a few months, after the summer of 1513. Chabod challenged Friedrich Meinecke and Oreste Tommasini, proponents of the dualistic thesis that only the first nine chapters of the work were written before 1513, while the others were completed later. For a summary and discussion of the issue and debate see Sasso (1993; 2015, pp. 60–69), and Chabod (1964).

[5] The idea that *The Prince* was the first moment of Machiavelli's reflection derives from the position taken by Lefort with respect to the vexed question of the date of the *Discourses* and the relationship between the two works. Lefort, in establishing his position, also refers to Hans Baron's studies. See Lefort (2012, pp. 87–88). On the influence of Baron on Lefort see Ménissier (2017).

also does not begin, as one might expect, with a definition of the state, and does not proceed to a comparison between regimes founded on princely authority and those based on other forms of political organization. Nor does the author appear to actually address a prince in order to teach him what is good, evil, or useful. The field of investigation, in short, does not allow itself to be clearly circumscribed, and the true object of the writing proves elusive (Lefort 2012, pp. 89–91).

To understand the work's singularity and penetrate its meaning, Lefort believes it is essential to approach it differently, by attempting to grasp what the author is proposing between the lines and beyond his explicit arguments. He believes it is necessary to connect the surface argument to the larger, hidden discourse in which it is contained, in order to understand what remains unexpressed and why it is essential that the "true" meaning is not immediately apparent (91).[6] Machiavelli's statement of his initial assumptions is already enough to generate surprise, when he declares that he wants to address two questions: "how many kinds of principalities there are and the ways they are acquired" (Machiavelli 2005, p. 7). While in keeping with the tradition of writings on government, this proposal is immediately jettisoned as the Secretary breaks with established tradition without providing any justification. He ignores the specific characteristics of different regimes and repudiates the classical opposition between legitimate and illegitimate power. In this way, the artifice through which *The Prince* is constructed is revealed: the work is presented as a classic treatise on government but this traditional appearance is

---

[6] Lefort's interpretation is also based on a comparison and reference to Leo Strauss's famous interpretation, to which he refers on several occasions. Nevertheless, there is no shortage of differences between the two. Both authors seek to lead the reader beyond apparent contradictions, errors, and surface discourse, and to reconstruct instead Machiavelli's underlying reasoning. However, Lefort does not set himself the aim of uncovering the "reality" of Machiavellian discourse and considers Strauss's work useful in so far as it confirms a preconceived thesis and unearths the true nature of politics which he, like Machiavelli, has totally mastered. For Lefort, moreover, the "work of the oeuvre" consists precisely in rejecting any idea of the author's true discourse, so much so that, within the framework of his theory of interpretation, not even the Florentine Secretary can be considered "maître absolu de sa pensée". Lefort also dwells on the German philosopher's work in the part of *Le travail de l'œuvre* devoted to "Interprétations exemplaires" (Lefort 1972, pp. 259–305). References to Strauss are also in Lefort (1978, pp. 259–285; 2000, pp. 172–206; 2007, pp. 551–568). Pierre Manent (1993, pp. 171–172) recognizes the proximity and at the same time the distance between Strauss's and Lefort's readings. On the relationship between the two thinkers and a comparison of their respective interpretations; see Louis (2016), Hilb (2013) and Labelle (2006).

specious, and the book's structure proves extremely fragile and elusive from the very first chapters. The text appears to be under the command of a double register built initially on customary classical references, which are then quickly sidestepped and used to assert something completely different (Lefort 2012, pp. 94–95).

This interpretation is confirmed in Chapter 6, devoted to "new principalities acquired by one's own troops and virtue (Machiavelli 2005, pp. 20–22)". Moses, Cyrus, Romulus, and Theseus are proposed as "grandissimi essempli" ("most illustrious examples") (20) of princes who became such by their own virtue and not by luck. Machiavelli admits that those who, like them, become princes through their own virtues, struggle to acquire their principalities as they must introduce new orders, but they are then able to keep control of them more easily. This logic then leads the author to assert the weakness of unarmed prophets and the need for the state to use force in order to guarantee its own preservation:

> However, if we desire to examine this argument thoroughly, it is necessary to consider whether these innovators act on their own or are dependent on others: that is, if they are forced to beg for help or are able to employ force in conducting their affairs. In the first case, they always come to a bad end and never accomplish anything. But when they depend on their own resources and can use force, then only seldom do they run the risk of grave danger. From this comes the fact that all armed prophets were victorious and the unarmed came to ruin. For, besides what has been said, people are fickle by nature: it is easy to convince them of something, but difficult to hold them in that conviction. Therefore, affairs should be managed in such a way that when they no longer believe, they can be made to believe by force. Moses, Cyrus, Theseus, and Romulus could not have made their institutions respected for long if they had been unarmed; as in our times happened to Brother Girolamo Savonarola, who was ruined in his new institutions when the populace began to believe in them no longer, since he had no way of holding steady those who had believed, nor of making the unbelievers believe. (22–23)

Lefort (2012, pp. 95–96) above all notes the eccentricity of this chapter, as the rigor and empirical analysis that underpins the reasoning up to this point seem to break down into a discourse that undermines the given points of reference. While Machiavelli does name the difficulties that afflict the founder of a new principality, he completely fails to specify what they consist of. The Duke of Milan, Francesco Sforza, who is named at the beginning of the book as an example of a new prince, is not even mentioned at this point. Instead, Machiavelli proposes certain mythical models and does not deem it necessary to offer any justification for them: any reference to the actions which they might be seen to typify are in fact absent. Even the evocation of Savonarola seems bizarre: as an unarmed prophet he is the opposite of the virtuous examples already named. And Brother Jerome is neither a prince nor a founder. The sense of confusion increases when one continues to the next chapter, devoted to new principalities acquired by foreign arms (mercenary armies) or by fortune (Machiavelli 2005, pp. 23–30). In contrast to those discussed in the previous pages, the domains examined here are easily obtained but prove very difficult to keep. Here mythical examples are eschewed in favor of the contemporary case of Cesare Borgia who, with the help of his father, Pope Alexander VI, and of his own cunning and ferocity, became lord of Romagna and of certain territories in central Italy.

The alternative that these two chapters seem to wish to present does not, however, stand up to any reading of the arguments that are developed. The example of Borgia in itself undermines the supposedly clear division between virtue and fortune and between the use of one's own army (one's own arms) or a mercenary army. Machiavelli, in fact, considers the Italian *condottiero* to be one of those who acquired their principality through fortune and without an army of their own. Nevertheless, he highlights how Borgia was able to create a new principality through his exceptional virtue and by relying on fortune and foreign arms only at the beginning of his venture. Not only that but despite what one might expect, Machiavelli considers Valentino a positive example and recommends that he be imitated in the same way as Francesco Sforza, despite the fact that he had been contrasted to the Milanese at the beginning of the chapter.[7] As the reasoning unfolds, therefore, the original definitions and oppositions established at the beginning are confused and complicated (Lefort 2012, pp. 96–99).

Despite the way they are presented and despite Machiavelli's own statements, Lefort does not believe that the two chapters are intended to outline several different and opposing ways of seizing control of the state. Beneath the superficial discourse separating virtue and fortune, and the use of one's own or of foreign arms, there appears a common point that

---

[7] In the final part of the chapter, Machiavelli does not hesitate to cite Valentino's behavior as an example to be imitated.

is the true focus of Machiavelli's interest, namely, the question of the basis of the state and of power (99). The Florentine Secretary invites his readers to discover a completely new discourse that examines the situation in Italy and the relations between its various powers in order to reconsider the entire foundation of politics and the rationale behind it. This is an unprecedented argument the pursuit of which involves a renunciation of the rigor of classical reasoning and the assumptions of tradition. *The Prince* thus warns the reader that understanding the situation contemporary to it requires a new vocabulary and way of thinking. In light of Machiavelli's "real" intentions, the opposition between virtue and fortune can therefore be understood as the contrast between actions that depend solely on the person carrying them out, and a subjugation to the desire of others, or in other words, a separation between the autonomy of mankind and political power on the one hand and its dependence on God or tradition on the other (124–125).[8] It is only in this context that the examples of Moses and Savonarola acquire their full meaning. While the former's politics is traced back to its "reality", and his virtue is likened to that of the other founders, the discredit that befalls the latter conveys a desire to criticize politics justified by a transcendent law, by reference to divine orders. Similarly, the real purpose of the defense of force that appears to be offered in Chapter 6 and reiterated in the celebration of Cesare Borgia's heinous acts is suddenly revealed: to free the reader from the impression of a history regulated by Providence (125).

For Lefort, Machiavelli thus invites the reader to question the foundations of politics, beginning by destroying the old truths established by the Christian tradition. Within this interpretative framework, Savonarola

---

[8] Lefort (2012, pp. 124–127) proposes a particular reading of the relationship between virtue and fortune presented in *The Prince*. Fortune, he says, referring to Chapter 25 of the treatise, is a power that is neither in the hands of the prince nor completely beyond his grasp. While in the first chapters it represents a power that is completely external—God or nature—and completely opposed to the virtue of the individual, this distinction is blurred as the work progresses. Thus, Lefort asserts, Machiavelli opposes the belief in an occult power capable of determining human actions with the virtue of acting in the context of inexorably uncertain knowledge. His reflection on fortune, then, merely showcases the similarities between the prince's relationship to power and man's relationship to time and Being. On Lefort's analysis of Chapter 25 of *The Prince* and his reasoning on the virtue-fortune relationship, see especially Lefort (2000, pp. 109–141; 2012, pp. 193–198). Thierry Ménissier (2010, pp. 318–322) is among the few authors who have devoted even brief comments to the virtue-fortune relationship in reference to Lefort's view. The debate on these issues has generated an endless volume of literature that we cannot address here.

appears to play a bigger role than that of an unarmed prophet, instead coming to represent the essence of what must be overcome. Machiavelli uses him to attack an idea of politics linked to the transcendent dimension that relies on prayer while forgetting that Moses took his kingdom by force. This is a politics that advocates the return to tradition and prevents the emergence of anything new. Fra Girolamo thus comes to represent the opposite argument to the one that Machiavelli is trying to develop in *The Prince*:

> Savonarola denounced the foolish and wicked who denied the possibility of governing by means of *pater nostres*, claiming to draw from the Old and New Testament proofs that cities had always been saved by prayer. According to Machiavelli, the fool is the one relies on prayer and forgets that Moses established his reign by force. According to Savonarola, it was the *unbelief* of men that was the source of Italy's woes; Machiavelli reemploys the same term with a different meaning: it is the lack of faith in the new things, not in the old image of protective God, that is the obstacle to a political reform; and his irony has a twofold effect when he suggests that Savonarola failed because he was unable to force men to keep their faith, not in God, but in him. (126)

It is at this juncture, therefore, that an even more interesting point emerges: Machiavelli does not offer any counterpoint to the truths proclaimed by Savonarola. He does not set out a new, certain knowledge of the nature of politics, of the state, or the relations between men. Instead, he roots political knowledge in a kind of non-knowledge. His discourse depends on the uncertainty that permeates the groundlessness of knowledge and reproduces the indeterminacy of politics. Lefort (127) argues that only from this perspective is it possible to understand the centrality of Chapter 15 of *The Prince*, in which Machiavelli proposes, against those who have sought to analyze utopian republics and principalities, "to search after the effectual truth of the matter (*verità effettuale della cosa*) rather than its imagined one" (Machiavelli 2005, p. 53). But according to Lefort, the Florentine Secretary uses this expression not to refer to the possibility of delving beneath the surface and grasping the mute forces and basic interests that govern politics. The "effectual truth" is not the name he gives to some notion of pure knowledge, but rather is a term he uses to convey the need to move beyond the republican and Christian ideologies proposed by tradition in order to confront politics as it actually emerges and unfolds in Florence and Italy. Lefort's Machiavelli, therefore, cannot play the role of the founder of political science, as he does not intend to oppose traditional knowledge with another kind of knowledge capable of explaining the essences, but proposes instead an "impure" knowledge,[9] one constructed on contact with events as they present themselves or, perhaps more accurately, represent themselves.[10] According to Lefort, it is this statement that determines "the tone of the work" (Lefort 2012, p. 93):

> We have been put on notice: the necessity of true discourse orders the writer to say what the others have kept silent about, just as the necessity of action orders the prince to do what the ordinary man is incapable of accomplishing. (ibid)

THE CONSPIRACY: A NEW POLITICS

If one accepts that *The Prince* offers a radical critique of traditional political thought and its theological foundation, one must then ask how this can be reconciled with the reflection presented in the *Discourses*. In other words: why, in that work, does Machiavelli issue a call to emulate the ancients, after having expressed his wish for a break with tradition in his treatise on principalities?

---

[9] I have borrowed this expression from Bode (2017).

[10] Effectual truth, Lefort argues, distancing the Florentine Secretary from the image of the founder of political science, is not an objective truth. He does not claim to grasp the essence or pure materiality of political elements but instead considers actions as they occur, as they are in movement. Machiavelli, in short, is not interested in "unveiling" the truth of political actions as a mere clash of forces taking place beneath the surface. Rather, for him, the task is to understand politics as it unfolds and is enacted, in its continuous interplay with human desires. To fully understand Lefort's intellectual operation, it is good to consider the debate of the time. In France of the first half of the twentieth century, the image of the Florentine Secretary as a theorist of the autonomy of politics was still widespread. According to this reading, politics was for Machiavelli a technical-operational sphere, separate from morality, in which cunning and deception prevailed and in which the end justified any means. Thus, *The Prince* and the *Discourses* were read as the texts foundational of modern political science or as the inspirational works of the new totalitarian regimes. The Italian thinker, as a result, could be celebrated as the first of the moderns or condemned as an adviser of tyrants. Leo Strauss helped spread the image of Machiavelli as a "master of evil". See Strauss (1958), but also Aron (1993) and Maritain (1953). On the French debate see, again, Sfez (2007) and Audier (2005).

In the preface to the first book of the *Discourses*—which, not coincidentally, takes up the opening sentences of Dante's *Monarchia*[11]—the Florentine secretary makes a plea for the imitation of Roman examples, expressing regret that this was deemed impossible by his contemporaries and that no prince, republic, or captain ever attempted to do so. To the naive gaze of the modern reader, these pages constitute an argument for rediscovering Roman history and emulating ancient customs, and are therefore in harmony with the humanist approach. Lefort, however, asserts that contemporary readers would have interpreted them quite differently (Lefort 2012, pp. 217–219). To them, the importance of the example of Rome in the Florentine political debate, and the high regard in which authorities such as Titus Livy, Plutarch, or Cicero were held, was perfectly clear. It would thus have appeared to Machiavelli's contemporaries that the preface was not so much an appeal for emulation as it was a fierce polemic against a certain interpretation of the Roman past, one that was commonly accepted and even enjoyed hegemonic status among the citizens of the Tuscan republic in those years. Not coincidentally, in the same pages Machiavelli acknowledges the popularity of Roman histories and appears aware of the "infinite number that read them" (Machiavelli 1996, p. 6). The point of the preface, Lefort argues, is therefore not to encourage a return to the example of the ancients, but to offer a critique of the interpretation of their ideas that prevailed in his own time (Lefort 2012, p. 219).[12]

The history of Rome thus becomes the battleground for his critique of the dominant ideology, that is, the humanist narrative that throughout the fifteenth century had located the historical and cultural roots and origins of Florence and its institutions in the Roman Republic. First and foremost, his discourse inveighs against the ideals professed by Salutati and Bruni, which still were highly influential in the Florentine political

---

[11] See Machiavelli (1996, pp. 5–6). For an analysis of Dante's presence in Machiavelli's work see at least Sasso (2015, pp. 205–222).

[12] Lefort (2012, p. 219) writes: "In affirming that no politician, no captain considers imitating the ancients, that the Roman model is unknown and that he himself will be the one to exalt it for the first time in its true form, the writer is no doubt letting it be known that he is preparing to subvert the Tradition that considered itself to be the guardian of an ancient heritage. In suggesting that the love of so many Florentines for Rome functions as a cover for their inability to confront the tasks of the present, he is no doubt letting the reader know that the significance of his interpretation of Livy and of Roman history is that of demystification".

and public debate as Machiavelli was setting out his own theories. The Secretary was steeped in these ideas, but he rejected the way they were used to justify the status quo, the established power, and the institutions of his city.[13] His polemical target, in short, is the very republican tradition that he himself emerged from, which has been transformed into a means of celebrating the current state—the restored lordship of the Medici[14]—and of concealing its inefficiency and lack of foundation. The republic has become an ideology, an illusion adopted by a society whose founding justification and origin have failed, and which therefore seeks to disguise the contingent origin of power and institutions by proposing other supposedly indisputable foundations, like tradition, history, and the myth of Florence's Roman origins. In this sense, then, ideology becomes a distinctly modern way of thinking.

According to Lefort, the preface to the second book of the *Discourses* offers further evidence in support of this thesis. In it, Machiavelli expresses his disapproval of the ways that the examples of the ancients are usually interpreted. Most writers, he says, devote themselves entirely to glorifying figures from the past without bothering to understand the truth of their ideas and their vital implications for the present. The text therefore contains a harsh but unspoken indictment of conservatism.[15] Far more radically, and unlike anywhere else in his work, in these pages Machiavelli is seeking to deconstruct the mechanism that leads men to dream up a mythical past to which they can submit. By attacking those who "praise ancient times and accuse the present" (Machiavelli 1996, p. 123), he is in fact attempting to strike against both a particular narrative of Roman antiquity that underpins the prevailing Florentine ideology, and a traditional way of thinking about the connection between knowledge, power, and tradition.

---

[13] The relationship between Machiavelli and civic humanism is not simple, and certainly cannot be reduced to a total rejection. As Lefort knew well, the Florentine Secretary remained strongly indebted to that tradition of thought and to certain republican ideals. The debate on the relationship between Machiavelli and humanism is still very much alive. See Hankins (2000, 2019), Black (2013), Garin (1970) and Gilbert (1965).

[14] On August 31, 1512, Pier Soderini, gonfalonier of the Republic, fled to Siena, and Giovanni and then Giuliano de' Medici took up residence in the Palazzo Vecchio, while formally retaining the city's republican institutions.

[15] The expression "procès general au conservatorisme", to refer to the content of the preface to the second book of the *Discourses*, is from Lefort (1978, p. 273).

Just as in *The Prince*, the Florentine secretary wishes to challenge the notion of a form of knowledge and power that is possessed by right and to break the commonly accepted link between tradition and truth. Another goal of the *Discourses* is therefore to propose a new way of thinking that reject both the hegemonic humanistic tradition, which is only able to justify the existing order of the Florentine Republic and any claim to a transcendent or religious foundation of power.[16] What he instead proposes is a reflection open to the indeterminacy of reality; an idea of power unsupported by any foundation. The abandonment of all tradition, in addition to entailing a critique of Florentine institutions, is a call to overturn any connection between power and knowledge and to open a channel to the dimension of contingency, while rejecting any heteronomous justification of the state and the community, whether this comes in the form of the divine. Word or in the guise of the mythical celebration of a glorious past.

> What is overturned is the idea that there is a rightful power and knowledge; that the place of the Subject coincides with that of the prince; that the locus of truth coincides with that of tradition. This overturning presupposes that the internal connection between power and knowledge in the institution in which the two crystallize and become petrified has been grasped. (Lefort 2012, p. 360)

From this polemical framework emerges the importance of the initial chapters of the Third Book of the *Discourses*, which are devoted to conspiracies and to the figure of Lucius Junius Brutus, who was able to pursue his political scheme through a conspiracy that elevated him to the mythical status of the founder of the Roman Republic. Feigning madness during the reign of Tarquinius Superbus in order to appear innocuous, Brutus waited patiently for the right opportunity to implement his revolutionary plan to bring down the monarchy. Later, having become consul, he approved the killing of his own sons, who were found to have been members of a plot to restore it.

In Lefort's interpretation, the figure of the conspirator and that of Brutus in particular is the prime example of the new political subject that

---

[16] For Lefort there is no caesura between Machiavelli's two major works, and no reason to suppose that he ever abandoned the path he first took with his work of 1513.

Machiavelli is keen to describe. Brutus acted without any external guarantees, could not rely on existing men or institutions, and struck against the power of the state and the convention. Thus at the moment that he acts, the conspirator faces the greatest possible indeterminacy and is left suspended, awaiting the moment of truth of his scheme. And this truth finds its full resolution in the unpredictable result of his actions.[17] These, in a nutshell, are the characteristics of the political subject that Machiavelli wishes to reveal below and beyond the veil of tradition, in the lack of foundation opened up by the rejection of all transcendent justification. He takes a step beyond humanism and presents an utterly modern form of power, that is, one separated from knowledge and law, free from the bounds of any indisputable origin, immersed in contingency and perpetually required, in its discourse and in the effect of its actions, to offer its own justification and prove its own legitimacy.

Thus is revealed the reason for the double register adopted in *The Prince* and the *Discourses*. Machiavelli must himself assume the guise of the conspirator in order to present this unprecedented and disruptive idea of power and politics, with its intensely critical attitude to authority. Just as Brutus feigned madness, he must use the classical structure of a treatise on government or the appeal for an emulation of the ancients to disguise his real message (414).

But who exactly is Machiavelli addressing? Who is the reader to whom he wishes to present his conspiracy? The answer, for Lefort, is clear: only the young can heed this lesson, as only they can establish the connection between knowledge and action needed to accomplish great political feats and create new orders.[18] Only the young men of Florence possess the

---

[17] The fact that there cannot be a universally valid norm means that the judgment of political actions can only be made when their outcomes are clear. Such outcomes, however, can be difficult to predict, so much so that, as the examples presented by Machiavelli show, similar actions can have completely different outcomes. This, ultimately, describes the entirely political problem of *riscontro*, that is, the difficulty inherent in the correspondence between human action and the "quality of the times", which is always exposed to contingency and subject to a great degree of chance. On this topic, see Marchesi (2017, pp. 66–68).

[18] See the article "Machiavel et les jeunes" (Lefort 1978, pp. 259–285). In it, Lefort condenses the consideration of the relationship between Machiavelli and the younger generation of Florentines that he had already set out more extensively but intermittently in *Le travail de l'œuvre*. In support of his interpretation, Lefort cites several pieces of textual "evidence" which can, at least partially, be outlined here. He first refers to the eulogy of youth proposed in Chapter 25 of *The Prince*. According to the philosopher, it

strength and desire needed for this revolutionary project, and it is therefore to them that the Florentine Secretary turns to execute his conspiracy. Machiavelli sets out to provide the youth with the means to understand the ideological function of tradition and perceive the lack of foundation of all power, and thus incite them to take part in a slow and patient conspiracy against the existing institutions, in particular the power of the Medici (Lefort 1978, pp. 282–284).[19]

In Lefort's view, Machiavelli's work therefore testifies to the change that, at the dawn of modernity and with the birth of the state, overcomes the representation of power and its connection to knowledge and law. It is witness to the emergence of a new ideological thought that attempts to make up for this loss and conceal the contingency. In other words, the Florentine Secretary moves beyond humanism to describe the consequences that the loss of the foundation—that is, the loss of the ability of religion to structure the social sphere, the dissolution of the bond

---

is also significant that one of the main examples of the new prince proposed is Cesare Borgia, who at the time of his exploits was in his early twenties. The treatise's stated recipients, Lorenzo and Giuliano de Medici, were themselves thirty-four and twenty-four years old respectively. As for the *Discourses*, the importance accorded to young people can already be detected in the period of the work's elaboration. Indeed, the meetings at the Orti Oricellari were attended by many young people (revolutionary republicans) eager for new ideas and initiatives. The relationship with young people then emerges most clearly, for Lefort, in the preface to the Second Book where the "conservatism of the age founded on submission to the world in which the fathers ruled" is denounced. The examples of Epaminondas and Xenophon, through which Machiavelli attempts to outline a new conception of politics that went beyond tradition, were also, according to Lefort, directed at younger readers.

[19] The idea of Machiavelli as a conspirator brings Lefort's analysis closer to that of other scholars, such as Harvey Mansfield and the aforementioned Leo Strauss. Many authors have opposed such interpretations by pointing out that Machiavelli frowns upon conspiracies because they are too dangerous and more often than not doomed to failure, even when they do not actually strengthen existing powers. I cannot stop here to examine in any depth the validity of Lefort's interpretation and how it differs from those of Strauss and Mansfield. I will therefore limit myself to pointing out that for Lefort this is not so much a matter of seeing any praise for conspiracies between the lines of Machiavelli's work, as it is of seeing the figure of the conspirator as the archetype of modern, contingent politics devoid of foundation and transcendent justification. Such an interpretation can be supported by the judgment of conspiracies contained in the *Florentine Istorie*. This theme is dealt with in Chapter 19 of *The Prince* and in Chapter 11 of the Third Book of the *Discourses*, which is in fact named "Of Conspiracies" (Machiavelli 1996, pp. 218–235). See Geuna (2015) (which offers a close critique of Mansfield's theses), Mansfield (1979), and Strauss (1958).

between theology and politics, and the disincorporation—has on the self-representation of the social.[20] It is because he has understood this radical change that Machiavelli turns against tradition and seeks a new political vocabulary and a new relationship with thought and with the world that is capable of being accountable to it.[21]

THE CONFLICT[22]

Chapter 9 of *The Prince* is devoted to the civil principality, whose protagonist is "a private citizen [who] becomes prince of his native city not through wickedness or any other intolerable violence, but with the favour of his fellow citizens" (Machiavelli 2005, p. 34), and, Machiavelli argues, rises to power through a combination of astuteness and Fortune, "either with the favour of the common people or with that of the nobility" (35). In support of this claim, he explains that:

---

[20] There are different positions regarding Machiavelli's relationship with Christianity, which I cannot discuss here. I therefore refer the reader to specific studies on this: Viroli (2012), Najemy (1999) and De Grazia (1989).

[21] On Machiavelli as the author, especially in *The Prince*, of an unprecedented piece of political art, see Zarka and Ménissier (2001).

[22] Since the 1960s and 1970s, various interpretative theories have been propagated that have emphasized the centrality of conflict in Machiavelli's work. One need only think of the studies of Antonio Negri (1999) or Louis Althusser (2000). Althusser himself, in the introduction to his *Machiavelli and Us* (Althusser 2000, p. 3), refers precisely to Lefort and writes: "Before launching into the risky venture of this essay, I should like to pay a well-deserved homage to a thesis on Machiavelli published three or four years ago: Claude Lefort's *Le Travail de l'oeuvre*. For I know of no analysis as acute and intelligent of an author who, from the time he wrote, has always perplexed his readers. And although Lefort denies offering an 'interpretation' of them, I am not aware of any commentary on *The Prince* and the *Discourses on Livy* that goes so far in understanding Machiavelli's cast of mind and turn of phrase–and never mind the transcendental philosophy a la Merleau-Ponty in which it is arbitrarily wrapped. Should it ever be discovered—as the outcome of an investigation of unprecedented meticulousness—for whom Machiavelli wrote, we owe it, in the first instance, to Lefort". In recent years, the debate on conflict in Machiavelli has expanded further, involving different authors and a variety of interpretations. An obligatory reference is first of all to the studies of Gennaro Sasso (1993), but see also: Pedullà (2018), Gaille (2018), Johnston et al. (2017), Del Lucchese et al. (2016), Del Lucchese (2011, 2015), and Vatter (2000). Roberto Esposito has dealt with the role of conflict in Machiavelli's thought on several occasions: Esposito (1984, 2012, 2023).

these two different humours are found in every body politic. They arise from the fact that the people do not wish to be commanded or oppressed by the nobles, while the nobles do desire to command and to oppress the people. From these two opposed appetites, there arises in cities one of three effects: a principality, liberty, or licence. (35)[23]

Commenting on this passage, Lefort first notes how the two conflicting parties cannot be reduced to an equal number of material conditions. Their fight is not one between two factual conditions, but between two desires that do not correspond to specific and divergent interests, but only exist in their opposition to one another. They are the two equally insatiable "appetites" that structure every political society and present an ontology of relation, an "opposition constitutive of the political" (140).[24] Secondly, the French philosopher highlights the profound asymmetry between the two humors: while the greats' desire to command is positive and tends toward a clear object, the humor characteristic of the people, pure negativity, is a desire without an object of its own. It follows that while the notion that expresses the desire of the great is that of "having", the idea of "being" instead governs popular desire. At this point, since this desire for a generic type of "being"—which is first and foremost expressed as the aspiration of "not being oppressed"—can be described as a desire for "freedom" or an absence of oppression, the conflict between the two humors, Lefort argues, acquires an essentially political character (140–141).[25]

These themes—social division, conflict—and the critique of tradition that they enable are considered in greater depth in the *Discourses*. In

---

[23] On Machiavelli's theory of the *umori* see: Gaille (2018), Zanzi (2013), and Parel (1992).

[24] Lefort repeatedly returns to the point that the two desires cannot be reduced to two factual conditions, to material or class interests, and speaks instead of a constitutive opposition within the political. This does not mean that he thinks that the economic dimension is not important. Rather, the two dimensions proceed in parallel, the economic determination occurs together with the so-called political determination (Lefort 1978, p. 222). Se the article "Machiavel: la dimension économique du politique" (215–237). However, there is no lack of authors who believe that the opposition of humors outlined by Machiavelli is only economic and social and therefore represents a mere clash of interests. See Marchesi (2018). The expression "ontology of relation" used to refer to Machiavelli's theory of conflict, is instead taken from Torres (2014).

[25] It is Machiavelli himself (1996, p. 18) who relates the people's desire for non-oppression to the idea of freedom.

that book, Machiavelli sets out to completely rethink Rome's institutional history and identifies the struggle between the two humors as the source of the greatness and liberty of the Roman Republic.[26] The starting point of this reasoning is contained in the second chapter of the First Book, which considers republics or principalities that "had a beginning far from all external servitude" (Machiavelli 1996, p. 10) and governed themselves through their own laws. Among them, Machiavelli distinguishes between states whose laws are the work of a single legislator and those whose laws are the result of chance, of accident. After stating that mixed government (which is shared between popular power, the power of the optimates, and the power of the prince) is the best form, since it is more stable and less prone to perversion and crisis, the Florentine analyzes two cases, those of Sparta and Rome. While in the Greek city a single legislator, Lycurgus, was able to create good laws that ensured that the state remained healthy for more than 800 years, Rome achieved the same result through disunity, particularly through the struggle between the plebs and the Senate. Rome and Sparta thus point to two different but apparently equally valid ways of ordering a republic through good legislation, that is, legislation capable of keeping the state alive and healthy. In the first example, good laws come about through stability and are suited to a society, like Sparta, that intends to remain unchanged. In the second, they are instead the result of a permanent instability that is positive for a society, such as that of Rome, whose ambition is to expand (10–15).

The subsequent two chapters (15–17) focus on the Roman case. While the earliest republican institutions could be considered "defective" (since in fact the three forms of government were not all represented there, as there were no tribunes of the people), it was in fact the "tumults"[27] or "conflicts" that created a "perfect republic", one endowed with orders and laws favorable to freedom.[28] Freedom, however, was not the only

[26] For different interpretations of the meaning of Machiavellian freedom, see Skinner (1998) and Sasso (1993).

[27] Machiavelli uses different terms, including "tumults", to refer to the phenomena we are considering here with the terms "conflict" and social "division". For a study of the cases involved and the difference between the various uses, see Pedullà (2018) and Geuna (2005).

[28] The period Machiavelli refers to in his eulogy of the freedom of Roman institutions is the one between the overthrow of Tarquinius the Proud in 510 B.C. and the killing of Caius Gracchus in 121 B.C. The riots that broke out in Rome following Tarquinius's exile are presented as the origin of Roman freedom and greatness.

"good effect" of the tumults of the Roman Republic. Conflict also underpinned its dynamism, drive for expansion, and military strength. Those who condemn social conflict, Machiavelli then argues, fail to understand how this was the source of Roman freedom and power:

> I say that to me it appears that those who damn the tumults between the nobles and the plebs blame those things that were the first cause of keeping Rome free, and that they consider the noises and the cries that would arise in such tumults more than the good effects that they engendered. They do not consider that in every republic are two diverse humors, that of the people and that of the great, and that all the laws that are made in favor of freedom arise from their disunion, as can easily be seen to have occurred in Rome. For from the Tarquins to the Gracchi, which was more than three hundred years, the tumults of Rome rarely engendered exiles and rarely blood. (16)

Here the idea of the law is separated from the idea of moderation, as the order is shown as emerging from conflict.[29] Through his interpretation of Roman history, Machiavelli sets out a veritable celebration of the virtues of discord, in opposition to the opinion of "the many", or in other words to representatives of the humanist tradition who locate the wisdom of the laws in their ability to reduce social conflict (15–17). Once again, Machiavelli returns and pays tribute to antiquity in order to put forward a damaging critique. This time, his target is the theory of good political rule as it was understood by classical authors, humanists, and the Christian tradition. This was a theory that in fact depended on a concord between citizens and the unity of the community. In this context, Machiavelli invokes the authority of Livy merely to endear himself to the reader, who he then incites to question the Latin historian's interpretation. Thus, in opposition to the "many", the Florentine secretary calls for the abandonment of any universal and transcendent principle that might be used to judge politics and governments, and instead recognizes only one principle, that of *verità effettuale*.[30]

---

[29] Flynn (2005, p. 50) writes: "The law cannot be thought of under the sign of measure, nor as related to a rational criteria which would put limits on the appetites of men; nor can it be conceived of as the effect of a natural regulation of the appetites imposed by the necessity of group survival".

[30] Machiavelli (1996, p. 16) writes: "I do not wish to fail to discourse of the tumults in Rome from the death of the Tarquins to the creation of the tribunes, and then upon

The celebration of tumults thus undermines an entire conceptual apparatus, linked to Aristotelianism, Christianity, humanism, and republican ideology, that had defined and continued to define the political thought of the era.[31] The first consequence of this approach, Lefort states, is a challenge to the conception of law, which can no longer be considered in relation to reason, but only to conflict. The law is no longer the most rational basis for bringing about the wellbeing of the whole community but is only the contingent and ephemeral product of tumult. The meaning of virtue must also change, with the search for good, wise, and rational institutions no longer being the yardstick with which to judge a regime. What determines the nature of a government is not the intentions of its rulers, nor the form of its institutions, but the relationship that the state, or, we might say, power, establishes with its subjects or citizens, with conflict. In other words, how the state responds to demands for legitimacy. On the other hand, internal conflict becomes the essential element of a society that no longer possesses a certain and indisputable foundation, that no longer presents itself as a unified body, and whose power is rooted in the social recognition of its own legitimacy.

According to Lefort, what *The Prince* and the *Discourses* propose, through the critique of the *concordia ordinum*, is therefore a new system of thought without foundation or stable points of reference. Machiavelli, in fact, does not identify any principle that might be used in opposition to the traditional reliance on social unity and harmony. His gaze is not that of a witness who, from a vantage point external to the subject matter, is able to identify abstract and universally valid criteria and norms. Instead, his goal is to make his reader understand how the law is embedded within the social space, in the struggle between "classes", and to encourage "him

---

some things contrary to the opinion of many who say that Rome was a tumultuous republic and full of such confusion that if good fortune and military virtue had not made up for its defects, it would have been inferior to every republic".

[31] Lefort is aware of Machiavelli's Aristotelian education and the importance of the Greek philosopher for humanism and sixteenth-century Florence. In his eyes, however, the reasoning in *The Prince* and the *Discourses* develops through an overturning of certain Aristotelian theories, beginning with the idea that it is possible to determine a notion of the common good applicable to society as a whole. Thus, while *The Prince* initially seems to expound a political dynamic that can be traced back to the dynamics of Aristotelian physics, whereby every body is seen as having the tendency of placing itself in its natural space and of returning to it if it is dislodged from this space by violence, these assumptions are later completely overturned by means of the idea of conflict.

or her to abandon the position as a witness to rejoin the cause of the people" (228).[32] To fully understand the importance and sheer radicalism of Machiavelli's reasoning, Lefort argues, one must therefore follow it as it unfolds in his writings on the people, whose viewpoint he invites us to consider.

The Role of the People

Machiavelli explicitly advocates for a politics that relies on the people in several passages of his work. When describing the civil principality in *The Prince*, for example, he states:

> He who attains the principality with the help of the nobility maintains it with more difficulty than he who becomes prince with the help of the common people, for he finds himself a prince amidst many who feel themselves to be his equals, and because of this he can neither govern nor manage them as he wishes. But he who attains the principality through popular favour finds himself alone, and has around him either no one or very few who are not ready to obey him. Besides this, one cannot honestly satisfy the nobles without harming others, but the common people can certainly be satisfied. Their desire is more just than that of the nobles – the former want not to be oppressed, while the latter want to oppress. (Machiavelli 2005, p. 35)

Concluding that "a prince must have the friendship of the common people. Otherwise, he will have no support in times of adversity" (36), he suggests the need for a bond between the prince and the people on which the health of the principality depends. This same bond emerges repeatedly

---

[32] Because of the importance of this theoretical passage, it is worth quoting it in its entirety: "Indeed, it does not suffice to dispel the illusion of the *unione*, to show the fecundity of the class struggle when it is expressed in broad daylight, for we could still give in to another illusion; we could imagine that the two adversaries occupy symmetrical positions and that their conflict is good *in itself*. The consequence of this would be the reestablishment, in a new way, of the image of a legislator who, placed outside the bounds of this conflict, would regulate its course, and the position of which would, by the way, coincide with that of the theoretician. It is therefore insufficient, in particular, to stop at the conclusion that all the laws favorable to freedom are born of the division of humors of the body politic. It must also be understood that is within the social space, in the experience of class struggle itself, that law is instituted; and it is necessary to find the meaning of the movement that requires it. Machiavelli leads the reader there, by obliging him or her to abandon the position as a witness and to rejoin the cause of the people".

in certain passages of the *Discourses* in which the interests of the prince and those of the people are almost indistinguishable. The prince's need to secure the support of the people is reiterated in Chapter 16 of the First Book, which discusses the ways the former might retain power (Machiavelli 1996, pp. 44–47). Moreover, Machiavelli states here that "the one who has the few as enemies secures himself easily and without many scandals, but he who has the collectivity as enemy never secures himself" (45). Chapter 58 further describes the multitude as being endowed with a peculiar form of knowledge that in fact makes it even "wiser and more constant than a prince" (115).[33]

Following Lefort, however, to fully understand the meaning of these passages it is necessary to return to *Discourses* I 5. Here Machiavelli asks "where the guard of freedom may be settled more securely, in the people or in the great" (17), and compares what the French philosopher calls the "democratic, liberal thesis" to the "aristocratic, conservative" one (Lefort 1978, p. 230). In these pages, the reader learns that the passion for conservation traditionally attributed to the great is in fact a fiction. Since no human desire can ever be fully satisfied, the great's thirst for power and possession should be considered insatiable. Besides, "it does not appear to men that they possess securely what a man has unless he acquires something else new" (Machiavelli 1996, p. 19). This irrepressible will to dominate is precisely the reason why the great are not suited to safeguarding the freedom of a republic. On the other hand, Machiavelli does not hide his belief that the people are also not inherently good and that its conduct can be driven by envy and hatred. The desire for freedom that distinguishes the people, however, being only a negative desire not to be oppressed, and thus a yearning that does not pursue any particular aim, cannot deteriorate into a desire for command, for power or for the subjugation of the adversary. Thus, Machiavelli states, if one looks at the multitude one will see that "a small part of them desires to be free so as

---

[33] Lefort devotes several passages of his *Le travail de l'œuvre* to understanding Machiavelli's use of the term "multitude" instead of "people". The Florentine Secretary's choice, the philosopher argues, should be interpreted as a further attack on traditional thinkers who use the term "multitude" precisely to emphasize the flaws of the people. Machiavelli uses the language of conservatives to counter their own theses more effectively. This becomes particularly clear, for Lefort, in Chapters 53 and 54 of the *Discourses*, which, as we shall see below, would superficially seem to support the traditional thesis of the inconstancy of the people but instead calls it entirely into question. See Lefort (2012, pp. 271–272).

to command, but all the others, who are infinite, desire freedom so as to live secure" (46).

The asymmetry between the two humors, already apparent in Chapter 9 of *The Prince*, here acquires its full meaning: conflict and its legislative utility are made possible by popular desire. As Lefort states:

> The Republic and its free institutions live only in the gap between the two desires. The fecundity of the law depends on the intensity of their opposition, and, since there is no doubt that the desire of the great, if they encounter no obstacle, does not cease to grow, the intensity of the opposition depends on the vigor of the people's resistance. (Lefort 2000, p. 136)

Only the adversarial relationship enables the creation of good laws that are conducive to the freedom, greatness, and prosperity of the state. And only the people can serve as the guarantor of this relationship. Only its desire not to be oppressed enables the conflict to continue and society to expand and prosper, just as it did in Rome. Only by relying on the dynamism of the people and on their demands can a society therefore maintain free institutions.

According to Lefort's interpretation, it is from this point of view that one must understand Machiavelli's support for politics that favors the people. His admiration for the people is explained precisely by the importance of its role in the preservation of the state: if only the people can maintain conflict, and if only it can allow the state to be great, free, and powerful, a republic must be founded on the recognition of the importance of the people and must rely on it, and on its desire for freedom, to keep itself in good health.

However, the example of Rome presents an additional difficulty. A pro-people policy appears to favor societies, like the Roman Republic or Florence, that wish to expand. But what about societies like Sparta or Venice, which strive to keep things the same? To answer this question, let us return to Chapter 6 of the First Book of the *Discourses*. Here Machiavelli envisaged two ways in which republics can be ordered: by eliminating internal conflict or by fostering it (Machiavelli 1996, pp. 20–23). Pursuing this analysis, he in fact presents the first approach as being the most suitable for societies that wish to remain small, such as Venice and Sparta. On the other hand, he deems internal conflict to be of use to those republics, like Rome, that wish to expand. As Lefort is quick to note, however, this distinction is immediately open to certain important questions. In fact, only a few lines later Machiavelli asserts that since "all things of men are in motion and cannot stay steady" (23)—that is, since the state, in order to maintain its liberty, must be able to cope with the contingent and unpredictable situations of reality, and since a middle path between stability and expansion is impracticable—only the Roman model can guarantee the health and survival of a republic. Thus, the Florentine Secretary appears to argue that only by accepting the existence of conflict can one respond to an ever-divided and constantly shifting reality. Only the expression of popular desire and the openness to change that derives from it can avoid the illusory unity that is ready to explode when the division of desires that runs through every human community inevitably presents itself. This is exactly what happened to Venice, which, like Sparta, arrogantly excluded the people from its own system and militia, and hid behind a fictitious unity and homogeneity, only to see its power crumble in a single day. Lefort therefore concludes:

> What gives the state its *raison* are not the concepts of equilibrium, security and conservation; it is the necessity in which it finds itself to face the accidents engendered within it by ambitions against its neighbors, or accidents others conceive against it. And it misunderstands that reason when, by artifices, it deprives itself of the strength of the people. (Lefort 2012, p. 233)

Here we are once again presented with a modern, unprecedented conception of the world and of society. Without transcendent principles, without foundations, the reality described by Machiavelli can be understood only in relation to events, in the incessant movement that prevents it from settling, and in the constant rerun of the battle for anything that is acquired. In this context, the only successful form of politics is one that is able to come to terms with the continuous movement of social life and remain open to circumstance, conflict, and indeterminacy (181–187). Only a politics that accepts the internal division expressed and guaranteed by popular desire can enable the state to prosper, with an important implication:

> Hence the political action that is justly founded is the one that takes class difference into account [...], the one that, in taking up an authority

that can only be located at a distance from the people, seeks its direction in popular consensus, that is, bears testimony to the desire for freedom. Freedom alone can keep the two halves of the social body from collapsing inward onto one another, from shutting down the swirling movement of appetite and fear, and thus maintain the division between civil society and the state. (271)

Any political project that makes unity and stability the guiding principles of its actions is doomed to failure. It is no longer capable of responding to the new institution of the social and is therefore illusory. Only by maintaining the internal conflict guaranteed by the popular desire for freedom can the state be in the best position to respond to external challenges, expand, gain power, and create laws that are worthwhile because they offer power and glory. Those who would instead seek to suppress internal conflict and attempt to place a limit on the expression of the desire for freedom condemn the state to fragility, to surrendering to the unexpected. The people are the engine and center of politics.

Machiavelli's ideas, however, proceed by means of continuous juxtapositions, by oscillating between opposing and seemingly irreconcilable justifications.[34] Thus after eulogizing the people and comparing the voice of the multitude to that of a god, after praising it as better able to respect agreements and for being less cruel than power deposited in the hand of an individual, in other parts of the work he turns this position upside down. While Chapter 44 of the First Book of the *Discourses* emphasizes the complete ineffectiveness of the multitude when left without guidance, Chapter 54 highlights its propensity to obey authority blindly, and points to the inconsistency of its knowledge. Popular decisions, driven by blind support for "great hopes and mighty promises" (Machiavelli 1996, p. 105), are unreliable, as demonstrated by various examples drawn from Roman and Greek history. Thus, when the Roman Senate approved Marcus Centenius Penula's campaign against Hannibal in response to popular demands, Rome met with a defeat as terrible as it was predictable. Similarly, the Athenian people's unwillingness to listen to Nicias's wise warnings not to intervene against Sicily led the city to defeat and ruin. Paraphrasing Dante, Machiavelli therefore concludes that "many times the people cries: 'Life!' to its death and 'Death!' to its life" (106).

---

[34] Numerous authors have emphasized Machiavelli's antinomian proceeding and have offered reflections on this theme. See Esposito (1984) or Chabod (1964, pp. 369–388).

Machiavelli's readers are no doubt left bewildered by such contradictions. The same subject, the people, which in some chapters of the *Discourses* is praised for its wisdom and stability is criticized in others for being unstable, driven by passion, and unable to make rational decisions. To clarify this point Lefort invites us to consider how in the critical passages the behavior of the people always depends on the nature of the bond it has established with authority. In Chapter 53, for example, after observing that the people, deceived by "mighty promises", and by a false image of good, sometimes desires its own downfall, Machiavelli adds:

> and if it is not aware that that is bad and what the good is, by someone in whom it has faith, infinite dangers and harms are brought into republics. When fate makes the people not have faith in someone, as happens at some time after it has been deceived in the past either by things or by men, it of necessity comes to ruin. (ibid)

The critique of the people's behavior is therefore inseparable from that of the ruling classes, the Roman Senate, or the politicians of Athens. This becomes clearer in the next chapter, which highlights the authority's inability to restrain an agitated multitude. The conduct of the people, in short, always appears to be linked to the credibility of the institutions. Their mistakes depend first and foremost on the inability of these institutions to make themselves credible and able to make good judgments. Their mistakes, their bad decisions, are inseparable from the crisis of authority. Likewise, the chapters enumerating the qualities of the people are not intended to highlight a supposed natural goodness. Even the people's wisdom, foresight, and loyalty in maintaining covenants are the result of a productive relationship with power. Lefort therefore asserts:

> In any event, their behavior depends on that of the men who hold political responsibilities. Considered as a mass of individuals, they have the same qualities and defects as every other human collectivity, but considered as a class, they do not make mistakes; for they are not the knowing subject; the knowledge they have is engendered from the twofold relation instituted with law and authority, and they remain ever caught up in sensible experience, tied to perception and divination—a knowledge of appearances and portents—whereas the knowledge possessed by those who govern, or more generally by members of the dominant class, implies calculation and foresight. Thus only the dominant class makes mistakes, for its members,

who are in a position to maneuver in the interests of their private ambition, are inclined to ignore the imperatives of the preservation of the state. (Lefort 2012, pp. 270–271)

In short, the people has no qualities of its own because it does not exist as an autonomous subject. It is the form of a relationship: not something objective, but the symbol of the desire that escapes the homogeneity sought by the dominant political discourse. It circumvents the fictitious unity imposed by political language, ideology, and any discourse that attempts to delineate a definition of community.[35] It is "the empty space", the residue, the thing that is always in a relationship with power and with everything that power opposes, and thereby opens up the possibility of an alternative. It is the symptom of the inability of any form of politics to understand society as a whole, to grasp the real, as Lacan might have put it.[36] It is a negative force but at the same time the remnant of a desire that is always built on a contrast in which the affirmation of

---

[35] This conception of politics and the role of the people has several affinities with that proposed by Jacques Rancière (2004) but especially by Ernesto Laclau who, not coincidentally, in his *The Populist Reason* (Laclau 2007), refers specifically to Lefort. A comparison between Lefort and contemporary theories of politics inspired by Lacan's thought would certainly be interesting. On these theories and a possible comparison with Lefort's work see, at least: Moroncini (2014), Marchart (2007, pp. 146–149), Stavarkakis (2007), Tønder and Thomassen (2005), and Mouffe (2005, 2006).

[36] It is within this theoretical framework that Lefort's reasoning most clearly reveals its proximity to Jacques Lacan's theoretical proposal. Lefort, who had attended Lacan's seminar at Rue d'Ulm, was well acquainted with the psychoanalyst's work and, as we have already noted, there are several aspects of his reflection where its influence can be detected: in the difference between the symbolic, the imaginary and the real; in the description of the originally symbolic social that calls to mind the mirror stage, in which the ego is already superego; up to the similarity between the concept of original division and that of original repression that makes the subject inaccessible to itself. However, the interpretation of Machiavelli's work and the role of the people offers a privileged perspective from which to understand this relationship. First, the dynamic of the social described here seems to faithfully reproduce, on another level, the constitutive dynamic of Lacan's subject. Just as the latter is the locus of an absence, of perpetual identification, of nothing but its own interpretation, and is a word in perpetual search of its own meaning, so Lefort's notion of the social is nothing other than the continuous relationship to the locus of power and the perennial demand for the latter's legitimacy. The subject theorized by Lacan, suspended between absence and presence, does not seem so distant from the description of a social that is continually questioning itself and unable to understand itself completely. The role of the people in this framework seems to be crucially indicative: in its dependence on power it never possesses the meaning of its own word, it represents a constant lack and at the same time the real, the impossible that exceeds symbolization and cannot be understood

freedom and the denial of oppression coexist. The people, in short, represent the experience of a void that no politics can fill. It is the symptom of the inability of the prince, the state, and political and ideological discourse to actually reduce society to unity. It is precisely this impossibility, on the other hand, that Lefort defines as the original division of the social. The task of sublimating it rests with power.

Power, Imaginary and the Foundation

It should be clear at this point that the task of power is not to end conflict and division but rather to govern it, that power should not aim to reconcile the various parties but must limit itself to keeping the dissent from transcending into a civil confrontation that would bring about the ruin of the state.[37] The prince thus finds himself in a delicate position, at the intersection between the desires of the people and those of the great.

---

in political discourse or in the symbolic dimension. Similarly, the role of the Name-of-the-Father in Lacan's theory, which, irreducible to an instance of repression, enables the stabilization of subjective identity, clarifies the dynamic described by Lefort between people and power, between conflict and law. For Lacan, as for Lefort, identification is impossible, and emancipation—understood as liberation from all identification, and the dissolution of the symptom—is a neurosis; there is no cure, either for the subject or for society. The similarities, in short, are not lacking, and this writer is strongly inclined to believe that Lefort was fully aware of this. However, the way forward may not be to interpret Lefort's theory as a direct attempt to politicize Lacan. Firstly, because it is Lefort himself who condemns the transposition of psychoanalytic concepts to the realm of politics (see Lefort 2007, pp. 257–258). Secondly, because the obvious similarity runs into the inaccuracies of the philosopher who, rather than faithfully reusing the concepts of psychoanalysis, instead appears to make rather careless use of them. It is true that Lacan's symptom and Lefort's power have a remarkable amount in common, but they nevertheless cannot be superimposed. What thus seems to emerge from an initial analysis, which would certainly need further and more precise investigation and which does not exclude a priori the effectiveness of Lacan's reading of Lefort's work, is not a direct affinity, so much as the air of a family relationship, a common way of reasoning whose roots, once again, could be found in the work of Merleau-Ponty whom, not by chance, Lacan himself knew well. On the possible relationships between the theories of Lacan and Lefort see Colonna d'Istria (2015) and Žižek (2008).

[37] Machiavelli is fully aware of the danger of conflict and the possibility that it can descend into civil confrontation. The cases of Florence and Rome are emblematic in showing how "healthy" political confrontations can degenerate into "discords" that produce not freedom but fear, disorder and weakness of the state. To be extremely succinct, we might say that for Machiavelli there are two conditions that social struggle must meet in order not to fall "out of all civil ways and customs": it must not take on a partisan and personal dimension, and it must not have the character of private interest.

Or, to put it better, he stands between the preservation of power and the unity of the community on the one hand, and the maintenance of internal conflict, of the openness toward the desire for freedom, on the other. While he cannot rely solely on the desire for domination without succumbing to corruption and weakening the state, it is also not possible for him to lean completely on the popular side without creating an "other people", an alternative form of desire capable of escaping the unity of political discourse. This is why, Lefort argues, Machiavelli states that the prince cannot rely on anyone:

> Not only can he not find in men taken as a group stable support, since their community covers over a wrenching apart, but he cannot even rely on a part of them, since one class only exists by the lack that constitutes it opposite the other. The necessary search for a point of attachment passes through the experience of a void that no politics will ever fill—through the recognition of the impossibility of the state's reducing society to a unity. (Lefort 2012, p. 140)

The continuous search for an impossible unity supports the dynamics of power/prince, which, as a contingent and precarious attempt to establish a relationship between humors, arises precisely in the space opened by that relationship. For this reason, in addition to producing the dynamics of society through the clash of its parts, conflict represents the very genesis of power, which can be established only because of it and because of the space it creates.

Here lies perhaps one of Lefort's greatest insights and one of the innovations of his interpretation of Machiavelli's work: separating himself profoundly from Cassirer's classical interpretation, he inscribes power within social relations but, at the same time, does not locate it entirely

---

Lefort never explicitly addresses these distinctions and does not analyze the possible degeneration of conflict. Moreover, what worries Lefort is not the excess but the lack of conflict in totalitarian societies and in the era opened up by globalization and the mass society. Thus in the article "Esquisse d'une genèse de l'idéologie dans les sociétés modernes" he does not hesitate to follow Marcuse and Baudrillard in denouncing a new logic of dissimulation that dominates contemporary societies and conceals the distance between representation and reality. See Lefort (1986, pp. 181–236). Breckman (2019) analyzes Lefort's idea of a new contemporary form of ideology.

within the social sphere.[38] Power and politics develop in the space specifically created by the game of confrontation, by perpetual conflict. This is not a transcendental place, as in the pre-modern form, but is one that exists within the dynamics of conflict. The prince belongs within the tumults. He does not possess any higher knowledge than the struggling classes but is affected by the same ambiguities and limits of political interplay and social and temporal division. His place is established by the same discourse that he must decipher in order to maintain himself, legitimize himself, and survive. At the same time, power is also not a completely immanent force. It is the third element that establishes society by regulating its conflict and giving it unity, albeit a provisional one. The prince differs from both the great and the people and symbolically reproduces the same division he seeks to overcome with an imaginary unity. On the other hand, if he failed to do this, if he failed to symbolize the unity of the community that transcends the division between the two humors, he would be considered merely an illegitimate coercive force. Space would then open up for the hatred of the multitude to grow, which would eventually lead to civil war and the break-up of the community.[39] Such a tyrant would also have the people as his enemy and would therefore not be able to survive the political game, the contingency, and the continuous movement of reality for long. In accordance with Machiavelli, it might be said that he would succumb either to foreign powers or internal conspiracies (Geuna 2015).

In this way, a particular definition of modern power emerges, one that sees it as internal but at the same time divorced from the social sphere, which, in turn, acquires a form of its own only by turning to power. The position of this new power is thus ambiguous: it is completely defined by the conflictuality that structures the community but at the same time it is separated from it due to its status as a third element, as a symbolic

---

[38] Ernst Cassirer expounds his theory of power and his interpretation of Machiavelli in *The Myth of the State*, published posthumously in 1946 (Cassirer 1961). He also considers Machiavelli's theory to be the beginning of political modernity. However, he sees the state as something autonomous and separate from society. See Lefort (1972, p. 205) and Audier (2005, p. 216).

[39] Lefort analyzes Chapter 21 of *The Prince*, devoted to the use of fortresses, very carefully (Machiavelli 2005, pp. 76–79). He once again highlights how the prince who thinks of maintaining power solely by force is doomed to failure. For Machiavelli, the best fortress is to avoid being hated by the people, and avoid imposing one's authority in the form of mere force. Only in this way can a prince think of ruling.

focal point of the imaginary unity of the community and the target of its continuous questioning, its continuous demand for legitimacy (Lefort 2012, pp. 188–189).[40] Like the castle village described by Franz Kafka, which takes form and meaning only in relation to the hill where the manor is located and is inaccessible to the protagonist, so modern society can exist only around a locus of power that is both internal and at the same time absent and never fully attainable. This is a power that has lost all transcendent justification and any organic consubstantiality with origin and community. As we saw in the previous chapter, it is the power of the modern state that splits from the society whose appearance, in so doing, it enables.

According to Lefort, this particular way of thinking about power and its relation to political reality and the humors becomes explicit in *The Prince*. The eighth chapter presents "those who have become princes through wickedness" (Machiavelli 2005, p. 30). The main example is Agathocles, who "was not only an ordinary citizen but also of the lowest and most abject condition" but eventually became King of Syracuse (31). When serving as the city's praetor and hoping to become its prince, one morning Agathocles assembled the people and the Senate and ordered his soldiers to kill all the senators and wealthiest citizens, thus winning control of the principality. Next comes the example of Liverotto, who also acquired his principality, the city of Fermo, through cunning and heinous murder. However, unlike Agathocles, Liverotto was unable to maintain power for more than a year. Through these two examples, Machiavelli distinguishes between effective and ineffective forms of cruelty. The former are those committed only once, demanded by the necessity of acquiring or securing power and subsequently converted into something of use to the subjects. Conversely, actions that trigger others by creating a climate of instability and fear represent misused cruelty. After celebrating the personal virtues of the prince, Machiavelli sets out the contours of a power that is completely dependent on the contingent context in which it operates and, above all, on the opinion of its subjects. Thus Agathocles was able to maintain control in part because of the honor he gained from his military exploits against Carthage and a dangerous expedition to Africa in which he defeated his enemies, bringing peace to Syracuse. The *imperio*, therefore, always appears connected to glory and authority. In

---

[40] See, Trindade (2013, p. 172) and Molina (2000, p. 72).

order to survive, power must gain continual recognition: it depends on the support of public opinion (Lefort 2012, pp. 138–139).

The importance of opinion and image is reiterated in the famous chapters of *The Prince* (15 to 19) that consider the qualities required of those who wish to maintain power. It becomes immediately clear that the individual in power does not actually possess these virtues—generosity and miserliness, cruelty and compassion—but has instead certain other qualities that are recognized by public opinion. In politics, only the latter has the status of reality. In fact, "it is not necessary for a prince to possess all of the above-mentioned qualities, but it is very necessary for him to appear to possess them" (Machiavelli 2005, p. 61). It is not important to be personally good, mean or cruel, but only to appear to be so. It is important for the prince to convey the image of his goodness, meanness, or, when necessary, cruelty, to his subjects.

The difficulty then lies in being able to respond to the humors and demands of the subjects, in offering the right image at the right time, and administering the various qualities so as to avoid the greatest danger to power: the hatred of the people. In short, since "men in general judge more by their eyes than their hands" (62), politics is the domain of appearance. It is an imaginary dimension in which the need to be is replaced by the need to appear to be. It is no accident that in the section of Chapter 18 relevant to this, Machiavelli presents the famous centaur prince, half fox and half lion, who must use cunning and force in equal measure and at the right time (60).[41] To survive, this ruler must constantly avoid incurring the hatred of the people and cannot afford to appear to represent pure and illegitimate oppression. Cunning, in this case, is not a synonym for vulgar deception. It is "the art of attaching every particular action and every image to which it give rise to a good image of the prince" (Lefort 2012, p. 169).

The Roman examples used in Chapter 19, and especially that of Septimius Severus, on which Lefort dwells at length, are particularly significant in this context. In addition to being ferocious and cunning in the pursuit of power, Severus was able to retain it through his "great and notable"

---

[41] Machiavelli writes that "a prince must know how to make use of the nature of the beast, he should choose from among the beasts the fox and the lion; for the lion cannot defend itself from traps, while the fox cannot protect itself from the wolves. It is therefore necessary to be a fox, in order to recognize the traps, and a lion, in order to frighten the wolves: those who base their behaviour only on the lion do not understand things".

actions and the glory he obtained from them. While other emperors, by committing the sins of brutality or cowardice, provoked popular hatred and lost their power and their lives, he was able to maintain a "great reputation" (Machiavelli 2005, p. 66) in the eyes of the people and the army. He was feared and revered by a satisfied populace and thus remained in power for a long period. Just like Agathocles, he succeeded in this way not because he was completely virtuous or entirely cruel but because, while committing heinous acts, he was able to establish his legitimacy with glory. In short, he was always able to surround his actions with a positive *imaginary* that legitimized them, albeit not one of which he was in full control, since it was constructed and constantly revised in accordance with his ongoing relationship with the people and their desires (Lefort 2012, p. 179).[42]

According to Lefort, the lesson to draw from this is that the prince is not free to mold his image at will and impose it, by force or by cunning, on the people. Instead, there is a dynamic operating between the desire of the people and the actions of the prince, between popular satisfaction and the virtuous and wicked actions of Severus, and a correlation that is closer than one might think. The reality of the prince, like that of the people, resides solely in the relationship. The act of wielding power does not take place in a separate space but in one created by popular desire and imagination and the interaction of these with the actions with which the prince seeks to respond to them. Everything unfolds in the symbolic space that separates and at the same time connects the people to power:

> Now, in this situation, the ambiguity of politics is found. The prince embodies the imaginary that has been assigned to him by his function in society, but at the same time *he is caught up in it*, he is this desire for power and glory into which the desire of his subjects is metamorphosed. Here resides the blind spot of his task: that he can only rejoin the others through the space that they set aside for him as his own. The very conditions that ensure access to the real disguise it from him. (189)

---

[42] Lefort writes: "Such is the rampart of Severus, an invisible rampart that is neither the result of force nor that of good works: a structure of the collective imagination (*sua grandissima reputatione*), which men construct themselves because he manages to make them want it". The translation, in this case, is not entirely clear. In the original Lefort (1972, p. 424) does not speak of a "structure of collective imagination", but simply of an imaginary (*un imaginaire*).

At the same time, the imaginary (or ideological) discourse promoted by authority cannot be managed directly by any of the actors involved in the political encounter. This, moreover, is also why the outcomes of political actions are always uncertain, unpredictable, and dependent on fortune. Neither the prince, nor the people, nor the great have direct access to reality.

For Lefort, the concluding sentences of Chapter 18 make this abundantly clear. Here Machiavelli compares two political perspectives. On one side there is the multitude, which is only able to judge through observation and has a relationship with politics mediated by images and appearance. On the other are the few, the great, who are able to feel and to perceive the actions of the prince at close quarters, to touch them with their own hands without relying on appearances. However, according to the French thinker, in these passages, Machiavelli is not inferring that politics is a mere deception. Any interpretation that views the people as being deceived by the ideology of the prince while the great understand the stark reality of the real mechanisms hidden behind the ideological veil is simply wrong. In fact, as we have already pointed out, not only does the cunning of the prince not run in only one direction and is something that only he must contend with, but the aforementioned "few" who manage to view the political action behind the ideological representation also do not grasp the "reality" of political fact. Rather, they simply possess another perspective, and their knowledge is no greater or more complete than the knowledge of the people. Indeed, the great fail to understand how the people's desire for freedom and power come together. The great, Lefort seems to argue, believe they can see beyond the symbolic horizon but in fact fail to see the general meaning that eludes them, as well as the way they are themselves already a part of this and are defined by it. They do not see that "the being of society gives itself in excess over all given reality", (461) and thus fail to grasp the dimension of the political.[43]

No one can lay claim to pure, unfettered action, unaffected by otherness and the imaginary, by representation; no one exists outside of the symbolic institution of the social. Neither the prince nor much less the great can be considered the sole proponents of an ideology that they can use to justify their own positions of domination at the expense of the people. There are no constituent subjectivities capable of pure creation,

---

[43] The great thus appear to make the same mistake as Marxism, which believes it can reduce politics to a mere clash of material interests.

but only instituting elements that always exist in relation to the world and to otherness, which defines these elements and whose relationship is the locus of their existence (Janvier and Mancuso 2013).[44]

The constitutive ambiguity of the people emerges here in the clearest possible way. It participates in the authority to which it submits and provides justification for power in order to satisfy its desire for non-oppression. The desire to be is reversed into a desire for servitude, a desire to "not know" what masks the connivances and atrocities of the prince.[45] This, Lefort notes, is allowed to happen because the violence which the prince is able to wield is not the same as that of the great. While the great are the people's direct adversaries, the prince, being obliged to rein in their insatiable desire for oppression, which would otherwise overwhelm him, in the eyes of the people represents a guarantee of a "lesser evil" than direct oppression from their adversaries. In this sense, Lefort speaks of an unusual reversal (*détour*), comparable to the Hegelian cunning of reason, whereby popular desire is welded to authority. But this *ruse de la raison* is yet another way of defining the co-implication that also intervenes in the relationship between the people and the prince.[46] The latter, in short, is the symbol and the symptom of the indeterminacy that runs through and defines modern society.

> Through that experience, the thought that the desire of the people contains within itself that of the Grandees, and vice versa, or that the state is nourished by the joint illusion of the dominated and the dominant,

---

[44] The reference is once again to Merleau-Ponty's writings and his definition of "institution". See M. Merleau-Ponty (2010).

[45] Lefort reflects at length on the theme of the voluntary servitude of the people, especially as it is presented in Étienne de La Boétie's work (1985).

[46] In an unpublished writing preserved in the *Archives Lefort*, titled "Machiavel et la loi" (Lefort 1966, p. 8), which analyzes the relationship between the prince and the people, Lefort states, "Tout se passe donc à considérer cette analyse comme s'il y avait une ruse de la raison, au sens hégélien du terme. Le Prince découvre que pour travailler à son intérêt ou à sa gloire, il doit échapper à la haine de ses sujets et donc satisfaire, pour une part, leurs revendications. Le peuple découvre que pour soutenir son désir de non-oppression, il doit accepter l'autorité du Prince et cette double découverte est à l'origine de l'ordre politique. Mais cette ruse de la raison ne doit pas nous faire oublier la raison de la ruse et c'est en ceci que Machiavel n'est pas Hegel, c'est que la société finalement ne vit que de son défaut; elle ne s'ordonne qu'autour de cette brèche par où s'engouffrent les appétits de classes. Autrement dit, la ruse de la raison s'origine dans une duplicité première qui est dans les choses et qui y demeure".

or that law itself interweaves the history of their passion—that thought is delivered from the artificialist conception, from the fiction of a universe in which there are nothing but effective or ineffective lies, in discovering at one and the same time its place of birth in the desire of the other and the measure of its power in the exercise of its reflection, in its action of disenchantment. The assurance that collective life bears the ongoing occultation of the work of desire and the continuous possibility of a dis-occultation is interrelated with the assurance that there is, in the spoken word, with the subjection of the collective language, implicated in the work of occlusion of thought, the resource of an opening to truth. (Lefort 2012, p. 464)

It is here that Lefort's conceptualization of "the political" as something different from politics emerges. The analysis set out up to now has defined power as the very heart of the social. It is the symbolic focal point through which the social can perpetuate its mechanism of division and recognition. It is the double game of power, its duty to divide and to unite, that gives society its dynamism, that allows it to express its being-in-itself, to engage in its continuous questioning, and at the same time protects society from clashing with itself in a way that would only lead to its dissolution, from descending into a battle of interests and civil war. As the political expression of the social's flesh and blood, the thing that gives meaning to society through an ongoing internal and external demand for legitimacy, power is the key to understanding the "political institution of the social", that is, the symbolic institution proper to a society—the modern society—that relates to itself only through the struggle for power. In other words, it is through the power that it becomes possible to understand the dimension of "the political" (*le politique*), the permanent conflict elaborated in a symbolic dimension that structures the community, that reveals and at the same time conceals the social's lack of foundation.

THE ORIGINAL DIVISION OF THE SOCIAL

As has been highlighted by the analysis of Lefort's reading of *The Prince* and the *Discourses*, at an initial level division takes the form of a clash between two energies, two desires, that of commanding and that of not being commanded, which are defined in relation to each other. While manifesting itself, at the economic level, as the opposition between the holders of wealth and the "bare arms", between the nobility and the people or, in the case of Rome, between the Senate and the plebs, this can nevertheless not be reduced simply to a class division (Lefort 1978, p. 234). It is not an objective division in which a cause and an effect can be recognized but is instead the modern form of the dynamic of the social, and determines the image of power and the self-representation of the social. In this sense, Lefort can say that Machiavelli does not view antagonism as a provisional moment in politics. Rather, he considers politics from outside of the natural law paradigm. He perceives the characteristics of the *polis* as something unconnected to the comparison between nature and culture that tends to contrast a natural state based on war to a social state in which generalized conflict comes to an end. Conflict in this understanding has a comprehensive and foundational dimension, not because it is the first principle or the root cause of the social but because of the fact that it is not possible to find the social before division. In short, at the "bottom" of the question of the political community described by Machiavelli, that is, the modern form of the social, there is no single generating principle, the "One", but a mechanism of perpetual difference, of continuous dispute. The theory of an antagonism that precedes society is immediately discarded: antagonism is already coexistence and coexistence is nothing if not antagonism.[47] This is why Lefort describes social division as "elusive", foundational, and insuperable. It is elusive (*insaisissable*) because it cannot be reduced to an opposition of fact or interest: it is never objectively determinable. It is original and insuperable because it is the very engine of the social, the *reality* to which the social "responds" by organizing itself.

At the same time, as we have seen, the approach that a given society has toward its own internal conflicts defines its relationship with the world, with the real, and with the other.[48] Two divisions, one internal (class division) and the other emerging from the difference with the rest of the world (reality and other states in particular) determine the direction and structure of political society, which appears to constitute itself

---

[47] In his "Note on Machiavelli", Merleau-Ponty (1964, pp. 211–223) had already considered the theme of conflict in the Florentine Secretary. Also of interest on the same subject are the reflections of Roberto Esposito, who, from his earliest work, emphasizes the presence of conflict in Machiavelli and highlights a binary ontology that provides no path to unity (Esposito 1984).

[48] In the fourth chapter of the fifth part of *Le travail de l'œuvre*, entitled "Sur la guerre et la différence des temps" (Lefort 2012, pp. 280–328), it becomes clear how the two divisions we have referred to are accompanied by a third division, temporal difference, which pervades political discourse and the discourse on war.

precisely through the articulation of these differences. Thus, far from being a mere clash of divergent interests, for Lefort the struggles between the different desires that make up the social are in fact the very process through which the social unfolds, they are its very dynamic, its development into a discourse of oppositions without possible synthesis. The different parts of the community and institutions confront and distinguish themselves specifically in the tumult. The law and the image of power are defined in this conflict, as is the relationship with the world and with reality, with the other. Thus, society's self-recognition always occurs indirectly, through a separation from itself, through confrontation. Likewise, its self-representation is forged through internal conflict between different self-representations. This dynamic reverberates internally and on all levels, and involves a continuous questioning of the social, its perpetual questioning of itself, of the image of power, and of its foundation.

This is why the loss of self is a continuous threat to the social, which, insofar as it is continually in question and unable to reach itself fully or directly, and insofar as it is the continual giving and establishment of itself, is characterized by the lack of stability produced by the mechanism of division. The social is in constant danger of losing itself in or out of the division, in civil war, or against the foreign enemy. In its modern form, it is the perpetuation of division itself. Its only meaning resides in the struggle between humors and with otherness to which only the locus of power, as the symbolic focus of questioning, can give meaning. What figure, then, better represents this idea of society and politics than Machiavelli's prince, who is alone, without certainties, under attack from the greats and the people, and at the mercy of fortune?

Lefort therefore did not discover, through Machiavelli, a kind of essence of the social "by its nature" divided between two opposing desires. Division is not an a priori, nor is it a founding principle, a preceding generative cause, or a law of history. This would be the result of the overarching thinking which, like Lefort, Machiavelli himself rejects when he views the truth of politics as the momentary result of the clash between human action and fortune. Beyond any "distortion of the original", beyond any *surplomb*, division instead appears to be a limit of thought, which is conscious of being embroiled in the same mechanism of the distortion of the social that it seeks to analyze. It is the limit of modern thought, power, and discourse, which are without foundation (Lefort and Gauchet 1971).

At the same time, division is not even just the attestation of a resistance that emerges as a backlash from the mechanisms put in place by a more or less oppressive power. Much more radically, division indicates the impossibility of thought coming into direct contact with reality and overcoming the dimension of interpretation and representation, without first getting lost in the differences between it and represented reality. Division, in other words, is the result of thought, politics, and society forced to come to terms with a lack of reference points and the impossibility of reaching the true origin: indeterminacy.

In this framework, the people do not represent a fundamental substratum, a pure subject, a no-rule event, the revolutionary explosion, or constituent power opposed to all institutions.[49] It is not enough simply to locate in the people the explosion of pure desire that will later be corrupted by contact with power, but one must break out of a dichotomous notion of the political in order to be able to grasp the deep sense of division, the "flesh" of the social and the indeterminacy on which it rests.[50] Lefort's Machiavelli, then, is not a "class" thinker, nor a proto-communist, nor the first anachronistic libertarian. Rather, he is the thinker who first recognized the loss of all foundations in modernity and, consequently, sought to understand politics starting from the notion of indeterminacy, and to confront a reality cleansed of universal principles. However, he did so without thinking that he could arrive at an objectivity that would restore an overarching thought. When singing the praises of the people Machiavelli does not take the side of a specific social class which, by its nature or because of the laws of history, would bring about freedom, constituent power or state power. Rather, his reflection must be interpreted as an idea *of the* political and not *about the* political, one that

---

[49] Lefort's interpretation thus goes in a different direction than that of the so-called "plebeian politics". See Breaugh (2013) and Vatter (2000). In this text the author, seeking to combine Lefort's thought with that of Hannah Arendt, interprets the people as a capacity for action, and in Arendt's sense, the production of the new as opposed to any constituted, as *no rule*.

[50] It is in this sense that we should read Lefort's statement that: "In a sense neither the wish of the Grandees nor that of the people can be fulfilled. They are not extinguished either under the sign of positivity nor under that of negativity. Nevertheless, the positions of the antagonists are different. The Grandees always want to have more; the more they possess, the more they are great. The people, on the other hand, in their desire not to be dominated, oppressed, make evidence of a radical impossibility, which destines it to that metaphor of the social whole that is the Law—and that is the State, insofar as it is constituted in the space of law" (Lefort 1978, pp. 230–231).

questions class division from within in order to understand how the unity of the community can be established from it, how power can establish itself in the vacuum created by conflict and in the furrow of division.

In response to this need, Lefort does not hesitate to reveal, in the unexpected conclusion to *Le travail de l'œuvre*, the internal split within the very desires of the people and the great. Every desire, he observes, does not stand the test of its definition, as it always reveals itself to be divided and coexisting with its opposite:

> To discover beneath the fact of appetite the break of desire is, in fact, to forbid oneself to suppose that there is a *real* separation between its two poles, unless it is to let it fall back once again to the level of nature; it is necessarily to agree that it relates to itself across separation, and that this relation can be manifested only in the form of a representation. It would be vain to pretend to reduce the desire of the Grandees to what constitutes its essence: in the experience of the instability of possession and power, it proves to be unsustainable, carrying within itself its opposite, the desire to be, at the same time that it attacks it in the other, and is condemned to emerge with the self-image of an effectively present totality, a "social nature" in agreement with itself at a deep level. [...] Similarly, it is impossible to make the desire of the populace coincide with the principle that constitutes it: the populace itself coincide with its opposite; to the extent that it is pure negativity, that it bears the infinite demand "not to be commanded, oppressed," and experiences the impossibility of its goal, it in turn proves to be unsustainable, riveted to the desire to have, at the same time that it discovers it in the other, and condemned to emerge with a self-image in which the substitute for what is withheld from it is offered. (Lefort 2012, pp. 459–460)

The distinction between the constituent and the constituted, between matter and form, between the great and the people, is ultimately illusory. All the elements which constitute the social, despite being opposed to one another, turn out at the same time to be caught up in the same story, in the same interweaving of meanings, in the same institution (459).[51] The relationship and the clash between the desires of the great and of

---

[51] Lefort writes: "Now it is the same thing to think the power of representation in the institution and to think the break in the continuum of desire implied by the rending of society into antagonistic classes; to read the contradiction of a re-connecting of the desire to have and the desire to be, which constitute, respectively, the essence of the desire of the Grandees and that of the desire of the people, and to read the ever-reenacted

the people participate, and continuously involve themselves, in the image of power that they never cease to question and redefine. Suspended in indeterminacy, in continuous division, they have always been part of the very "flesh" of the social. They are stuck within the dynamics of the institution of the social.[52] In this dynamic, division and foundation run after each other. The contingent foundation hopelessly proposed by any dominant political discourse, from the least to the most emancipatory, is always affected by otherness and challenged by what escapes it, by what is not understood. It is a "remainder" that we called the people and which in turn puts forward various meanings. It is traversed by an internal and elusive division.

The modernity described by Machiavelli is thus neither the emergence of an autonomous society nor that of a society essentially without foundations. Rather, modern society is the society of otherness and indeterminacy in which the foundation, far from disappearing, is continually re-proposed and questioned.[53] Thus,

> when we ask ourselves what, for Machiavelli, constitutes the foundation of politics, we are confronted with the idea of an ultimate division, in the sense that it does not cease repeating its dividing with the shifting of terms. It is division of classes, division of desire, or, if we would leave the causal side for that of the effect, division between state and society, division between the desire of the prince and collective desire… But the question of the foundation is not annulled in the experience of division; rather it makes itself heard with increasing strength, like that of instauration. In the instauration of the authority of the prince, or of the authority of Rome,

enterprise of the figuration of a social identity in which difference is abolished" (Lefort 2012, p. 459).

[52] In this way, Lefort pursues Merleau-Ponty's proposal of thinking about instituting subjectivities, which are always related to otherness and the world and not constituent, or detached from the world and otherness by an illusory solipsism. See Merleau-Ponty (2010).

[53] Referring to the example of Severus, Lefort notes how foundation is always accompanied by preservation, and this by the repetition of the founding act (Lefort 2012, p. 178). The return to principles, in short, takes the form of a return to the original spirit of the law, which must, however, be reinterpreted according to current circumstances. This is a move that retains within itself both the dimension of change and that of preservation. Lefort thus distances himself from those authors who have seen the return to the beginning as a straightforward regression to the original movement without any institutional reference, to the pure act of the foundational force.

the sign of foundation is legible. But in such a way as to receive division, to open themselves up to the play of differentiation of terms, in giving free rein to the work of conflict, the prince or Rome show themselves capable of founding an enterprise—of opening a passage to history. Such is the indetermination connected with foundation that it is always possible to blind oneself in such a way as to read the justification of the arbitrary in it, to maintain that the prince is free to do whatever he likes, provided he wins power and security. (464–465)

Only in this theoretical framework, in this symbolic institution of the social characterized by division and indeterminacy, can one understand the democratic form of society.

REFERENCES

Althusser, Louis. 2000. *Machiavelli and Us*. London: Verso.
Aron, Raymond. 1993. *Machiavel et les tyrannies modernes*. Paris: Editions de Fallois.
Audier, Serge. 2005. *Machiavel, conflit et liberté*. Paris: Vrin.
Black, Robert. 2013. *Machiavelli*. London: Routledge.
Bode, Remo. 2017. Una filosofia della ragione impura: il pensiero italiano. In *Effetto Italian Thought*, ed. E. Lisciani Petrini, G. Strummiello, 55–70. Macerata: Quodlibet.
Breaugh, Martin. 2013. *The Plebeian Experience: A Discontinuous History of Political Freedom*. New York: Columbia University Press.
Breckman, Warren 2019. Retour sur «l'idéologie invisible» selon Lefort. *Raison Publique* 23: 37–54.
Cassirer, Ernst. 1961. *The Myth of the State*. New Haven: Yale University Press.
Chabod, Federico. 1964. *Scritti su Machiavelli*. Torino: Einaudi.
Colonna d'Istria, Pauline. 2015. La division originaire du social. Lefort lecteur de Lacan ? *Politique et Sociétés* 34/1: 131–147.
De Grazia, Sebastian. 1989. *Machiavelli in Hell*. Princeton: Princeton University Press.
de La Boétie, Étienne. 1985. *Le discours de la servitude volontaire*. Paris: Payot.
Del Lucchese, Filippo. 2011. *Conflict, Power, and Multitude in Machiavelli and Spinoza: Tumult and Indignation*. London: Bloomsbury.
Del Lucchese, Filippo. 2015. *The Political Philosophy of Niccolò Machiavelli*. Edinburgh: Edinburgh University Press.
Del Lucchese, Filippo, Frosini, Fabio, and Morfino, Vittorio. 2016. *Radical Machiavelli. Politics, Philosophy, and Language*. Leiden: Brill.
Di Pierro, Mattia. 2018. Claude Lefort e l'interpretazione di Machiavelli. Una riscoperta del politico tra potere e conflitto. *Filosofia politica* 32/1: 133–150.

Di Pierro, Mattia. 2020. *L'esperienza del mondo: Claude Lefort e la fenomenologia del politico*. Pisa: ETS.
Esposito, Roberto. 1984. *Ordine e conflitto. Machiavelli e la letteratura politica del Rinascimento italiano*. Napoli: Liguori.
Esposito, Roberto. 2012. *Living Thought: The Origins and Actuality if Italian Philosophy*. Stanford: Stanford University Press.
Esposito, Roberto. 2023. *Vitam instituere. Genealogia dell'istituzione*. Torino: Einaudi.
Flynn, Bernard. 2005. *The Philosophy of Claude Lefort: Interpreting the Political*. Evanston: Northwestern University Press.
Gaille, Marie. 2018. *Machiavelli on Freedom and Civil Conflict: An Historical and Medical Approach to Political Thinking*. Leiden: Brill.
Garin, Eugenio. 1970. *Dal Rinascimento all'Illuminismo: Studi e ricerche*. Pisa: Nistri-Lischi.
Geuna, Marco. 2005. Machiavelli e il ruolo dei conflitti nella vita politica. In *Conflitti*, ed. A. Arienzo and D. Caruso, 29–57. Napoli: Dante & Descartes.
Geuna, Marco. 2015. Machiavelli e il problema delle congiure. Rivista Storica Italiana, 127/2: 355–410.
Gilbert, Felix. 1965. *Machiavelli and Guicciardini: Politics and History in Sixteenth Century Florence*. Princeton: Princeton University Press.
Hankins, James. 2000. *Renaissance civic Humanism: Reappraisals and Reflections*. Cambridge: Cambridge University Press.
Hankins, James. 2019. *Virtue Politics. Soulcraft and Statecraft in Renaissance Italy*. Cambridge: Harvard University Press.
Hilb, Claudia. 2013. Claude Lefort as Reader of Leo Strauss. In *Claude Lefort: Thinker of the Political*, ed. M. Plot, 71–86. New York: Palgrave Macmillan.
Janvier, Antoine, and Mancuso, Eva. 2013. Peuple(s) et subjectivation politiques chez Claude Lefort. Une lecture du Machiavel. *Tumultes* 40/1: 145–162.
Johnston, David, Urbinati, Nadia, and Vergara, Camila. 2017. *Machiavelli on Liberty & Conflict*. Chicago and London: The University of Chicago Press.
Labelle, Gilles. 2006. Can the Problem of the Theologico-Political be Resolved? Leo Strauss and Claude Lefort. *Thesis Eleven* 87/1: 63–81.
Laclau, Ernesto. 2007. *On Populist Reason*. London: Verso.
Lefort, Claude. 1966. Machiavel et la loi. *Archives Claude Lefort*, EHESS-CESPRA, CL. 72, boîte 13.
Lefort, Claude. 1972. *Le Travail de l'œuvre Machiavel*. Paris: Gallimard.
Lefort, Claude. 1978. *Les formes de l'histoire: Essais d'anthropologie politique*. Paris: Gallimard.
Lefort, Claude. 1986. *The political forms of modern society: Bureaucracy, democracy, totalitarianism*. Cambridge: MIT Press.
Lefort, Claude. 2000. *Writing. The Political Test*. Durham: Duke University Press.

Lefort, Claude. 2007. *Le temps présent. Écrits 1945–2005*. Paris: Belin.
Lefort, Claude. 2012. *Machiavelli in the Making*. Evanston: Northwestern University Press.
Lefort, Claude and Gauchet, Marcel. 1971. Sur la démocratie: le politique et l'institution du social. *Textures* 2/3: 7–78.
Louis, Adrien. 2016. Voir et comprendre la politique moderne. Leo Strauss et Claude Lefort. *Archives de Philosophie* 79/3: 485–498.
Machiavelli, Niccolò. 1996. *Discourses on Livy*. Chicago, London: University of Chicago Press.
Machiavelli, Niccolò. 2005. *The Prince*. Oxford: Oxford University Press.
Manent, Pierre. 1993. Vers l'œuvre et vers le monde. Le Machiavel de Claude Lefort. In *La démocratie à l'œuvre: Autour de Claude Lefort*, ed. C. Habib and C. Mouchard, 169–190. Paris: Éditions Esprit.
Mansfield, Harvey. 1979. *Machiavelli's New Modes and Orders: A Study of the Discourses on Livy*. Ithaca: Cornell University Press.
Marchart, Oliver. 2007. *Post-Foundational Political Thought: Political Difference in Nancy, Lefort, Badiou and Laclau*. Edinburgh: Edinburgh University Press.
Marchesi, Francesco. 2017. *Riscontro. Pratica politica e congiuntura storica in Niccolò Machiavelli*. Macerata: Quodlibet.
Marchesi, Francesco. 2018. *Cartografia politica. Spazi e soggetti del conflitto in Niccolò Machiavelli*. Firenze: Olschki.
Marcotte-Chénard, Sophie. 2015. Qu'est-ce qu'une oeuvre de pensée? Réflexions sur l'art de lire lefortien. *Politique et Sociétés* 34/1: 149–171.
Maritain, Jacques. 1953. *L'homme et l'État*. Paris: Bibliothèque des Sciences Politiques.
Ménissier, Thierry. 2010. *Machiavel ou la politique du centaure*. Paris: Hermann.
Ménissier, Thierry. 2017. Lefort lecteur de Machiavel: le travail continué de l'œuvre. *Revue Française d'Histoire des Idées Politiques* 46/2: 9–32.
Merleau-Ponty, Maurice. 1964. *Signs*. Evanston: Northwestern University Press.
Merleau-Ponty, Maurice. 2010. *Institution and Passivity: Course Notes from the Collège de France (1954–1955)*. Evanston: Northwestern University Press.
Molina, Esteban. 2000. Maquiavelo en la obra de Claude Lefort. *Metapolítica* 13/4: 64–81.
Moroncini, Bruno. 2014. *Lacan politico*. Napoli: Cronopio.
Mouffe, Chantal. 2005. *On the Political*. Abingdon, New York: Routledge.
Mouffe, Chantal. 2006. *The Return of the Political*. London: Verso.
Najemy, John. 1999. Papirius and the Chickens, or Machiavelli on the Necessity of Interpreting Religion. *Journal of the History of Ideas* 60/4: 659–681.
Negri, Antonio. 1999. *Insurgencies: Constituent Power and the Modern State*. Minneapolis: University of Minnesota Press.
Parel, Anthony. 1992. *The Machiavellian Cosmos*. New Haven: Yale University Press.

Pedullà, Gabriele. 2018. *Machiavelli in Tumult: The Discourses on Livy and the Origins of Political Conflictualism*. Cambridge: Cambridge University Press.
Poltier, Hugues. 1998. *Passion du politique. La pensée de Claude Lefort*. Genève: Labor et Fides.
Rancière, Jacques. 2004. *Disagreement. Politics and Philosophy*. Minneapolis: The University of Minnesota Press.
Sasso, Gennaro. 1993. *Niccolò Machiavelli*. 2 vol. Bologna: Il Mulino.
Sasso, Gennaro. 2015. *Su Machiavelli. Ultimi scritti*. Roma: Carocci.
Sfez, Gérald. 2007. Machiavel en France et la seconde moitié du XXème. In *Machiavelli nel XIX e XX secolo. Machiavel aux XIX et XX siècle*, ed. P. Carta, X. Tabet, 309–369. Padova: Cedam.
Skinner, Quentin. 1998. *Liberty Before Liberalism*. Cambridge, Cambridge University Press.
Stavrakakis, Yannis. 2007. *The Lacanian Left. Psychoanalysis, Theory, Politics*. Edinburgh: Edinburgh University Press.
Strauss, Leo. 1958. *Thoughts on Machiavelli*. Glencoe: Free Press.
Tønder, Lars, and Thomassen, Lasse. 2005. *Radical Democracy: Politics between abundance and lack*. Manchester: Manchester University Press.
Torres, Sebastian. 2014. La trama politica del desiderio: Machiavelli. *Consecutio Temporum. Rivista critica della postmodernità* 6: 174–191.
Trindade, Gleyton. 2013. Maquiavel e a dimensão simbólica do poder: fundamentos da teoria democrática de Claude Lefort. *Revista Brasileira de Ciência Política* 12: 155–180.
Vatter, Miguel. 2000. *Between Form and Event. Machiavelli's Theory of Political Freedom*. Dordrecht-Boston: Kluwer Academic Publishers.
Viroli, Maurizio. 2012. *Machiavelli's God*. Princeton: Princeton University Press.
Zanzi, Luigi. 2013. *Il metodo di Machiavelli*. Bologna: Il Mulino.
Zarka, Yves Charles, Ménissier, Therry. 2001. *Machiavel, le Prince ou le nouvel art politique*. Paris: PUF.
Žižek, Slavoj. 2008. *In Defense of Lost Causes*. Verso: London.

CHAPTER 7

The Political and the Institution of the Social

Structure or Institution

Before considering Lefort's theory of democracy and totalitarianism in the next chapter, I believe it will be useful to reflect on the theoretical framework in which this develops and takes its stand, in order to fully understand the meaning and scope of his proposal. I will therefore take a small step back and return to the French debate of the late 1940s and early 1950s.

The year 1949, when Lefort and Castoriadis founded Socialisme ou Barbarie, also saw the publication of Claude Lévi-Strauss's *The Elementary Structures of Kinship*, the book that sanctioned the birth of the theoretical current that would dominate for decades to come: structuralism. Its author became a vital figure in the French intellectual world in those years, and his publications were veritable publishing sensations, selling thousands of copies and having a direct and disruptive effect on scholarly debate (Dosse 2018, pp. 373–378). The release of *Tristes Tropiques* in 1955 was a particular success, and a genuine intellectual shock, with its hybrid character, pitched somewhere between an autobiographical narrative and a scholarly essay, enabling it to reach an extremely broad and diverse audience (378–385; Nora 2010). Intellectuals, journalists, and scholars from various disciplines—from Raymond Aron to

Georges Bataille and Lucien Febvre—welcomed the event with enthusiasm, and the success highlighted and reaffirmed the emergence of a new relationship between theory and the humanities. The book represented the establishment of anthropology as the leading discipline in the social sciences, and the rise of structuralism as the hegemonic theory of the period.

The mid-1950s in France were in fact marked by what François Dosse has called the "moment ethnologique" (Dosse 2018, pp. 373–397) In this period "intellectuals believe they find new allies in the tropics, among the primitives, the Nambikwara and the other Bororo peoples" who offer "the image of an unperverted humanity" from which to imagine a new form of emancipation, which in that historical and political context also meant decolonization (309). Anthropology and structuralism thus supplied new tools to political theory, to the critique of power and society, and to Marxism itself.

In 1950 Lévi-Strauss wrote his famous introduction to the work of Marcel Mauss, which first and foremost acclaims him as the father of modern ethnology. For Lévi-Strauss, Mauss's main achievement was that he grasped the symbolic origin of society. In addition, by defining social life as "a world of symbolic relations", he was able to highlight the profound interrelationship between the individual and society, the complementarity between the individual psyche and group culture (Lévi-Strauss 1987, pp. 19–21). In other words, he saw how individual behavior must be understood within a collective symbolic system (12–13).

In this context, Lévi-Strauss emphasizes the importance of Mauss' idea of "total social fact". This indicates the correlation between economic, religious, and cultural phenomena, between agricultural techniques and rituals, between the form of households and the distribution of products. However, much more than this, Mauss uses the concept to overcome the dichotomy between subject and object, between thing and representation, to perceive how "in a science in which the observer is of the same nature as his object of study, *the observer himself is a part of the observation*" (29). In short, Mauss suggests society should be analyzed as a symbolic totality, in which the observer is obviously included.

It is at this point, however, that the crucial passage of Lévi-Strauss's interpretation makes its entrance. For him, this awareness does not trap anthropology in a hermeneutic dead end, facing an unattainable object within an analysis that stubbornly breaks down only on the subject. Rather, analyzing society as a totality means simultaneously also being able to see it from the outside, in its entirety. And this is possible because every subject, although it can never totally come out of itself, can see itself *as if* from the outside *as* an object of study. And so ad infinitum: even the subject that objectifies itself can be objectified. The subject, in short, can be objectified countless times, though never completely. In turn, sociological observation is able to break out of the antinomy between subject and object due to the fact that it experiences concretely the unlimited process of objectification of which the subject is capable, but which for the individual is difficult (31–32). This objectifying capacity makes it possible to overcome the distance between subject and object.

As a result, Lévi-Strauss continues, following Mauss' theory of *mana*, it is possible to find a common ground where subject and object can meet and understand each other. This is a pre-subjective space, a deeper reality, a simpler and hidden infrastructure that explains and brings reality to the phenomenal data of society. And while Mauss turns to the unconscious in order to grasp this dimension, Lévi-Strauss instead proposes that we look to language and perceive the formal structures of which the unconscious is only an effect. Thus, by applying the findings of structural linguistics to Mauss' theory, Lévi-Strauss illuminates an unconscious structure of which subjects are a part, and through which it is possible to relate social phenomena to each other so as to study society and its relations within the framework of a single comprehensible system. Not only that, but Lévi-Strauss wagers that these structures can be understood mathematically, that is, that they constitute a universal and knowable formal logic capable of revealing the invariable aspects of human societies. In short, he believes that this formal structure makes it possible to pursue a science of the social by treating it as an object, as if one were analyzing it from the outside to perceive its essential infrastructure. Here then lies Mauss' great discovery and the importance of his essay "The Gift":

> What happened in that essay, for the first time in the history of ethnological thinking, was that an effort was made to transcend empirical observation and to reach deeper realities. For the first time, the social ceases to belong to the domain of pure quality—anecdote, curiosity, material for moralizing description or for scholarly comparison—and becomes a system, among whose parts connections, equivalences, and interdependent aspects can be discovered. First, it is the products of social activity, whether technical, economic, ritual, aesthetic, or religious (tools, manufactured products, foodstuffs, magical formulae, ornaments, chants, dances, and

myths), which are made comparable to one another through that common character they all have of being transferable; the modes of their transferability can be analyzed and classified, and even when they seem inseparable from certain types of values, they are reducible to more fundamental forms, which are of a general nature. (38–39)

Lévi-Strauss' analysis presents Mauss as a proto-structuralist, a kind of unwitting father of structuralism who opened a path that he did not follow to the end. He stopped right on the threshold of the discovery of structure and the immense possibilities that it brought, "like Moses conducting his people all the way to a promised land whose splendour he would never behold" (45).

Maurice Merleau-Ponty also fell under the spell of the new structuralist theory, and in the early 1950s attempted to bring his philosophy closer to linguistics and the new human sciences (Dosse 2018, pp. 385–387). As early as 1954–1955, in a course on institution and passivity at the Collège de France, he considers and discusses Lévi-Strauss's view, highlighting the problems with the anthropologist's "difficult position", which seems to yield to the illusion of *surplomb*, of an objective knowledge of the real (Merleau-Ponty 2010, pp. 73–75). His judgment is less harsh in an article published slightly later, in 1959, entitled *De Mauss à Lévi-Strauss* (Merleau-Ponty 1964, pp. 114–125). In it he essentially accepts the interpretation of Mauss proposed by Lévi-Strauss nine years earlier, and hails the structuralist project as a "great intellectual endeavor" (125). According to Merleau-Ponty, the idea of structure is a useful tool for overcoming the dichotomy between subject and object and for understanding the web of relations and symbolic meanings that constitutes the social. This is the same web that he had already tried to point to with the concept of *institution* a few years earlier. The phenomenologist affirms:

> This notion of structure, whose present good fortune in all domains responds to an intellectual need, establishes a whole system of thought. For the philosopher, the presence of structure outside us in natural and social systems and within us as symbolic function points to a way beyond the subject-object correlation which has dominated philosophy from Descartes to Hegel. By showing us that man is eccentric to himself and that the social finds its center only in man, structure particularly enables us to understand how we are in a sort of circuit with the socio-historical world. (123)

7 THE POLITICAL AND THE INSTITUTION OF THE SOCIAL

Merleau-Ponty's untimely death prevents us from knowing what direction his ideas would have taken, how and how far he would have continued to use the notion of structure, and to move toward structuralism and the human sciences. However, the 1959 text seems almost to obscure the fact that he was replacing the concept of institution with that of structure, which he seems to consider equally capable of describing the social.

In this sense, Lefort separates his thought from that of his master, although he does so out of a greater sense of loyalty to the idea of phenomenology proposed by Merleau-Ponty than Merleau-Ponty himself. Of course, as I have already shown, even Lefort is not immune to the "moment ethnologique". He too is "forced" to confront the disruptive rise of structuralism and the questions underlining it, the "exigency of the spirit"[1] that led to its emergence. In the early 1950s he repeatedly considers Lévi-Strauss' theses and makes use of some of his studies in parts of his own work (Lefort 1978). However, he certainly does not share Merleau-Ponty's enthusiasm for the anthropologist's work and, especially, for the concept of structure.

The 1951 article "The Exchange and the Struggle among Men", which I have already considered in chapter two, in fact analyzes specifically Mauss' theories about gifts, and clashes openly with Lévi-Strauss' reading (21–45). In this text the interpretation of Mauss' work thus becomes a genuine battleground in which two different ideas of society and as many conceptions of the relationship between the social and the theoretical come into conflict. According to Lefort, Mauss was attempting to understand the immanent intentions of the subjects engaged in the exchange of gifts. His focus was on meaning and representation and not on the symbolic dimension. Gift exchange for him is a human and social act rather than a natural fact, and as such cannot be separated from its representation. Mauss therefore did not intend to reduce social phenomena to their nature as symbolic systems, nor did he wish to establish a pre-subjective logical order that would justify real-world behavior. He in fact took the reverse approach, attempting to understand the relationship between meaning and behavior. It is therefore here, according to Lefort,

---

[1] In English it is translated as "intellectual need" (Merleau-Ponty p. 123): "This notion of structure, whose present good fortune in all domains responds to an intellectual need, establishes a whole system of thought".

that the error in Lévi-Strauss' reading and the limitation of his structuralism lies: proceeding in an entirely opposite direction from Mauss, Lévi-Strauss goes in search of a deeper reality than social meanings, a meaning of which the latter would in fact merely be the effects: he seeks the real and objective cause that explains social meanings. Not only that, but he believes that this underlying "reality" may be a mechanical law from which the reciprocity of the gift is derived; a mathematical structure that determines the empirical game of exchanges and relationships.

For Lefort, Lévi-Strauss' rationalism therefore occupies the intersection of two opposite and identical forms. On the one hand it is a Kantian-type idealism in search of general and universal laws of the human spirit and its innate and immutable structure. On the other, this rationalism is a scientistic objectivism that believes it can study society as an object, through an absolute science that reduces social representations to objects (35).

However, Lefort continues, the price of this analysis is that it denies the existence of the social and is unable to understand it. By reducing the whole of the social, its meanings and relations, to the result of an earlier structure, Lévi-Strauss strips all meaning from it, failing to recognize the productivity of the representations that animate it. The meaning of the social, its reality, is thus always placed before and outside the social itself. In this way, he not only succumbs to an illusion of being able to see the whole picture, but does not even recognize the dimension of experience. He turns society into a mere effect of a meaning located elsewhere, so much so that his study of the empirical dimension, the analysis of concrete reality, has no value in itself, but is only of use in the construction of an earlier symbolic logic. He, we might say paraphrasing Hegel, reveals nothing more than the skeleton, from which all flesh and blood have been stripped away. Lefort therefore concludes:

> In short, we question Lévi-Strauss for having identified in society *rules* rather than *behaviors*, to borrow Mauss' expressions; for having artificially posited a total rationality from which groups and men are reduced to an abstract function, rather than grounding it in the concrete relations that actually bind them to one another. (34)

For Lefort, in order to analyze the social it is instead necessary to move in exactly the opposite direction: to perceive the reciprocity that governs the game of gift exchange, and the fact that the lived experience of a plurality of consciousnesses is encountered in it. In other words, understanding the dimension of the social means understanding its reality through its representation, which is real, experienced, and produces relationships, or meanings that are not only effects but are themselves also causes. Anticipating a concept that Lefort would develop a few years later, one might say that the social must be understood as experience, in the inextricable interweaving of actions, thoughts, history, and ideology.

This position is a crucial element in the development of Lefort's thought, which continues to engage with structuralism even, and especially, in the following years, by which time it has taken a hegemonic position in French debate. It is no coincidence that he came back to the critique of Lévi-Strauss in the text that, in 1976, opens the first issue of the journal *Libre*, whose editorial board included, alongside Lefort, also Castoriadis, Miguel Abensour, Pierre Clastres, Marcel Gauchet, and Maurice Luciani (Lefort 2007, pp. 275–300). This text, written by Lefort but left unsigned, as if to retain a collective identity, aims to position the group's theses within the theoretical-political debate of the time. It is a veritable manifesto of what, at this point, it is possible to call "the theory of the institution of the social": a description which one could use to refer to a theory that, as I am presenting it here, is first and foremost elaborated by Lefort but is also shared and interpreted in more or less different, if not conflicting, ways, by the aforementioned group.

The essay's opening lines declare its intentions and approach. The year 1968 is chosen for its symbolism, and the previous eight years and the eight preceding those will be considered in order to take stock of the state of philosophical and social theory in France. Those before 1968 are described as having been characterized by a renewed scientific spirit in the humanities, by the reformulation of modern empiricism and objectivism. Structuralism is the undisputed protagonist of this phase, and it is therefore on this that the critique is focused (276).

Lefort reiterates that the concept of structure first proposed by Lévi-Strauss has emptied out the social, its dynamics, its action, and its productivity of all meaning. It has served to conceal the distinction between the use of knowledge and the object of knowledge. It has concealed the division that runs through the social and fuels its dynamics:

> What is being erased is not the real itself, but the very horizon of reality. What is destroyed is what Merleau-Ponty called the "flesh" of the social or the "flesh" of history. What is disappearing is the notion that fact and representation can be reversed, that what is at stake is the institution, whose form commands the process of the differentiation of functions and opposition of actors, and which arises simultaneously from this process. (278)

This same problem, he continues, is particularly clear in the work of Louis Althusser, who uses structuralism to "translate into rigorous language the confused intuitions of the mode of production" (279). Lefort's critique is not so much directed toward the distinction, which he nevertheless considers arbitrary, between the writings of Marx's youth and those of his maturity. Rather, the problem with Althusser's theory lies in the fact that it abolishes discourse on the oeuvre and the discourse of the social. His aim is not to propose another interpretation of Marx's texts, but rather to replace the debate on the oeuvre with "an object of knowledge sufficient unto itself and which makes the reading of Marx superfluous (or authorizes it only within the limits of its 'reproduction')" (280). In other words, Althusser turns Marx's work into the discourse of a science, in which all interpretation is disallowed. His analysis of the social suffers from the same error: the depth of the social, like that of the oeuvre is erased. The social no longer acts upon itself, and there is no more history, no more relationship with otherness and division. Each element of history, of the social, becomes merely the effect of an earlier objective structure.

Lefort's sentence is harsh: according to him, structuralism, Althusser and the language of the new sciences lead to the endorsement of a more sophisticated version of ideology, which, being the "logic of an idea", succeeds in excluding otherness, the impact of work and history, and the indeterminacy of interpretation, thus effectively leading everything back to a closed, objective and unmodifiable system (280). As a result, the philosopher concludes:

> The effectiveness of the discourse of the 1960s lies in its critique of ancient illusions—a critique born earlier, within the framework of science and philosophy, which it appropriates for its own ends. It thus rejects the idea of a genuine barrier between knowledge and reality. And therefore it seems to break with scientism, with the naive faith in a universe governed by laws in the service of good observation. But the barrier has now been brought

down in order to be able to bring everything within the limits of the object of knowledge, to adapt it, let us say, to the operations of its production, to save knowledge from the inconveniences of experience. (281)

From this perspective, structuralism is ultimately seen as an ideological discourse that criticizes the old metaphysical illusions, the foundations, and claims that the real and the subject do not exist only in order to force them, along with knowledge, into a new foundation: that of structure, a network of operations whose coherence is the evidence of its validity.

Lefort and those working around him in those years—Castoriadis, Gauchet, Abensour, Clastres, but also Marc Richir or Robert Legros—thus intend to circumscribe an alternative theoretical area opposed to that of structuralism.[2] Within this, the concept of the institution is a useful tool that serves as an alternative to the term "structure", and one which they in fact use to refer to a symbolic dimension of the social that is not, however, independent of and prior to the social itself. The institution is a symbolic framework that is created in experience but at the same time escapes the full control of social agents. It is both acted upon and endured. It is not a fixed, universal and mathematizable structure: it is a dynamic, continuous refoundation.

Interpretation or Archaeology: Lefort and Foucault[3]

The theory of the "institution of the social" that emerges in the 1960s and 1970s is established in part as a polemical alternative to structuralism, post-structuralism, and the ideology of immanence that they conceal. Two different "factions" of French political philosophy are pitted against each other, in a situation that blurs together theoretical, political,

---

[2] For more on the role of the publications *Texture* and *Libre* in the French debate of the period, see Berthot (2007). The author highlights the continuity between *Socialisme ou Barbarie* and these two journals, which he sees as part of a rediscovery of political philosophy in France. Valuable comments on these publications are also offered by Marcel Gauchet (2008, pp. 197–220) and Miguel Abensour (2014). In these same years Castoriadis was developing his theory of the imaginary institution of the social (Castoriadis 1987)

[3] I have previously analyzed the relationship between Lefort and Foucault more broadly and slightly differently in Di Pierro (2022).

and academic motivations,[4] with each camp offering alternative ways of thinking about structure, the social, and the relationship between theory and politics. This becomes clear when one brings to light Lefort's relationship with the work of a thinker renowned precisely for being the spearhead of structuralism and then post-structuralism: Michel Foucault.

In the first half of the 1960s Foucault is engaged in a total historicization of forms of knowledge (Foucault 1988, 2003). After the publication of *The Order of Things* in 1966 (Foucault 2001) he sets out to define his method of inquiry more clearly and to defend it against criticism. It is in this context that in 1968 a short paper entitled "Response to the Circle of Epistemology" (Foucault 1998, pp. 279–296) appears in the *Cahiers pour l'analyse*, in which Foucault responds to certain requests for clarification on his conception of historical transition and on the origins of his analysis.[5] The response consists of a few dozen pages which, far more than offering an explanation of his own past research, set out the parameters of a new method of inquiry. Foucault asserts that history has been and still mostly is read through the lens of continuity, of permanence, through descriptions of long periods, of regularities that it is supposedly possible to identify beneath the apparent disorder of events.[6] From this perspective, fracture and inconsistency are a problem that historians must overcome in order to re-establish a broader and more stable underlying structure. This way of thinking about becoming relies on a series of notions—tradition, teleology, causality, development, the mentalities—that are accepted without proper examination and justification. Foucault, on this point following the analyses of Gaston Bachelard and Georges Canguilhem, therefore proposes a deconstruction of such notions designed to escape the "fiction of continuity". This involves above all accepting that "we are

---

[4] It may be interesting to recall that the Centre Universitaire Expérimental in Vincennes, near Paris, was founded in 1969. In it leading figures of French "critical thought" (many of them linked to the PCF) worked together, including Deleuze, Alain Badiou, Jacques Ranciére, Étienne Balibar and Foucault, who was the director of the philosophy department. For a history of this institution see Soulié (1998).

[5] The name Circle of Epistemology refers to the group of authors who coordinated and promote the journal's work: Alain Badiou, Alain Grosrichard, Jacques-Alain Miller, Jean-Claude Milner, and François Regnault.

[6] Foucault is referring here to the *Nouvelle Histoire* of the *Annales* historians and, in particular, to the work of Fernand Braudel. For more on Foucault's distinctive approach to history see O'Farrell (1989), Flynn (2003, pp. 29–48, 2005a, b), and Falzon (2013, pp. 282–298).

dealing in the first instance only with a population of dispersed events" (Foucault 1998, p. 303), in order to analyze only subsequently how these relate to each other to produce established knowledge. Instead of identifying the course of a unified history hidden underneath the plurality of events, one must begin from fragmentation and determine how the various elements interact with each other. This means deconstructing discourses on specific sectors of knowledge in order to trace their constitution from the interaction between the discursive elements that compose them (O'Farrell 1989, pp. 44–64). It involves putting difference above unity: a mantra that remained a constant in Foucault's work (Revel 2003, pp. 59–63).

According to Foucault, the elements on which one must suspend judgment are first and foremost those which impose themselves most immediately: books and, above all, the oeuvres of particular authors. No book actually exists by itself, but rather each one is a node in a network of references on which its very definition and physiognomy depend. However much it may present itself as an object that it is possible to hold in one's hands, its uniqueness depends on a broader sphere of discussion which is in fact what makes its existence possible (Foucault 1998, pp. 303–304). In Foucault's eyes, the notion of an author's oeuvre raises similar, if not greater, problems. On the surface this is simply the sum of texts that can be connected to the name of an author, but as soon as one tries to clarify what exactly this name refers to, the idea falls apart. The link between a text and the author's name is not at all obvious and immediate: alongside texts that an author has published under his or her own name there may be others printed under a pseudonym. Moreover, while some writings were meant to be given to print in the authors' lifetime, others might have remained in draft form, not being intended for publication and perhaps published only posthumously. In short, even a superficial investigation of the definition of an "oeuvre" appears to involve a number of theoretical choices. One solution to this might of course be to connect the coherence and uniqueness of a given work to a certain "function of expression", or, that is, simply to refer all its component elements to an author's thought. However, even in this case it is not difficult to note that unity is not immediately evident but rather is constituted by a preliminary operation of interpretation that defines the thought in question.[7] An author's oeuvre, Foucault thus concludes, is neither an immediate unity nor a homogeneous unit. In short, the author and his work are two clear examples of unreflected unity: through them discourse appears pre-arranged by a preliminary datum, an unattainable and always presupposed origin (305).

In Foucault's eyes, the analysis of the author and his/her work thus brings to light how it is precisely the idea of origin that lies at the root of any continual interpretation. There is a fallacious relationship to the origin that can be expressed through two postulates. The first is that the irruption of an actual event into the order of discourse can never be fixed to a particular point. The continuity of events and discourses is thus guaranteed by the common reference to a hidden and unattainable origin. The second postulate is directly related to the first and states that every manifest discourse is always dependent on something that has already been said but is at the same time unsaid. In short, anything formulated in a discourse can already be traced back to a preceding semi-silence residing in the recess of what has already been expressed. Thus there is once again a constant, silent, and original flow of meaning to which all discourse is connected that ensures that a continuity persists beyond any apparent dispersion (305–306).

Foucault intends to reverse this perspective by examining discourses from the interplay of their particular instance, and perceiving them as events rather than in reference to a hidden principle or foundation.[8] He seeks to deconstruct the unreflected units, not to trace the actual origin of a given piece of knowledge, but to show how below the "oeuvre function" and the "author function" there is nothing more than a discursive field composed of individual statements. The renunciation of origin and of presupposed continuities thus opens up a whole new field of research consisting of the totality of all spoken or written utterances, understood in their dispersion, as events. This project aims at providing a pure description of the facts of discourse in which the latter is understood as a finite, limited, and completely immanent set of purely linguistic sequences that have been formulated. In other words, Foucault's intent is to trace

---

[7] On these themes and the deconstruction of the author figure see also the essay "What is an author?" (Foucault 1998, pp. 205–222). The text is a transcription of a speech given at the Collège de France in 1969.

[8] It is well known that Foucault's critique of origin was influenced by reading Friedrich Nietzsche. In this regard, see at least Foucault (1998, pp. 369–392).

the series of rules which determine in a culture the appearance and disappearance of statements, their retention and their destruction, their paradoxical existence as events and things. To analyze the facts of discourse in the general element of the archive is to consider them, not at all as documents (of a concealed significance or a rule of construction), but as monuments; it is—leaving aside every geological metaphor, without assigning any origin, without the least gesture toward the beginnings of an *arché*—to do what the rules of the etymological game allow us to call something like an archaeology. (310)

In *The Archaeology of Knowledge* (Foucault 2002), published in 1969, Foucault illustrates this project in its entirety, discussing in greater depth the themes addressed the year before in the "Response to the Circle of Epistemology". He now explains that the archaeological method consists in reading history by means of difference, by describing the discourses and statements on which they depend as specific, exact, and immanent practices, as events that reveal themselves in fragments (31). To adopt this methodology is to set aside all transcendentalism in order to analyze statements and discourses as they actually occur, as dispersed elements that are organized as they actually appear and not according to rules external to them.[9]

For Foucault, however, statements do not appear on the discursive scene *ex nihilo*. They are not a pure or chaotic emergence but must respond to rules. Not everything can be said and formulated at any time. Enunciations depend first and foremost on a "historical a priori" that constitutes their condition of reality, on a law that circumscribes what can be said. This a priori, far from being an external and universal structure, is implied in the very elements it regulates (142–143).[10] Taken as a whole, the various systems of statements constitute what Foucault proposes might be called the "archive", or the "law of what can be said", "the general system of the formation and transformation of statements" (146). This is a schema in which we are embedded, and which we speak out from, and which it is therefore impossible to describe in its entirety. The final element that frames the appearance of discursive

---

[9] The study of Dreyfus and Rabinow (1983) continues to be important for understanding Foucault's archaeological method.

[10] Foucault's historical a priori reworks, by historicizing it, the notion presented by Edmund Husserl in the *Origin of Geometry*. On this, see Han (2002).

systems is that of *episteme*, that is, "the total set of relations that unite, at a given period, the discursive practices that give rise to epistemological figures, sciences, and possibly formalized systems" (211).[11] However, none of these concepts are meant to re-propose a transcendent dimension capable of bringing unity and continuity to history. Rather, they refer to a fully historicized framework of rules which, while governing relations between utterances and discourses, are at the same time consubstantial to those relations. In a nutshell, Foucault uses the historical a priori, archive, or episteme to attempt to determine the conditions of historical possibility immanent to phenomena, to develop a fully historical framework that adds nothing to what "actually exists", that is, to what has actually been pronounced or written.

The possibility of describing this epistemic framework obviously depends on the particular position of the observer. While he is undeniably embedded in the episteme and the archive, he seems at the same time to be capable of an objectifying gaze, capable of grasping the contingent rules through which the epistemic framework is constituted, much like the subject described by Lévi-Strauss. We see here the emergence of the theme of the "outside", of the search for the possibility of an external place, or rather an external movement, from which to conduct a critique, the pursuit of the point of rupture, which is of fundamental importance in Foucault's reflection.[12]

In 1970, a year after the release of *The Archaeology of Knowledge*, Lefort published a short article, mostly ignored by critics, with the significant title "L'interprétation de l'œuvre de pensée" (Lefort 1978, pp. 238–258). Not coincidentally, the article appears in the *Cahiers de Psychanalyse*, the journal of the Association psychanalytique de France, the faction opposed to that of Jacques Lacan's disciples, who instead rallied around the *Cahiers pour l'analyse* and who included Foucault

---

[11] The notion of *episteme* had already been presented in Foucault (2001).

[12] This theme arises in Foucault's early reflections on literature, in which he attempts to thematize the space of the Dionysian. It is then translated into the otherness of reason in *History of Madness*, and then into the pure materiality of order and language that precedes all discursive formation. Chevallier (2014) traces this mode of thought throughout Foucault's entire journey, in relation to reflection on power, up to his final writings. There are varying opinions between interpreters on the importance and the very presence of this theme in Foucault. See at least Revel (2010).

himself.[13] The goal of the essay is to provide a clear definition of the "work of thought". The argument in fact is built precisely on a juxtaposition with the theses advanced by Foucault in the "Response to the Circle of Epistemology". Lefort's position is clear: although the questions raised by Foucault are certainly valid, his conclusions are disappointing, as his analysis stops just as it reaches the threshold of the real problem.

> Let the deception be denounced one more time. It will be said that we are imprisoned within a vicious circle and that to escape it we must first admit the evanescence of the work and immediately exchange it for a reflection. But it is once we have rejected this circle that the question of the work arises: once we recognize that the identity of the work implies the search for its identity; once we accept the paradox that the work is nothing outside the movement that leads us to it, and that this movement—interpretation—originates from the work itself. (240)

In short, while Lefort accepts that it is not a mistake to point out the artificiality of the oeuvre and of the author to reveal how they lose consistency when tested by an analysis that seeks to establish their limits, it is precisely this inconsistency that needs to be understood. What needs to be clarified is precisely their persistence despite their absence. The oeuvre, the work of an author, exists only through the "questioning of itself", when the reader, the interpreter asks what it is, or what it says. It is precisely this question about itself that overwhelms the reader and in turn forces him to question himself, to propose an identity of the work that is invariably partial and fictitious. It is precisely this paradoxical "effect", caused by an element (the oeuvre) that is nothing other than its questioning of itself, that represents the heart of the problem that deserves clarification, but which Foucault instead avoids, rejecting it on the pretext that it would be metaphysical. Furthermore, this same question emerges in every interpretive practice in which the interpreter is included in a critical discourse that towers over him, in a collective enterprise that precedes him and continues after him and of which he cannot be the master, the *maître*. Moreover, the production and preservation of oeuvres, and the very status of the author, are not autonomous. They presuppose a certain consensus and require a

---

[13] The Association psychanalytique de France emerged in 1964 from the split in the Société française de psychanalyse due to the opposition between the majority current that included, among others, Jean-Bertrand Pontalis, and the minority current whose main representative was Jacques Lacan.

continuous effort of reference and verification. Critical discourse is thus not accidental: comments and interpretations prove inseparable from the oeuvre, as constituent elements of a certain culture, of a given institution of the social (241).

Only by becoming aware of the symbolic dimension of the oeuvre, by discovering that the elements of which it is composed refer back to each other and together to a bigger picture is it possible to truly understand what it means to interpret and what each interpretation brings into play. It is therefore not possible to discover the elements that make up an oeuvre of thought in the form of single, scattered events, or pure and unrelated sentences. They are already caught up from the beginning in a series of cross-references or dimensions of meaning from which they are not autonomous. The interpreter himself cannot escape the symbolic dimension of which he has always been a part. A pronouncement does not exist in itself as an objective reality, a completely immanent pure element, or mere practice. Lefort therefore concludes:

> Critical discourse, as it principally expresses itself, entails a certain kind of unity and style which is not the sum total of particular representations where the influence of historical circumstances or ideologies can be clearly discerned. Instead, it refers back peremptorily to the author's discourse, it allows us to consider it and attests to the presence of the work, the presence which some call ineffable and therefore illusory. (243–244)

While according to Foucault it is possible to look beneath fictitious unities and continuities and unearth a series of particular statement events and then follow their differentiation, for Lefort it is not possible to access any completely immanent rule or pure utterance. It is true that Foucault, through the notions of the historical a priori, the archive and especially the episteme, also refers to a general framework in which sentences have always been embedded and by which they are to some extent defined. However, while the episteme is a completely immanent structure equivalent to its constituent elements, the institution of which Lefort speaks admits externality, recognizes a non-explicit dimension that eludes the interpreter and makes interpretation itself not only possible but indispensable. In other words, beneath the unity of the oeuvre lies neither emptiness nor the dispersion of enunciative events but the very issue that fosters the work, namely indeterminacy: the reference to the same absent origin that Foucault dismisses. Discourse, in short, always relates itself to otherness, to the impossibility of defining the boundaries of the work, and of objectifying it by overly generalized thinking. This is why Lefort, when criticizing Foucault's analysis, states:

> Rather, it seems to us that overlooking the question of the oeuvre—its insistence that its interpreter must produce the unquestionable guarantees of the work's identity and the conclusions that derive from the lack of such guarantees, the trust placed in the laws that would govern the distribution of utterances within an anonymous discourse—attests to a singular desire to ward off uncertainty, the uncertainty that has always been the mainspring of interpretive work and that distinguishes it from the operations of geometry, however capable it too may be of conceiving new dimensions. (240–241)

It is therefore no accident, nor a small matter, that the 1972 work, *Le travail de l'œuvre*, opens with a section titled "la question de l'œuvre" (Lefort 2012, pp. 3–60) and that the entire third part of the French first edition (more than 150 pages) is devoted to the "exemplary interpretations" of Jean-Félix Nourisson, Francesco De Sanctis, Augustin Renaudet, Ernst Cassirer, Gerhard Ritter, Leonhard von Muralt, Antonio Gramsci, and Leo Strauss (Lefort 1972, pp. 153–310). Before applying himself directly to the reading of *The Prince* and the *Discourses*, Lefort believes it is first necessary to engage with the critical literature precisely because Machiavelli's work is inseparable from the critical thinking it provoked and provokes in those who interrogate it. For although it is to be understood in the historical context in which it arose, it has no other existence than in an open exchange with those who read it. This means both rejecting a naive realism that believes itself capable of reaching back to the truth of the work as it would have been understood in its time (late fifteenth-century Florence) and avoiding assigning the work the status of a spiritual artifact the sense of which can be felt beyond history and context. In other words, while one must not stop investigating the context and period in which the work was written, one must never forget that the position occupied by the interpreter always brings into play a political experience linked to his own time and society. In this way, Lefort continues, the oeuvre confronts each interpreter with temporal and social division, with an indeterminacy that is not a vacuum, but which, when we decide to investigate it, is ultimately productive. The work is not fully under the control of the interpreter, but involves and exceeds him. The presence of the oeuvre becomes a reality only when it withdraws, changing continuously in the face of interpretation, as division and continuous interpretations interact in a hermeneutic circle that, not by chance, follows the movement of the institution. Indeed, Lefort asserts:

> Convinced that the oeuvre only gives itself to us on condition that we give our thoughts to it, I am also persuaded that it never had any other existence than in an open exchange, that is, an existence of such a nature that the answer does not cancel out the question but requires new ones—by the institution of a collective discourse, at the heart of which the words of each are intertwined or articulated while at the same time mutually governing one another's advent; and thus—in questioning that exchange, that *institution*, at the very moment when my work in turn brings me to participate in it—it is already the oeuvre that I question. (Lefort 2012, p. 21)

There is therefore a fundamental analogy between the question of the oeuvre and the question of the social. Just as the oeuvre is nothing more than the continuous interpretations that define it, but at the same is time able to have an effect on the interpreter, even overwhelming him when he questions it, the social is a permanent definition of itself, the perpetual creation of a discourse of which it is not completely the master. Just as the oeuvre confronts the interpreter with a productive indeterminacy, the division of the social fuels its movement. The social, like the work, is never closed in absolute immanence. Neither are the sum of its enunciative elements or the power relations that run through them. They are always influenced by an exteriority. A "fictitious" exteriority (as no transcendence can be expected outside the social or the oeuvre) which points to the impossibility of escaping interpretation, of reaching a dimension of reality beyond or below the symbolic. This is an exteriority that, as I have shown, Lefort calls Power.

The direct critique of Foucault on the "question de l'œuvre" is therefore not marginal, but defines the profiles of two contrasting theories, two alternative visions of the social and the relationship between philosophy and politics.[14]

---

[14] On the importance of the theory of interpretation in Lefort's thinking and, in particular, its relation to the interpretation of Machiavelli, see Flynn (2005b, pp. 59–79) and Marcotte-Chénard (2015, pp. 149–171).

Against Theories of Immanence

In the courses he taught at the University of Vincennes between 1969 and 1970, Foucault anticipated some of the propositions that would guide his research in the following decade—his encounter with Nietzsche, sexuality, and the management of illegality and punishment—and which would pour out first into *Discipline and Punish* and then into the first volume of *The History of Sexuality: The Will to Knowledge* (Foucault 1978, 1995). In this period Foucault begins to deal with something that until then had remained in the background of his ideas: the relationship between discourses and power. Here we witness the transition from the archaeological to the genealogical method. In relative continuity with the previous discourse, Foucault now wants to bring into the light the set of relations, of devices, of discourses, of historical and contingent norms that form the relations of power. As he had done with unreflective unities, he now considers it necessary to deconstruct the unitary and transcendent image of power in order to discover how it is nothing other than a relation (Foucault 2016, p. 8).[15] Underneath the idea of Power are thus found only a myriad of dispersed relations, of which it is possible to make a microphysics.

> It seems to me that power must be understood in the first instance as the multiplicity of force relations immanent in the sphere in which they operate and which constitute their own organization; as the process that, through ceaseless struggles and confrontations, transforms, strengthens, or reverses them; as the support that these force relations find in one another, thus forming a chain or a system, or on the contrary, the disjunctions and contradictions that isolate them from another; and lastly, as the strategies in which they take effect, whose general design or institutional crystallization is embodied in the state apparatus, in the formulation of the law, in the various social hegemonies. (Foucault 1978, pp. 92–93)

---

[15] In the foreword to the Italian edition, Foucault affirms sexuality is only an example of a more general problem that he has been pursuing for more than 15 years, i.e. how in modern Western societies the production of discourses and truth is linked to institutions of power. The coherence or discontinuity of Foucault's discourse is still a matter of debate. However, I agree with the thesis that it is possible to detect an internal torsion that Roberto Esposito recently described as a shift from an inquiry into forms to an investigation into the forces behind the emergence of knowledge. See Roberto Esposito (2018). On the question of continuity or discontinuity in Foucault's approach, see at least Revel (2005, 2010), and Han (2002).

Here Foucault once again highlights the dispersion beneath continuity. Rather than looking to a single core of sovereignty as the point from which scattered relations in society might radiate, he investigates the unstable local power relations that make up the discourse-power nexus. Instead of viewing power as the locus of the rationality of dominion and the structuring of society, he investigates how the ensemble device is formed from the implication of singularities of dispersed tactics, such as governmentality (Foucault 1995, pp. 27–28). From this perspective, power is a completely immanent relation of force and knowledge; a productive and not merely oppressive relationship to which, however, there is always a corresponding resistance. As Foucault himself states, in words that it is not misleading to interpret as a polemic targeted specifically at Lefort, "if it is true that Machiavelli was among the few [...] who conceived the power of the Prince in terms of force relationships, perhaps we need to go one step further, do without the persona of the Prince, and decipher power mechanisms on the basis of a strategy that is immanent in force relationships" (Foucault 1978, p. 97). In short, while Lefort elevated Machiavelli to the status of a key figure through whom to understand contemporary society and the role of power and conflict within it, for Foucault the Florentine Secretary became a character who could be set aside. While Lefort pointed to Power as the symbolic pole around which, passing through otherness, society recognizes itself as a totality, Foucault insisted that power relations immanent to social matters should be investigated.

The different readings of Machiavelli's work thus correspond to two different interpretations of power and the social. The two paths thus continue to develop and diverge during the 1970s.[16] Foucault's insistence on immanence and dispersion is matched by Lefort's conception of the symbolic institution of the social and of power as a symbolic pole. In this context, in 1971 Lefort co-authored, with Marcel Gauchet, the opening article in the second issue of the journal *Textures*,[17] which they

---

[16] Alain Brossat (2021, p. 146) notes that Foucault's anti-Machiavellianism is unsatisfactory, superficial, and responds to an argumentative and tactical requirement. The real target should in fact have been Lefort.

[17] After their separation and the demise of Socialisme ou Barbarie, Lefort and Castoriadis continue to have discussions in the weekly meetings of the Cercle Saint-Just, together with Edgar Morin and Pierre Vidal-Naquet. In 1971, they also returned to collaborate on the editorial board of the journal *Textures*, in conjunction with a group of younger

devoted to the concept of the political (*du politique*) and titled "Sur la démocratie: le politique et l'institution du social" (Lefort and Gauchet 1971).[18] In their text, the two authors present a theory of a democratic regime that was an alternative both to liberal rationalism, which is based on the metaphysical idea of an autonomous subject, and Marxism, which fails to recognize the symbolic dimension of the social and therefore sees the political as subordinate to the economic. Their proposal is that the logic of a given political regime, and the democratic one in particular, is a response to the advent of the social. In these terms, any political regime would actually be understood as a particular "form", an institution determined by the way in which the social, as a symbolic space, responds to the question about itself, to the very fact that society exists (8–9). It is here that the distinction, to which I have already referred, arises between the political (*le politique*) and politics (*la politique*), the former referring to the symbolic and instituting dimension of the social that enables, contains, and gives meaning to the latter, which is understood as the specific field of action of subjects vying for power.

Lefort and Gauchet's essay reiterates the symbolic function of power: it is a point of convergence in which the social is simultaneously recognized, divided, and united. It is the site of an absent but always necessary foundation; it is the origin on which the social questions and that "acts" upon the social. It is the symbol of division, of the indeterminacy that runs through the social, of the impossibility of complete immanence. The social is nothing but a continuous self-interpretation that is carried out through otherness, that is, through the symbolic place of power.

The year 1976, in which Foucault's *The Will to Knowledge* was published, is also the year in which the first issue of the journal *Libre* appears. As mentioned, in the opening article Lefort offers an account of the French theoretical-political debate over the previous sixteen years (Lefort 2007, pp. 275–300). After considering the eight years leading up to 1968 and critiquing structuralism, he goes on to consider the eight

---

scholars: Marcel Gauchet, Miguel Abensour, Robert Legros, and Marc Richir. The journal was actually born two years earlier in Brussels, but the second issue, dedicated to the concept of "the political" (*Du politique*), was a kind of relaunch. See Dosse (2014, p. 269) and Berthot (2007).

[18] Signed by Lefort and Gauchet the text is a revised transcript of the course taught by Lefort between 1966 and 1967 at the University of Caen. The same text is also the source of a polemical discussion between the two authors, who disagreed about the authorship of the ideas presented within it.

years that followed the May protests. Alongside the continued claim to scientificity that had characterized the previous years, Lefort sees in this second period the emergence of a different discourse that appears to overturn and reject all scientific method. This discourse calls into question the ideas of science and theory (282–283). In it the concept of knowledge coincides with that of power and the latter can be reduced to coercion. However, despite its totally innovative aspect, and despite its apparent critique of established knowledge and modern ideology, this new discourse merely takes modern objectivism to a different level. After all, it is characterized by the same avoidance of interpretation that had distinguished structuralism. In Lefort's eyes, it in fact also attempts to reduce knowledge to the known object, to power, and the latter to relations based on force. The targets of the polemic are Wilhelm Reich's and Herbert Marcuse's theories of desire, which juxtapose the explosion of positive emancipatory social desire with the oppression of every institution, every power, but above all the work of Gilles Deleuze and Felix Guattari and, again, of Foucault (283–285).[19]

Although the latter is never explicitly named, his theory of power is the main object of criticism. According to Lefort, Foucault's interpretation, whereby power is the name given to relations distributed at every level of the social, fragments and pulverizes the institution of the social and fails to capture how the being of the social is always in play in political society. By claiming that power is nothing more than the relations that are imposed in hospitals, in schools, in the army or in discourse about sex, Foucault remains blind to the symbolic dimension of the social, or, rather, he forgets that society is its own institution and that every relation is always included in it. His theory of relationships.

> does its best to create a vacuum, and then installs a set of operations carried out by agents who would be mere crossover points between different networks, or, rather, of which there would be no agent: everyone finds himself, at a given level, involved in a technique that makes him into a controller or the controlled, and, as a man, subdivides him into an indefinite number of excitations to produce power or resistance. (285)

[19] It is necessary to emphasize how Lefort's critique confronts and polemically aggregates reflections that retain important differences between them. See, for example, Foucault's own critique of Marcuse's theory of desire in the first chapter of *The Will to Knowledge* (Foucault 1978).

Foucault, Lefort thus concludes, eliminates all reference to society and history in favor of the artificial vision of a fragmented social evenly divided between desire and repression. In his theory, the social is crushed by a network of immanent forces that exclude the action of the subject and the action of the social on itself. He thus re-proposes the same error committed by structuralism by eliminating the indeterminacy, otherness, and activity of the social in favor of an immanent and mute structure. He forgets that every relationship is always mediated and interpreted, and always takes place within the dynamics of the institution.

In Lefort's eyes, the works of Gilles Deleuze and Felix Guattari intensify the problems of this completely immanent interpretation of the social. He refers here first of all to *Anti-Edipus*, which they had published only a few years earlier, in 1972 (Deleuze and Guattari 2009). In this celebrated text, the two authors above all sought to criticize Freud's psychoanalytic theory. Although he had the undisputed merit of having discovered the unconscious and the libido, Freud subjected these discoveries to the law of Oedipal representation and came to conceive of desire out of absence. In contrast, Deleuze and Guattari propose an interpretation of desire not as a lack but as an affirmation. One never desires, as Freud believes, a specific object, but always a multiplicity of them, a set of interconnected objects, a context, an environment. Moreover, desire does not only involves representing something missing, but it also produces a relationship, the production of the network of heterogeneous elements. Thus, the unconscious is not the theater in which the characters who populate the unconscious act. It is rather a factory, which "produces" life, which constructs the real. Beneath the illusory unity of psychoanalytic symbols the manifold productivity of the immanent "flow of desire" is revealed. Here the concept of the "desiring machine" plays a role as Deleuze and Guattari intend to use it to replace the static unity of structure. Through this concept, which refers to the continuous flow of a desire only momentarily interrupted by a cut that produces the object of desire, they describe a social dimension completely immanent to itself and immediately productive. In their crusade against representation all mediation is banished.

But this is nothing new in Lefort's eyes: once again the imperative of modern discourse is fulfilled, that is, both the notion of thought and thought objects are dissolved into self-production. In Deleuze and Guattari's plane of immanence, division is welded together, otherness removed, and the social is immediately political, immediately true (Lefort 2007, 284–285).

In opposition to the theories of Foucault and Deleuze, and against the theories of immanence and desire, Lefort and the *Libre* group put forward an alternative proposal, namely a rediscovery of the symbolic dimension of the social, that is, the dimension of the political.[20]

> Once more bringing back to light the dimension of the political, the historical dimension: this is the one task. The political defines neither a set of institutions in society, nor a network of relations extracted, like a good object, from multiple networks of equal use to matters of scientificity. If we cling to this word, despite the perversion of its use, it is because it allows us to consider the whole of the social, not a substance, but this differentiated environment that is open to the generality of representation and opens up to itself in the work of representation, arranged in such a way that it is a matter of identity and at the same time a matter of external reality, where individuals find their identifying references and gain access to the same reality. (294)

The total immanence argued for by Foucault, by Deleuze but also by Marcuse, that is, the rejection of the question of origin, otherness and opacity, results in knowledge and the known object being crushed together in a way that eludes interpretation, the oeuvre, that indeterminacy on which the social arises and to which it is always referred. In Lefort's eyes this coincidence, reaffirmed by the rejection of the dimension of the political, reintroduces the foundation that these authors do not seem ready to give up. Also crushed on this immanent plane of absolute horizontality, conflict is reduced to a sterile opposition between power and resistance in which the "gap" is either impossible or is to be found in a total exteriority. If 1968 had ushered in wild thought, a knowledge free insofar as it was open to indeterminacy, to the acceptance of groundlessness, the theories of Marcuse, Foucault, and Deleuze exploit the fragments of contestation to re-establish an order that is hidden under the banner of the new. Through the complete immanence of structure, of

---

[20] Foucault (2010, p. 149) refers and criticizes Lefort's theory of the political in the February 2, 1983 lecture at the Collège de France. According to him, *le politique* is an unnecessary dimension of transcendence that covers the comprehension of politics in its relationship between *dunasteia* and *politeia*. See Di Pierro (2022, p. 434).

the immediately affirmative flow of desire, they actually conceal social and historical experience, proving themselves incapable of accommodating indeterminacy.

Against this ontology of immanence, which becomes an ideology, i.e. a masking of the contingency and instability of the foundation, Lefort proposes a political ontology that wishes to take into account the negative and otherness. The idea of the symbolic institution of the social and the related idea of the political (*le politique*), with which he critiques structuralism and post-structuralism, precisely suited this need. Through them Lefort seeks to understand a society that has renounced transcendence, that has located its origin in itself, but which at the same time can never coincide with itself, can never be truly autonomous. This is a society that is conscious of always being a self-representation: the democratic form of society.

REFERENCES

Abensour, Miguel. 2014. *La communauté politique des «tous uns». Entretien avec Michel Enaudeau.* Paris: Les Belles Lettre.

Berthot, Franck. 2007. Textures et Libre (1971–1980) Une tentative de renouvellement de la philosophie politique en France. In *Les revues et la dynamique des ruptures*, ed. J. Baudouin, F. Hourmant, 105–129. Rennes: Presses Universitaires de Rennes.

Brossat, Alain. 2021. Oublier Machiavel. In *Foucault et…Les liasons dangereuses de Michel Foucault*, ed. A. Brossat, D. Lorenzini, 127–155. Paris: Vrin.

Castoriadis, Cornelius. 1987. *The imaginary institution of the society.* Cambridge: Polity Press.

Chevallier, Philippe. 2014. *Michel Foucault. Le pouvoir et la bataille.* Paris: Puf.

Deleuze, Gilles, and Guattari, Felix. 2009. *Anti-Oedipus. Capitalism and Schizophrenia.* New York: Penguin.

Di Pierro, Mattia. 2022. Archaeology or Interpretation: Michel Foucault and Claude Lefort. *Constellation* 29: 434–446.

Dosse, François. 2014. *Castoriadis: une vie.* Paris: La Decouverte.

Dosse, François. 2018. *La saga des intellectuels français 1944–1989. I. À L'Epreuve de l'histoire 1944–1968.* Paris: Gallimard.

Dreyfus, Hubert, and Rabinow, Paul. 1983. *Michel Foucault: Beyond Structuralism and Hermeneutics.* Chicago: Chicago University Press.

Esposito, Roberto. 2018. *A Philosophy for Europe: From the Outside.* Cambridge: Polity Press.

Falzon, Christopher. 2013. Making History. In *A Companion to Foucault*, ed. C. Falzon, T. O'Leary, J. Sawicki, 282–298. Malden: Wiley-Blackwell.

Flynn, Thomas. 2005a. *Sartre, Foucault and Historical Reason, vol. 2 A Poststructuralist Mapping of Foucault History*. Chicago: University of Chicago Press.
Flynn, Bernard. 2005b. *The Philosophy of Claude Lefort. Interpreting the Political*. Evanston: Northwestern University Press.
Flynn, Thomas. 2003. Foucault's Mapping of History. In *The Cambridge Companion to Foucault*, ed. G. Gutting. 2nd edition, 29–48. Cambridge: Cambridge University Press.
Foucault, Michel. 1978. *The History of Sexuality. Volume I: An Introduction*. New York: Pantheon Books.
Foucault, Michel. 1988. *Madness and Civilization. A History of Insanity in the Age of Reason*. New York: Vintage.
Foucault, Michel. 1995. *Discipline and punish. The Birth of the Prison*. New York: Vintage Books.
Foucault, Michel. 1998. *Essential Works of Foucault, 1954–1984*. New York: The New Press.
Foucault, Michel. 2001. *The Order of Things. An Archaeology of the Human Sciences*. London/New York: Routledge.
Foucault, Michel. 2002. *The Archaeology of Knowledge*. London/New York: Routledge.
Foucault, Michel. 2003. *The Birth of the Clinic: An Archaeology of Medical Perception*. London/New York: Routledge.
Foucault, Michel. 2010. *The Government of Self and Others. Lectures at the Collège de France 1982–1983*. New York: Palgrave Macmillan.
Foucault, Michel. 2016. *La volontà di aspere. Storia della sessualità 1*. Milano: Feltrinelli.
Gauchet, Marcel. 2008. *La condition historique*. Paris: Gallimard.
Han, Béatrice. 2002. *Foucault's Critical Project: Between the Transcendental and the Historical*. Redwood City: Stanford University Press.
Lefort, Claude. 1972. *Le Travail de l'œuvre Machiavel*. Paris: Gallimard.
Lefort, Claude. 1978. *Les formes de l'histoire. Essais d'anthropologie politique*. Paris: Gallimard.
Lefort, Claude. 2007. *Le temps présent. Écrits 1945–2005*. Paris: Belin.
Lefort, Claude. 2012. *Machiavelli in the Making*. Evanston: Northwestern University Press.
Lefort, Claude, and Gauchet, Marcel. 1971. Sur la démocratie: le politique et l'institution du social. *Textures* 2/3: 7–78.
Lévi-Strauss, Claude. 1987. *Introduction to the Work of Marcel Mauss*. London: Routledge & Kegan Paul.
Marcotte-Chénard, Sophie. 2015. Qu'est-ce qu'une œuvre de pensée ? Réflexions sur l'art de lire lefortien. *Politique et Sociétés* 34: 149–171.
Merleau-Ponty, Maurice. 1964. *Signs*. Evanston: Northwestern University Press.

Merleau-Ponty, Maurice. 2010. *Institution and Passivity. Course Notes from the Collège de France (1954–1955)*. Evanston: Northwestern University Press.
Nora, Pierre. 2010. Tristes tropiques, un moment de la conscience occidentale. *Le Débat* 158/1: 3–8.
O'Farrell, Clare. 1989. *Foucault: Historian or Philosopher?* London: Palgrave-Macmillan.
Revel, Judith. 2003. *Michel Foucault. Un'ontologia dell'attualità*. Soveria Mannelli: Rubbettino.
Revel, Judith. 2005. *Michel Foucault. Expériences de la pensée*. Paris: Bordas.
Revel, Judith. 2010. *Foucault, une pensée du discontinu*. Paris: Fayard.
Soulié, Charles. 1998. Histoire du département de philosophie de Paris VIII. Le destin d'une institution d'avant-garde. *Histoire de l'éducation* 77: 47–69.

CHAPTER 8

Democracy

THE DEMOCRATIC FORM OF SOCIETY

According to Lefort, democracy cannot be reduced to a political regime, nor to a set of institutions and rules. Rather, it must be understood as a "form of society": a particular way of making sense of the social and of shaping and staging it, reflected first and foremost in the representation of the sphere of power.[1] Democracy is the result of modern symbolic change, of a new institution of the social that brings together the sensibility and experience of individuals, the arrangement of institutions, and the modalities of thought. In Lefort's description, modern society is characterized first and foremost by the fact that it is no longer structured by religion, by the disintegration of the organic or corporeal form, and by the consequent split between power, knowledge, and law. Modern society organizes itself around change, and separates itself from its past and its future in the context of a progressive human history. It is the political institution of the social.

---

[1] On Lefort's democracy see: Thériault (2015), Demelemestre (2012) and Dallmayr (1993).

> The modern democratic revolution is best recognized in this mutation: there is no power linked to a body. Power appears as an empty place and those who exercise it as mere mortals who occupy it only temporarily or who could install themselves in it only by force or cunning. There is no law that can be fixed, whose articles cannot be contested, whose foundations are not susceptible of being called into question. Lastly, there is no representation of a center and of the contours of society: unity cannot now efface social division. (Lefort 1986, p. 303)

While medieval monarchs were the embodiment and connection to unquestionable divine power and knowledge, modern power, having lost its religious justification, is without foundation. It separates itself from its origin and discovers itself to be *empty*, to no longer be consubstantial with any community or law, or embodied by any person. It can only be represented temporarily by political subjects forced to seek legitimacy in the eyes of society. Those who govern occupy the locus of power for only a short and precarious period, and remain suspended in the constant search for popular support and glory, and in the spasmodic maintenance of their own appearance. The legitimacy of modern power is always subject to revocation and dependent on its own representation. A new, political discourse therefore emerges from this, one that is disconnected from absolute knowledge and tied instead to the legitimization or critique of power. The humanists, chiefly Coluccio Salutati and Leonardo Bruni, were among the first to put forward this discourse authoritatively.

In this context, all definite points of reference are lost, and all political definitions—of subjectivities, state, territory, the nation, the people, values, tradition, and history—that were previously kept in place by their link to the foundation are now the subject of continuous debate and conflict. Even the very definition of the community, of its internal structure and its relations with the outside world, leads back to exactly this type of debate and conflict between its members. No situation is beyond question, and no authority remains uncontested. The distinction between the symbolic and the real, which remained hidden by the connection between power and transcendence, society and origin, is now recognized. Thus a fully historical society is inaugurated, one that has no fixed points of reference but is instead open to indeterminacy and to its own division (Lefort 1988, pp. 9–21).

In short, democracy unfolds through the social's continuous self-questioning—of its own definition, its own meaning, and of the legitimacy of its claim to power—in a dynamic that does not allow any definitive answer to emerge. It is the perpetual movement of questions about an absent origin, about a missing foundation. The dynamic of democracies thus appears to follow the movement of the Being, with its continuous experience and continuous questioning, presented in the ontology of Merleau-Ponty and contained in his idea of institution and of phenomenology as a constant questioning of its own presuppositions.

What Lefort sets out to describe is therefore something beyond an awareness of the contingency of the social order, its historicity or even its self-establishment. The indeterminacy which he discusses is in fact something far more radical. He is not describing the discovery of the absence of foundation but rather the fact that this absence cannot be discovered, cannot be reached. Democracy is not defined by the way that the social is reduced to its immanent characteristics, to the "reality" of the crude relations of force and interest, and modern democratic society does not eliminate all otherness. On the contrary, democratic indeterminacy is the impossibility of society being sufficient to itself, coinciding to itself in full autonomy. It is the realization that the social is created through the openness to an otherness that continuously evades it. Absence, we might say, is itself continually elusive.

> Are we therefore to believe that modern democracy opened the era of autonomy? The disincorporation of power—the fact that those who are entrusted with it depend on popular suffrage and enjoy only a legitimacy granted to them—does not mean that the site of power is limited to the interior of society. If it becomes forbidden to occupy that site, it is always from it that society acquires a representation of itself, as differentiated as that society may be and as manifold the oppositions that shape it. (Lefort 2007a, b, p. 143)

It is precisely the unattainability of emptiness exposed by the loss of the foundation that opens democratic society to the indeterminacy revealed in the locus of power. Its emptiness is in fact the name of the unrepresentable; it is the symbol of an unreachable and indefinable otherness which structures society as if from the outside, but without transcending it. Likewise, the fact that the imaginary, the symbolic, and the real do not identify with each other, just as power is not embodied by those who exercise it, translates into the social's inability to coincide with itself, or with its own meaning. In short, the emptiness that characterizes democratic power reveals not immanence but indeterminacy. The structure of democratic society is thus like that of a vortex gravitating around an absent center. Its movement and physiognomy are determined by continuous questioning, while the absence around which it defines itself continually exposes it to things other than itself, to the lack and excess of meaning.[2]

According to Lefort, the characteristics and meaning of the democratic society can only be grasped within this symbolic framework. It is only when it is understood to be a form of society that the sense or essence of its institutions can really become clear. Popular sovereignty, therefore, emerges as the political designation of the division and emptiness that characterizes democratic power. It constitutes the fundamental point of reference of democratic institutions and political actions, but only on the condition that it remains indeterminate (Lefort 2007b, p. 613). In short, "Democracy inaugurates the experience of an ungraspable, uncontrollable society in which the people will be said to be sovereign, of course, but whose identity will constantly be open to question, whose identity will remain latent" (Lefort 1986, pp. 303–304). Like the sovereign people described in the works of Machiavelli, the democratic sovereign people is actually an absent subject. It is never One and homogeneous, but is riddled by division. It is both affirmation and negation and exists only through its continuous redefinition. Unable to attain its unity, the people falls apart just when it should appear in its purest form: in elections its

---

[2] About democratic community Lefort writes: "The idea that power belongs to no one is not, therefore, to be confused with the idea that it designates an empty place". The former idea may be formulated by political actors, but not the latter. The first formulation in fact implies the actors' self-representation, as they deny one another the right to take power. The old Greek formula to the effect that power is *in the middle* (and historians tell us that it was elaborated within the framework of an aristocratic society before being bequeathed to democracy) still indicates the presence of a group which has an image of itself, of its space and of its bounds. The reference to an empty place, by contrast, eludes speech insofar as it does not presuppose the existence of a community whose members discover themselves to be subjects by the very fact of their being members. The formula "power belongs to no one" can also be translated into the formula "power belongs to none of us" (and in historical terms, this appears to be the earlier of the two). The reference to an empty place, on the other hand, implies a reference to a society without any positive determination, which cannot be represented by the figure of a community". (Lefort 1988, pp. 225–226). See also Lefort (2007b, p. 991). From this point of view, this description of democracy can be related to the debate conducted by authors who have attempted to develop theories or descriptions of community that go beyond substantivist semantics, beyond any idea of ownership and essence. See Esposito (2009), Blanchot (2006), Nancy (1991), and Agamben (1993).

unity is divided into a multiplicity of anonymous and individual votes. The choices of individuals thus replace a subject—the people—which always remains unfinished, divided within itself by a series of contradictions, oppositions and desires (Lefort 2007b, p. 466).

The very principle of representation, which is the lifeblood of democratic institutions, is not only the means by which representatives accept political authority on behalf of the citizens who appointed them. Much more than this, representation is what guarantees society its visibility (613):

> A particular type of symbolism is always required in order to ensure the idea of the unity and continuation of the Nation. But while the holders of monarchic or aristocratic power do not allow themselves to see that to preserve the mystery of power, to accept the secret of which they are the guardians and which confers them the supreme right to make decisions, the establishment of democratic representation must—at least at the beginning—exhibit for all to see the motives and results of public deliberation, and make plain the competing concerns generated by the diversity of interests and opinions within society. Representation establishes a space within which debate has no other goal but to tease out the general interest from particular interests, the interests of this or that social category that are the object of controversy. (614)

In the same way, all aspects of identity, every precarious rallying point for the representation of the unity of society—the idea of the nation, of the community, of the state—and even law and history are dependent on public discussion and debate. Definitions follow one after the other, and it matters little that some attempt to be universal, to represent the totality of the social. What matters is that none can actually do so. None can actually breach the division, bring an end to conflict, close the circle of interpretation. Every political definition is always traversed by division, by negation, by the very conflict that produces it. Any totality, cut off by division and internal oppositions, remains unattainable.

This dynamic clarifies the profound meaning of another element that characterizes democratic societies: rights.[3] Critiquing the positions expounded by Marx in *On the Jewish Question*, Lefort asserts that rights

---

[3] On this topic see Lefort (1986, pp. 239–272 and 2007, pp. 405–421). Pranchère (2019), Couture (2019), and Simard (2015) highlight the importance of rights in Lefort's theory and in his conception of democracy.

are not merely a veil used by the bourgeoisie to hide social differences, nor do they belong solely to the bourgeois individual (Lefort 1986, pp. 245–259). Declared in 1789, human rights go beyond the narrow meaning of the rule of law; they are the lintel of democratic politics, the rules that underpin the clash that governs its dynamic, its continuous transformation. They do not divide individuals from each other according to their own private interests, as Marx believed. On the contrary, rights invite men to step out from themselves and to bond with others through speech, public discourse, writing, and debate. They do not describe the bourgeois man but the democratic one, who is made only in the continuous redefinition of himself, without foundation (239–272).

Not only this, but for Lefort the 1789 Declaration of the Rights of Man and of the Citizen defines the modern physiognomy of power and the dissolution of the link between power, knowledge, and law (250–251). Indeed, claims made in the name of rights are always stronger than political power, which is unable to control and limit them. Rights elude any foundation. They are in fact not rooted in any natural foundation or in a common and universal human essence. They exist only in their momentary and contingent expression. Their meaning can be determined solely by their effects. In other words, human rights are the proof of indeterminacy, of the fact that power cannot define society as a whole. They express the inevitable contestation of the legitimacy of power, and represent the continuous proposal of new political definitions (Lefort 2007b, pp. 418–419).[4]

In this dynamic, the act of claiming one's rights is linked to the opposition toward definitions acquired through political discourse and social representation, to the demand for recognition and to the potential redefinition of a given political discourse and the subjectivities that interpret it.[5] Rights, in short, express the dispersed and disordered conflict of a

---

[4] Marcel Gauchet (2002, pp. 1–26) strongly criticized the Lefortian theory of rights. For an in-depth discussion of Gauchet's position and relationship to Lefort's ideas see Moyn (2012) and Couture (2014).

[5] Lefort (1986, p. 258) writes: "From the moment when the rights of man are posited as the ultimate reference, established right is open to question. It becomes still more so as the collective wills or, one might prefer to say, social agents bearing new demands mobilize a force in opposition to the one that tends to contain the effects of the recognized rights. Now, where right is in question, society—that is, the established order—is in question." And, he continues a few pages later: "These rights are one of the generative principles of democracy. Such principles do not exist in the same way as positive

society that has lost its center and unity; a society that no longer orders itself around the One, but which starts out from a point of division. We can therefore conclude, in Lefort's words, that:

> A politics of human rights and a democratic politics are thus two ways of responding to the same need: to exploit the resources of freedom and creativity which are drawn upon by an experience that accommodates the effects of division; to resist the temptation to exchange the present for the future; to make an effort, on the contrary, to discern in the present the signs of possible change which are suggested by the defense of acquired rights and the demand for new rights, while learning to distinguish them from what is merely the satisfaction of interests. (272)

Modernity and Democracy

As we have stated, according to Lefort the democratic phenomenon can be understood only as a symbolic revolution that overturns the principles of the *ancien régime* and inaugurates the "dissolution of the markers of certainty" (Lefort 1988, p. 19). It consists of society's obligation to face a radical indeterminacy that is above all the result of the loss of the link with transcendence and of religion's ability to structure the symbolic dimension. In short, from this point of view democracy is, in a way, consubstantial with modernity. It is the political rendition of modern symbolic change.[6]

The signs of this shift can be traced throughout centuries of European history: in the works of Dante, in humanism, in Machiavelli's thought, in the secularization of the two-body image of the king, and so on. Within

---

institutions, whose actual elements can be listed, even though it is certainly true that they animate institutions. Their effectiveness stems from the allegiance that is given them, and this allegiance is bound up with a way of being in society, which cannot be measured by the mere preservation of acquired benefits. In short, rights cannot be dissociated from the awareness of rights: this is my first observation. But it is no less true that this awareness of rights is all the more widespread when they are declared, when power is said to guarantee them, when liberties are made visible by laws. Thus the awareness of right and its institutionalization are ambiguously related" (260).

[6] In Di Pierro (2020) I wrote about the internal tensions within the idea of the democratic institution of social. On democracy and modernity in French contemporary though see Chevrier et al. (2015).

this framework, Lefort notes how from the sixteenth century onward religion and politics began to split conspicuously, in a modern reflection that considers the foundations of the civil order "as a result of the combined effects of the collapse of the authority of the Church, and of the struggles that accompanied Reformation; as a result both of the assertion of the absolute right of the Prince and of challenges to that right (213)".[7]

According to Lefort, it is important to keep in mind that the meaning of this symbolic change is not inherent in power from the beginning, as if it emerged gradually over the centuries in a form that is already predetermined from the outset. It does not mark out the sequential stages of a teleologically oriented history. Nor is it a conscious change, planned and pursued by societies from the thirteenth century to the present day. Rather, it occurs in the background, in contingency but also without the actors being aware of it.[8] It is the contingent outcome of human actions but at the same time escapes human control. More importantly, it can be recognized only ex-post, from a perspective that at that point is rooted in the modern, democratic symbolic institution. It is only from this vantage point that the signs of democracy in history can be seen, or rather interpreted, not because they exist in themselves as ahistorical and imperishable essences, but because they are the meaning that emerges from an established, already democratic way of thinking. In other words, this is what Castoriadis called the antinomy of historical knowledge (Castoriadis 1987, pp. 162–163). From this second perspective, then, democracy is the *current* symbolic institution, the context in which contemporary institutions and thought (at least Western ones) exist. This is the perspective from which it is possible to perceive a history of democracy. The question that follows, therefore, is: Since when has the possibility of this view been possible?

Although it is not possible to write a history of the symbolic, Lefort does not hesitate to admit that in the nineteenth century the "path" of modern democracy appears to reach a breaking point before exploding. And the explosion is loud and violent: the French Revolution is its most obvious manifestation (59–114).

---

[7] It is clear that one of the main points of reference in the passage is the reflection of Machiavelli.

[8] This intertwining of activity and passivity, the dynamic that eludes and overrides human actions and consciousness, is a specific element of the meaning of the institution, as Merleau-Ponty had already conceived of it. See Merleau-Ponty (1988).

Indeed, it is precisely in this revolution that one can see the signs of a profound and radical change that disrupts the preceding symbolic system. The fall of the monarchy compels society to observe its loss of foundation and disincorporation. The beheading of Louis XVI forces it to contend with a new vacuum that consumes any attempt at foundation, eliminates the possibility of defining the identity of a community, and sweeps away the ordering principle of the social. This void is the result of the end of the theological-political mechanism and the beginning of a new ordering principle of the social. It is the fulfillment or the radicalization of the democratic symbolic revolution. It is the void around which the new form of democratic society swirls.

In short, the storming of the Bastille inaugurates a new symbolic institution that relegates the *ancien régime* to history. So much so that the more or less chaotic attempts in this handful of years to reestablish the security of a lost foundation actually respond to an entirely new need. They are already shaped by a new institution of the social: they are the response not to the void created by the end of monarchy but to the one opened up by the beginning of democracy. The Jacobin Terror itself can be seen in this light. It is a completely new, democratic power, and the evidence of profound disorientation, a failed attempt to give order to a social that has now radically changed in its symbolic dimension.

> The events we thought we observed taking place within the space of the Convention are a reflection of what had been happening on a larger scale throughout society since August 1792. The Terror gave rise to a multiplicity of positions of power by giving those who had won them an opportunity to conceal from others and, if need by [sic], from themselves the fact that they were exercising their omnipotence. That, however, would have been a banal phenomenon, had it been solely a matter of using principles for purposes of dissimulation. It becomes extraordinary if we note that the dissimulation is a result of the obligation, which is incumbent upon everyone, to leave the place of power apparently empty. Robespierre's ploys are no more psychological than those of the other terrorists, great or small. The Terror is revolutionary in that it forbids anyone to occupy the place of power; and in that sense, it has a democratic character. (86)

This is why the Terror and the Committee of Public Safety that promoted it fell to pieces when they tried to institutionalize the religion of the Supreme Being: "Revolutionary Terror or modern terror cannot accommodate itself to a theocratic institution" (88). This failure to establish this new cult makes it clear that the recovery of the theological foundation is now impossible: it is revealed as an illusion, it resolves itself as a tragedy.

In short, the defeat of the monarchy produces deep uncertainty in the symbolic points of reference and brings with it the threat of social dissolution. The beheading of Louis XVI overturns a symbolic apparatus that had held up for centuries. The body disintegrates. Society loses its foundation and fragments. The political-theological principle of the One dissolves and survives only in the imaginary notions of disoriented politicians or thinkers who are forced to use old categories to cope with radically new circumstances. This is why both revolutionaries and thinkers of the most diverse backgrounds, such as Michelet, Quinet, Guizot, Tocqueville, or even Leroux, in the years following the revolution attempt to recover the religious dimension, to reestablish the rallying post of a lost unity in order to avert dissolution (249). But the transcendent foundation is now lost. Henceforth the religious will no longer be able to order the social; it will split from the political and survive only in the private dimension. Quinet understood this when he criticized the deification of some of the key concepts of the Revolution and asserted that "if we are to learn the truth about history, the nation or the people, we must undertake the revolutionary task of demystifying them" (133).

In this way, however, Lefort is offering us yet another perspective from which to interpret democracy. From here it becomes clear that at the core of the modern *tourbillon*, of the slow process of secularization, is a theological and political scheme that continues to operate almost undisturbed for centuries, only to erupt in the nineteenth century and with the French Revolution in particular.[9] According to this, "any attempt to explain the contours of social relations implies an internalization of unity; that any attempt to define objective, impersonal entities implies a personification of those entities" (254). Everything, in short, continues to be divided and to be reconnected to the figure of the One who safeguards the community. This is a pattern of representation of the social whose terms change with the centuries, but whose principle of opposition is preserved until the nineteenth century. The absolutism of the sixteenth century, for example, can be seen as a key stage in the emergence of the

---

[9] See the article "The Permanence of the Theologico-Political?", originally published in 1981 and now in Lefort (1986, pp. 213–255).

modern. Indeed, through this innovative political construction the state splits from the social and identifies itself with a specific territory, with the nation from which it is called to legitimacy (Lefort 1977, pp. 1–4). Its justification, however, remains religious. The king represents divinity, as both his power and the nation remain linked to a transcendent dimension, to the figure of the One. This same principle also emerges in the French Revolution, in the continuing search for a firm and unquestionable principle around which the community can recognize and ground itself. It is therefore at this point that the nation is deified, and comes to replace the figure of the monarch, and it is also why, in 1794, we see the institutionalization of the cult of the Supreme Being promoted by Robespierre.

From this other perspective, then, symbolic change is not a centuries-long process but a sudden upheaval with no definite time or cause. From this viewpoint, "the democratic revolution, for so long subterranean, burst out when the body of the king was destroyed, when the body politic was decapitated and when, at the same time, the corporeality of the social was dissolved" (Lefort 1986, p. 303). This is why Alexis de Tocqueville saw democracy not only as a regime change but as a revolution, a radical shift in the collective mindset. He was able to discern the French Revolution as the result of the irreversible shift from the hierarchical society to the society of equality.[10]

At this point, however, the meaning of democracy diverges from that of modernity: democracy becomes more specifically the social form that in the nineteenth century emerges from a genuine symbolic revolution—the democratic revolution—that follows the French Revolution. Democracy in a sense represents the fulfillment of modernity or, to remain truer to Lefort's view, comes to represent the symbolic institution that appeared or was invented in the seventeenth century and from whose perspective modernity can be interpreted as a stage in its fulfillment.

Are we then witnessing the rearticulation of the canonical periodization in new terms? The emergence of the origin narrative of the French Revolution, of the end of the modern age in 1789 and start of the contemporary age in 1815? Perhaps, in part. But we cannot stop there

---

[10] For an in-depth interpretation of Lefort's reading of Tocqueville, see Lefort (1988, pp. 183–210; 2000, pp. 35–66; 2007b, pp. 907–913). On Lefort's interpretation of Tocqueville see Bilakovics (2013), Audier (2004), and Guellec (2001).

if we wish to follow the whirlwind of Lefort's ideas to its end. His definition of democracy has not yet unraveled and it is necessary to make another detour in order to view it in full. Indeed, to continue to follow the Frenchman's line of thinking, it would be as useless as it is wrong to look to the French Revolution for the precise point of this upheaval as if it were an *ex nihilo* event interrupting the flow of historical time. A closer look reveals that the discontinuity we have just pointed to is illusory: revolutionary events are shown to be intimately linked to what went before. It is no coincidence that Michelet, Tocqueville and later François Furet were able, without being mistaken, to note the elements of continuity between the Revolution and the *ancien régime* (Tocqueville 2011; Furet 1981; Michelet 1967). They could point out how the monarchy itself prepared the ground for the Revolution, how the signs of a radical change in social relations were evident before 1789. Lefort, who is familiar with the works of Furet, is also fully aware of the difficulty of tracing the precise contours of the Revolution, of dating it. When does it begin? When does it end? In 1789? Does it continue until the execution of Robespierre in 1794? Or until the *coup d'état* of Brumaire 18, 1799? Or does it survive and continue even with Napoleon? In short, the history of the symbolic democratic revolution appears complicated, to say the least. It does not allow itself to be reduced to a precise point, time and event, nor even to be explained in the terms of cause and effect. It permits itself to be glimpsed only in the unresolvable tension between continuity and discontinuity, between event and process: it is evidence of a decidedly singular shaping of society (*mise en form*), "and we would try in vain to find models for it in the past, even though it is not without its heritage" (Lefort 1986, p. 225).

> In my view, the important point is that democracy is instituted and sustained by the *dissolution of the markers of certainty*. It inaugurates a history in which people experience a fundamental indeterminacy as to the basis of power, law, and knowledge, and as to the basis of relations betweel [sic] *self* and *other*, at every level of social life (at every level where division, and especially the division between those who held power and those who were subject to them, could once be articulated as a result of a belief in the nature of things or in a supernatural principle). It is this which leads me to take the view that, without the actors being aware of it, a process of questioning is implicit in social practice, that no one has the answer to the

questions that arise, and that the work of ideology, which is always dedicated to the task of restoring certainty, cannot put an end to this practice. (Lefort 1988, p. 19)

Democracy thus remains an enigma. It is consubstantial to modernity as a symbolic institution, but at the same time it is its fulfillment and also a different, unprecedented social form. It appeared and was invented in the nineteenth century and certain institutions are linked to it. It is a process and an upheaval, an occurrence and an invention. It is the result of human actions and at the same time something that eludes them: an almost independent and at times even necessary symbolic framework, which proceeds unbeknownst to the actors, but is linked to their actions.

This internal tension in Lefort's thought is surprising: it is one of the most interesting aspects of his work but at the same time reveals some of its limitations. For example, his definition of democracy as a long-running process betrays the signs of a philosophy of history to which the philosopher has always been opposed. Similarly, although the idea of remaining open to an otherness which humans cannot completely master is one of the most interesting features of the definition of democracy proposed by Lefort, the dimension of otherness seems to contradict the assumptions of his thought when it appears to be completely unconnected to human actions, as if it were a normative ideal, an ultimate horizon, the end of history.[11] In short, attempting to define the democracy set out in Lefort's work also means running into its enigma, into the aporias of his work. It means taking charge of the political nature of his thought, without therefore neglecting its contradictions and limitations.[12] Doing this means first of all understanding how the definition of democracy is intimately linked to that of another form of society: the totalitarian one.

---

[11] It is Lefort himself, in a few surprising if not in fact perplexing lines, who defines the democratic symbolic dimension as a necessary dimension unrelated to the economic and technical ones. See Lefort (2007b).

[12] For Lefort, all thought is always situated and always political. His own thinking must therefore also be considered a stand against totalitarianism and in favor of democracy.

Totalitarianism

Lefort's interest in deciphering the totalitarian form of society in a sense coincides with the beginning of his reflection, or rather with his need to understand and define the Soviet regime.[13] He had already engaged in a strong critique of the USSR during the Socialisme ou Barbarie period, in conjunction with Castoriadis.[14] As I show in the first chapter, the two thinkers, arguing against the ideas of Trotsky, pointed out the absolute novelty of that regime, which they considered an unprecedented social formation led by a new ruling class: the bureaucracy. The preliminary outcome of this work was the definition of bureaucratic society that they elaborated in the early 1950s, using the testimonies of early Russian defectors as the principal material on which to base their analyses (Lefort 1986, pp. 89–121). For Lefort in particular, this society was distinguished by certain precise characteristics: the integration of every sphere—the law, the economy, knowledge—into a single authority personified by the party and those who control it, the consequent imposition of a single dominant model on all activities, the use of terror, the elimination of all opposition, and the ideology of history (Lefort 1979, pp. 117–144).

First of all, bureaucracy unveils a unique way of managing and legitimizing power and a specific relationship with the other spheres that make up society: it reduces everything to its own internal logic and to its self-perpetuation. The administration of justice, for example, is completely subordinated to the interests of bureaucratic power. Guilt or innocence is not determined by the actions of the defendants but only by the needs

---

[13] Therefore, the interpretations that I criticized and that see Lefort's ideas as a continuous attempt to understand and critique Soviet society cannot be considered wrong. See Molina (2005) or Poltier (1997). The philosophical reflection on the concept of totalitarianism is too extensive to be considered in a footnote. For an in-depth and comprehensive overview on the subject see at least Forti (2024). As far as our study is concerned, it is sufficient to note that Lefort's reflection is part of a broad debate that in France originated as early as the 1930s with the interventions of Raymond Aron, Georges Bataille, and Simone Weil, and which reached its greatest extent in the 1960s and 1970s. These years, in which Lefort produced his best definition of a personal theory of totalitarianism developed as a response to the democratic revolution, are the same in which the question of totalitarianism explodes in the political sphere and in the media. The journals *Libre* and *Textures*, of which Lefort was among the liveliest contributors, along with Marcel Gauchet and Miguel Abensour, contributed profoundly to this debate in 1970s France. For a critical examination of this discussion see Christofferson (2004).

[14] Castoriadis' production on this theme in the 1950s and 1960s is extensive. See at least Castoriadis (1988a, b, 2018).

of the apparatus. Similarly, economic planning ends up being completely irrational, as the goal to which it responds is not the increase of production and industrialization, but the preservation of the bureaucratic class and the increase of its power (140–141).

Bureaucratic rule is also characterized by terror, a term that Lefort applies to something rather different from the admittedly extreme fear that ran through despotic societies like the regimes of Mussolini, Franco, and even Hitler.[15] The terror that Viktor Kravchenko speaks of in his *I Chose Freedom* pervades the whole of society, right down to personal and emotional ties, and at the same time is a characteristic of party relations. It expresses itself both on the subjective level, in the party's policies, for instance in the campaign against the *kulaks* or in the purges, and on the objective level, as an anonymous and autonomous movement of the system of which the self-destruction of the ruling class is the clearest effect (131–137). Terror is thus not simply a tool of the bureaucratic class, but a force over which no one has complete control. Lefort identifies the driving force of this dynamic in the "ideology of history", that is, the idea of a historical and logical necessity that is realized independently of individual people, who merely serve it as instruments or momentary emanations (143). This is the ideology that gives meaning to all acts of terror, that legitimizes the power of the bureaucratic class and the decisions it makes, including its planning, the elimination of the kulaks, and the targeting of external and internal enemies. The bureaucracy, moreover, is nothing more than the direct expression of this necessary process, and adherence to the ideology is thus at the same time the instrument through which the bureaucracy also takes over the sphere of knowledge. No knowledge contrary to or even independent from the dictates of the bureaucratic apparatus is possible. The bureaucracy and the official knowledge connected to it present themselves as the direct expression of necessity; they are the historical truth.

The party immediately emerges as a key element, as the seat of revolutionary leadership. Once it comes to power all authority is concentrated in its hands, including the functions of the police and the justice system, and the organization of the economy (135). It is the point of encounter and of confusion between the social and political spheres. It is the means by which the bureaucratic society seeks to organize itself and, at the

---

[15] In these years Lefort still distinguishes the bureaucratic Soviet regime from traditional forms of despotism, which include Nazism.

same time, is the instrument of government for the new ruling class. The party is the custodian of knowledge about the course of history and the place from which the bureaucracy can direct that progress. The extreme centralization of authority in the hands of the party and then in the supreme leader (for example Stalin), the purges, and the use of terror as a method of government are no more than the extreme expression of the bureaucratic society (133).

However, Lefort quickly considers this analysis inadequate, and even before the end of his participation in SouB, he attempts to understand the novelty and the meaning of the USSR from another point of view.[16] Moreover, he finds that once Marxist economism is abandoned, once the symbolic dimension of the social is recognized, Soviet society is no longer only a political regime but rather a specific "form of society" that must be understood in its symbolic dimension. In this context, the significance of Soviet society can only reveal itself within the broader framework of reflection on modern change.[17] Only against the background of this symbolic upheaval is it possible to perceive the radical innovation of totalitarian oppression, and to grasp fully its essence and characteristics, as the significant difference between it and dictatorial or authoritarian regimes emerges clearly. It is at this point that the term "totalitarianism" replaces that of "bureaucratic society", while the analysis simultaneously moves beyond the boundaries of Soviet society to also include at least the Nazi regime.

This change in terminology thus reveals a profound shift in the theory. While the elements that described bureaucratic society remain, they do so in a changed theoretical framework, and thus acquire new meaning. For Lefort, totalitarianism is in essence best understood not as a bureaucratic society but as a form of modern society. More precisely, it is first and foremost a *response* to modernity: to indeterminacy, to the lack

---

[16] His 1956 article "Totalitarianism without Stalin" (Lefort 1986, pp. 52–88) is of decisive importance to this development. As Abensour (1993, pp. 79–136) rightly notes, this essay marks a theoretical turning point, shifting from the critique of bureaucratic society to the conceptualization of the totalitarian form of society.

[17] Miguel Abensour argues that Lefort's work puts forward two different theorizations of totalitarianism. The first, still essentially Marxist, is contained in a series of texts from the late 1940s and early 1960s that present a minimal definition of the form. In the 1970s, however, Lefort arrived at a maximal definition rooted in the context of democratic revolution and beyond the scope of Marxism.

of foundation, to disincorporation and division (Lefort 1986, pp. 292–306). In other words, the totalitarian form of society can be seen as an attempt to recover, in a by now irrevocably changed symbolic horizon, the foundation that characterized the societies of the *ancien régime*. After the democratic revolution dismissed the image of the body, totalitarian society attempts to restore the lost organicity by integrating all the spheres that compose the social into a single unit. A series of identifications thus rebuild corporeality and, at the same time, rejects the division of the social. The proletariat identifies itself with the people and the party, which in turn identifies with its own apparatus and then with the top executive, the "Egocrat".[18] This figure (whose best example is once again Stalin) sums up and represents the whole of the social body, and the principles of knowledge and of the law. Knowledge and law are thus reintegrated into power, which regains an incontestable legitimacy and foundation. As a result, power is no longer empty, indefinable, and ungraspable, but is embodied by an incontestable subject and knowledge, that of a leader and a ruling class who personify the totality of the social and possess the knowledge required to rule it. The distinction between the imaginary, the symbolic, and the real is again eliminated, abolished, or hidden. The origin returns, and society can once again present itself as united and homogeneous. All internal conflict, all opposition is abolished, and the division of democracy can be said to be resolved.

The figure of the people-as-One represents this unity at the imaginary level (287 and 297–299).[19] For the totalitarian society, the people is a

---

[18] Lefort derives the term "Egocrat" from Aleksandr Solzhenitsyn's famous *The Gulag Archipelago*, the publication of which contributed profoundly to the debate on Soviet totalitarianism in early 1970s France. Lefort discusses this essay in depth in his *Un homme en trop* (Lefort 1976). See Solzhenitsyn (1974). The egocrat describes, for Lefort, the unprecedented form of totalitarian power. He is not simply a despot who rules above the laws but his function is to embody the entire social body. He is the image of power, and his body represents the entire extent of society.

[19] For Lefort, the idea of a united and homogeneous people is a fundamental aspect of totalitarianism. The philosopher argues that this is not a contradictory relationship but rather one of mutual consensus between the party, the ruling class, and the egocrat. See Lefort (1986, pp. 298–299), where Lefort states: "It should also be observed that in totalitarian ideology, the representation of the People-as-One is in no way contradictory with that of the party. The party does not appear as distinct from the people or from the proletariat, which is the quintessence of it. It does not have a specific reality within society. The party is the proletariat in the sense that it is identical with it. At the same time, it is the guide or, as Lenin put it, the consciousness of the proletariat; or, as I

homogeneous, compact, undifferentiated subject. It has a unique identity and will, it negates all divisions and represents the identity of all of society, the community of blood, the political community, and the historical community. The people-as-One is thus the means by which the totalitarian society responds to democratic division and indeterminacy. Society can now harmonize with itself. It is a stable, homogeneous, and united community that rests on a new foundation:

> From this point of view, may not totalitarianism be conceived as a response to the questions raised by democracy, as an attempt to resolve its paradoxes? Modern democratic society seems to me, in fact, like a society in which power, law, and knowledge are exposed to a radical indetermination, a society that has become the theater of an uncontrollable adventure, so that what is instituted never becomes established, the known remains undermined by the unknown, the present proves to be undefinable, covering many different social times which are staggered in relation to one another within simultaneity [...] With totalitarianism an apparatus is set up which tends to stave off this threat, which tends to weld power and society back together again, to efface all signs of social division, to banish the indetermination that haunts the democratic experience. (305)

However, this does not mean that totalitarianism represents an attempt to return to the past. The totalitarian response is one that is now carried out on a modern basis and in a symbolic horizon that has irrevocably changed. Religion has still lost its ability to structure the social field, and the body remains disintegrated (304). It is not possible simply to return to the *ancien régime*, and the totalitarian society will therefore not recover the foundation and unity it seeks by rediscovering a religious dimension, which by now has been relegated to the private sphere. They are located

---

would say, using an old political metaphor, to which I shall come back, it is its head. And, similarly, the representation of the People-as-One is not in contradiction with that of an omnipotent, omniscient power, with, in the last analysis, that of the *Egocrat* (to use Solzhenitsyn's term), the ultimate figure of that power. Such a power, detached from the social whole, towering over everything, merges with the party, with the people, with the proletariat. It merges with the body as a whole, while at the same time it is its head. A whole sequence of representations is to be found here, the logic of which should not escape us. Identification of the people with the proletariat, of the proletariat with the party, of the party with the leadership, of the leadership with the *Egocrat*. On each occasion, an organ is both the whole and the detached part that makes the whole, that institutes it".

instead in the terrain of immanence and complete autonomy. In other words, totalitarianism "accepts" the modern idea of a completely human and contingent society, and indeed intends to follow this path to its ultimate extreme, eliminating all traces of otherness in favor of a society that is completely autonomous and transparent to itself. The origin makes itself present once more, but this time it resides within the social. The unity of the machine replaces the organic body. In short, once the transcendent foundation has been dispensed with, everything passes into the hands of men, who can now shape their society as they please. The locus of power moves down to the social sphere. Similarly, knowledge, no being longer transcendent, is completely manageable and knowable. Once God has left the scene the immanent laws of History or Nature that provide legitimacy to power and institutions take his place. In this sense, according to Lefort, totalitarianism radicalizes some of the characteristic elements of the modern institution while attempting to expel its indeterminacy.

Therefore, if democracy marks the advent of a purely human society devoid of transcendental justification, totalitarian society presents itself as completely self-possessed, coincident with itself, and able to shape itself as it wishes. While democracy celebrates the sovereignty of an undefined people, totalitarianism seeks the real sovereignty of an actual, homogeneous people with a definite identity. While democracy rejects the transcendent legitimization of power, totalitarianism conceives of power as completely immanent and internal to the social field. In short, all the elements that in the democratic form appear subject to continuous discussion—the community, the people, power, the nation, the state, history—become actualized and substantive. Indeterminacy and conflict are circumvented.

According to Lefort, it is precisely at this point that the fragility of the totalitarian can be discerned and the grounds for its critique opens up. Indeed, it is clear from the analysis of Soviet society and the testimonies of dissidents that the unity and self-transparency of totalitarian society is actually a deception. The ostentatious homogeneity of the social is imaginary; it merely conceals the division created by the presence of an unchallenged ruling class entrusted with enormous powers. The affirmation of unity is matched by the emergence of a state apparatus separate from society. Organic unity is actually torn apart by the actions of a new ruling class and a state apparatus that is separate from society and beyond its control. The identifications between the people, the party, the bureaucracy, and the egocrat only conceal the divisions between these different elements. In the same way, the homogeneity of the people conceals otherness: the continuous production of an internal enemy that is expelled from the unity of the community as an outsider. The supposed unity of the people-as-One is thus closely connected to a separation from an enemy that takes on different guises at various times: forces from the old social order (the kulaks, the bourgeoisie), the emissaries of external enemies (spies), internal parasites (the Jews, the gypsies, the counterrevolutionaries). Division may not be allowed, but it nevertheless keeps recurring (298). These enemies are therefore continually expelled, being considered a danger to the community, a disease that must be eliminated. The move to affirm an identity thus produces the radically different other: a dimension into which any threat to the negation of internal division is projected. The otherness that is suppressed in this way then resurfaces in a more radical form that is then met with even greater brutality: in the terror, the prison camps, and the concentration and extermination camps. The self-correspondence and transparency that are supposed to characterize totalitarian society turn out to be untenable and illusory.

Thus while totalitarianism, as a form of society, possesses an internal coherence, the democratic background in which it is set, the political institution of the social in which it is forced to act, drags its contradictions into the light. Totalitarian society, Lefort concludes, is an illusory response to the democratic revolution. It relies on the chimera of a unity that cannot be realized and which conceals and makes more extreme the denied division. If totalitarian society is a means to avoid confrontation with indeterminacy, its failure reveals that this is in fact impossible. Totalitarianism is thus not a different institution of the social, but is a failed attempt at one. Instead it is a perversion masquerading as modern democratic society.

Lefort therefore adopts this perspective to criticize totalitarianism without resorting to overhanging thinking and normative ideals, and without seeking to recover an anachronistic and in any case impossible idea of good governance. The totalitarian society is objectionable precisely because it is "false": it is incapable of responding effectively to the modern symbolic institution or even of actually changing it. The ways of "making sense" (*mise en sens*) of it and of "staging" it (*mise en scene*), we might say, are ideological: they conceal a completely different and contradictory way of "enacting" it. The division that this society boasts of expelling in fact runs through it even more comprehensively. Totalitarian discourse, then, is not acceptable precisely because it is impossible, as it produces even worse, more profound, and more dangerous distortions than those it deludedly claims to eliminate. Besides, Lefort observes, what else do human rights make clear, on the other side of the Iron Curtain, if not the fallacy of the totalitarian response to the democratic dynamic?

> What makes the criminality of Nazism so unique, what makes it impossible simply to say: "This is another society, this is another type of political society"? [...] What is it that mysteriously stops a democrat, a tolerant person, someone who respects the freedom of others, from being able to say: "this regime is perverse"? And I say, for example, that the regime in Tehran is perverse. I insist on this "I" because, as soon as there is a man, a ruler, an all-powerful group that claims to bend to his rule, to the norms of a belief, or to the people as a whole, I say: "this is perverse and criminal". I do not say it because of my own values, or those of my environment, but because of the universal values that arose with democracy. (Lefort 2007b, p. 654)[20]

Despite Lefort's efforts, however, does democracy not simply continue to be a regulative ideal against which totalitarianism can be judged? Does the idea that the democratic institution of the social is an indisputable truth to which we must necessarily comply not transform this very institution into the object of an overhanging thought? Once again we see the emergence of the same tension that innervates Lefort's work and his conception of democracy, which was highlighted in the previous section. In this case, however, we can sketch out two answers. First, for Lefort the falsity of totalitarianism is not a theoretical issue but a political one. It is a matter of *experience*: it is clear from the accounts provided by Soviet defectors, from the terror, the death camps, and the gulags (Lefort 1994, pp. 179–331; 2007b, pp. 309–321, 369–374, 495–504, 625–610, 667–678). The failure of totalitarianism is obvious from the accusations of human rights abuses emerging beyond the Iron Curtain, and from the Prague and Budapest uprisings (179–184). From this point of view, there is no need for any normative ideal before totalitarianism can be condemned. On a more theoretical level, moreover, an initial,

---

[20] On this point, little debated by critics, see Lefort (2007b, pp. 631–655). This essay is a transcript of a speech delivered by the philosopher during the Rencontres internationales de Genève held in the Swiss city between October 5 and 6, 1989, and of the debate that followed.

albeit partial answer, can be sought by analyzing more closely the relationship between the totalitarian and democratic forms of society, while trying not to reduce either to a reductive normative model or a simplistic separation. For the Parisian thinker, in fact, the task is not to set the ideal of a democratic society against totalitarian degeneration, or institutions that maintain a minimum level of democracy against illiberal regimes. The relationship between the two forms of society is far more complex than this. Democracy is not entirely different from totalitarianism, but in fact retains the potential to drift toward totalitarianism. In other words, there is no clear division or boundary between democracy and totalitarianism. Once again we find that there is no bipolarity capable of defining the political sphere: the two forms of society permeate each other all the time. Totalitarianism is the radical countermeasure put in place to stem and resolve the inherent weakness of democracy, to resolve its inability to define itself and its component elements. We might say that it is the attempt to contain an indeterminacy that in its most radical implications even proves to be untenable. After all,

> There is always a possibility that the logic of democracy will be disrupted in a society in which the foundation of the political order and the social order vanish, in which that which has been established never bears the seal of full legitimacy, in which differences of rank no longer go unchallenged, in which right proves to depend upon the discourse which articulates it, and in which the exercise of power depends upon conflict. When individuals are increasingly insecure as a result of an economic crisis or of the ravages of war, when conflict between classes and groups is exacerbated and can no longer be symbolically resolved within the political sphere, when power appears to have sunk to the level of reality and to be no more than an instrument for the promotion of the interests and appetites of vulgar ambition and when, in a word, it appears *in society*, and when at the same time society appears to be fragmented, then we see the development of the fantasy of the People-as-One, the beginnings of a quest for substantial identity, for a social body which is welded to its head, for an embodying power, for a state free from division. (Lefort 1988, pp. 19–20)

Following this interpretation, it could even be argued that democracy is nothing more than a continual effort to avert its own drift toward totalitarianism, a perpetual questioning of the answers that from time to time seek to conceal indeterminacy.[21]

Moreover, democracies themselves are continually subject to ideological discourses that attempt to give form to the social, to propose foundations, however contingent, and to define the limits and contours of a community. Of course, not every ideology is totalitarian, but the perversion of democratic logic, Lefort warns us, is never far away. To survive it democracy must keep the locus of power empty. And to do so it must establish a particular relationship with change and foundation.[22]

ON REVOLUTION: CHANGE AND FOUNDATION IN DEMOCRATIC SOCIETY

The end of Lefort' participation in SouB coincides with his abandonment of militancy and the revolutionary perspective, after which he no longer accepts the idea of revolution as a radical interruption of the historical continuum, as a pure emergence of the new, as a total refounding of a society (Lefort 1979, pp. 9–10). Why might this be? The thesis I propose is that this change of view is another that depends on his conception of democracy, modernity, and totalitarianism.

Lefort's decision to distance himself from the revolutionary mindset is connected to his critique of the ideal of the virtuous, undivided society that will be ushered in by revolution. Even as early as the 1950s he repeatedly attacks the idea, widespread in communist circles, that the socialist revolution would establish a completely new, peaceful society free of class divisions, exploitation, the state, and politics (33–113). For Lefort, this ideal was the result of overhanging thinking that could even be identified in the work of Marx, for whom the proletarian revolution would be a pure, completely immanent act, capable of abolishing the level of representation, politics. According to the French thinker, it was precisely these

---

[21] See, for example, the pages devoted by Lefort to the "invisible ideology" in Lefort (1986, pp. 224–236). On this topic, see Breckman (2019).

[22] On the relationship between democracy and ideology, see Olivier Mongin's (2019) lucid analysis. Issue 451 of the journal *Esprit*, in which Mongin's text is published, contains a section devoted to Lefort named "L'inquiétude démocratique. Claude Lefort au present".

distortions of thought and revolution that paved the way for the Soviet bureaucratic and totalitarian society. The ideal of a completely just society, master of itself, coincident with itself, and without contradictions led the Russian revolution to Stalin. And on closer inspection, Lefort asserts, this same idea of revolution and society continues to operate in the background of the ideas of the majority of SouB led by Castoriadis in the late 1950s (98–113). The significance to be attributed to the revolution, its organization and its outcome is therefore at the heart of his abandonment of the movement in 1958.

During the 1970s, in the context of Lefort's mature framework of theories on the symbolic institution of the social and modernity, the terms of the critique once again take on new meaning, as it becomes clear that the significance of revolution must be grasped in its connection with modernity. After all, the roots of its characterizing elements—the rupture between the old and the new, and the creation of a society that projects itself beyond any transcendent principle in accordance with reason and principles that are considered universal and valid for all mankind—are to be found in the idea of politics and society that was being constructed in the fifteenth-century by Florentine humanism. In short, the idea of revolution as the foundation of a new era, of a *novus ordo seclorum*, is made possible by the modern conception of politics and the representation of power and the state. Only in this new symbolic context does the revolutionary ideology built on an absolute foundation of a fully human, fully self-possessed society make sense. A society that coordinates itself in the here and now, in the present, that looks to its future rather than its past and is self-organizing in all its aspects and spheres. The will of individuals and the application of reason are a sufficient basis for its foundation, while the transcendent principle is abandoned.

Therefore, according to Lefort, this definition of revolution actually corresponds to an ideology already evident in the most important upheaval of the modern era: the French Revolution in which the people embodies the will of the nation and, in the imagination, occupies the locus of power (Lefort 1988, pp. 57–162; 2000, pp. 159–171; 2007a, b, pp. 267–273 and 535–549).[23] The people becomes the symbol of a humanity divorced from transcendence, which finds the legitimacy of

---

[23] Lefort carries out his reflection on revolution in discussion with authors such as Quinet (1987), Michelet (1989), and Furet (1981). On Lefort's reading of Quinet and Michelet see the articles by Baczko (1993).

its actions within itself and establishes a new order on this basis. In a "doubly absurd" idea the people asks the Convention, which belongs to the people, to generate the people itself (Lefort 1988, p. 79). The revolutionary ideology is thus built on the illusion of the unity of the people and its identity, which then forms the basis for the legitimacy, truth, and creativity of history (107). The people is embodied in the Convention and its representatives, and thus becomes One: it is an illusory representation of a united, homogeneous society with a single, rational and objective will, capable of designing itself in every aspect and doing so with a view to finally creating a pacified, self-possessed society.

From this point of view, revolutionary ideology still suffers from its reliance on the theological-political mechanism, and can be interpreted as an attempt to bring about and at the same time contain the democratic revolution (86–88).[24] As we have seen, revolutionaries are also unprepared for the vacuum opened by democratic modernity, being forced to confront a totally new symbolic horizon with outdated categories still influenced by old concepts that responded to a symbolic institution that has now been overcome. They then design a totally historical and human society while also attempting not to abandon the One, and in so doing seek to build a stable human foundation on which society can recognize and divide itself. In short, the modern revolution or, to put it better, the ideology of modern revolution, delivers politics into the hands of men but at the same time brings with it potential distortions and illusions typical of the democratic institution of the social, the first of which is the attempt to restore a lost foundation that is no longer in the mind of God but also not in the hands of men.[25]

This is where revolutionary ideology meets totalitarian ideology and almost seems to anticipate it. Both are ideological and illusory discourses that seek to eliminate division and to find the One, the foundation. Both are doomed to failure. As such, just as will happen with totalitarianism, the people evoked by the ideologues of the French Revolution also pay for

---

[24] See Lefort (1988, pp. 115–134). In these pages Lefort analyzes the theory of Edgar Quinet, for whom terror is a response to the void left by religion. In 2000, pp. 159–171, he argues that both Michelet and Quinet grasp the very essence of revolution in religion. It is precisely this belief that differentiates them from Tocqueville.

[25] During the 1980s in France, this also meant rethinking the French Revolution and its founding role for the French Republic. See Furet (1981). On revolutionary ideology see Howard (1993).

their illusory unity with an impossible identification and with the incessant creation of new enemies. Revolutionary power manages to present itself as being internal to the people only at the price of having to define an external aggression, a threat or aristocratic plot aimed at erasing its position, which always risks appearing to serve particular interests. Division continually resurfaces under the veil of unity. Every embodiment of the people in a new form of power reveals an unjustified gap between the instituting and the instituted (107–108).[26] "The image of a society which is at one with itself and which has been delivered from its divisions can only be grasped during the administration of the purge, or, better still, during the work of extermination" (84). The will to establish a foundation thus leads to the Terror.

> The idea of revolution as an absolute event—as the foundation of a world in which men dominate institutions entirely and are in complete agreement over their activities and aims; as the establishment of a world in which power gives way to the flow of collective decisions and law gives way to the current of wills, and in which conflict is eliminated—this idea is part of the totalitarian representation. The belief in a society that will organically order and arrange itself from within itself refers back to an entirely external referent, to the position of a powerful Other who encloses the whole and constitute it as the One. (Lefort 2007b, p. 268)

This begs the question of whether, according to Lefort, revolutions are by their essence totalitarian. Not at all. In fact, immediately after the passage above, he asks "can criticism stop at this point?" Do the distortions of revolutionary ideology disqualify all revolution, as Marc Richir or François Furet believe (Furet 1976; Richir 1976)?[27] Lefort does not share this idea at all but on the contrary believes that "the critique of

---

[26] Lefort (1988, p. 107) affirms: "Revolutionary ideology is constituted by the insane assertion of the unity, or indeed the identity, of the people. The legitimacy, the truth and the creativity of history are assumed to come together in the people. Now this primordial image contains a contradiction, for the people appear to conform to their essence only if they are distinguished from the empirical popular masses, only if they institute themselves as – and display themselves as being – legislators, as actors conscious of their ends".

[27] The article I refer to here (Lefort 2007b, pp. 267–273) originally appeared in issue no. 9 of the journal *Esprit* in 1976. In this issue, entitled "Révolution et totalitarisme", a number of authors, including Lefort, Furet, Richir, and Paul Thibaud (1976), discuss the question of revolution. This is why Lefort directly criticizes the positions of Furet and Richir.

revolutionary mythology, of the ghost of the 'good society', of the society without divisions, leaves open the question of revolution" (Lefort 2007b, p. 272).

It is for this reason that even in the 1950s the French thinker is already looking with interest and sympathy at the uprisings in the streets of Prague and Budapest, which he believes might contain the meaning of modern revolution. His attention is drawn particularly to the Hungarian Uprising of 1956 against the leadership of the ruling Communist Party and the corruption of the ruling apparatus that has subjugated itself to the policies of Moscow (Lefort 1994, pp. 193–260; 2007b, pp. 261–273, 301–308). This erupts in the streets of Budapest on October 23 and is led by students and intellectuals before spreading to the whole of society. It begins as an attempt at reform but soon becomes a mass event and explodes into a genuine revolution, a plural, dispersed, "wild process" (*processus sauvage*) that develops on the shop floor, in the universities, and in the cultural and information sphere (Lefort 2007b, p. 272). It is an anti-totalitarian, anti-bureaucratic, anti-capitalist, and anti-state revolution. The insurgents demand independence, free elections, new socialist and democratic institutions, the withdrawal of Soviet troops, and the return of the former president, Imre Nagy. They demand the construction of a socialist republic in which a system of councils will replace centralized bureaucratic power and take control of business activity and the economy (Lefort 1994, p. 203), and intend to replace the power of the party with "institutions in which the rights of each individual are guaranteed and which would escape the division between the rulers and the ruled" (Lefort 2007b, p. 264).[28] The Hungarian revolutionaries thus seek a much more radical and extensive socialist democracy than the bourgeois democracy. Learning from the mistakes of the past, they have abandoned the idea of the people-as-One, of the absolute foundation, and of a completely self-possessed society embodied in power (265). For this reason, the Hungarian Revolution is a historical revelation, it is the first to accept the multiple, the heterogeneous, the conflicting in order to reinvent democracy by standing within it. It represents the complete rejection of the One. It is a revolution in the democratic institution of the social, one that does not aim to recover the foundation and which has abandoned the theological-political mechanism. It accepts and supports

---

[28] The council system meets this particular need. On this issue, see Ask Popp-Madsen (2021) and Muldoon (2018).

fragmentation and division. In this sense, this revolution does not contradict the symbolic institution of societies, such as democratic societies, that have lost their center and their unity, and which contain only division, parcelization, and disorder. It has lost the political-theological core and ushered in radical indeterminacy. And in this respect it nurtures similarities with the "new disorder" that would detonate in Paris in May 1968.

In short, in democratic society conflict is no longer centered around an overall vision of the social, and no longer organized on the basis of the One. It is multiple, dispersed, and without center. It moves in unpredictable and uncontrolled directions and never involves the totality of the social. It does not aim at absolute refoundation, at hegemony. That is why, according to Lefort, rights establish the grammar of democratic social conflict: they bring the possibility of dispersed contestations that always go beyond power and are unrelated and opposed to each other, and directed toward different goals (Lefort 1986, pp. 239–272). Rights do not construct an overall image of society, nor do they aim to reestablish an irrefutable foundation. At the same time, they do not reduce the social to a plane of immanence that is by its essence contrary to the state, but instead articulate dispersed representations. They represent both the continuous proposition and the critique of contingent identities, and are beholden only to their expression and claim, being divided and subject to criticism at the very moment they are asserted. They are the instrument of conflict in a society that has lost its center, that is no longer a community, that resolves itself into a continuous critique of itself and its assumptions (272).[29]

We are now confronted once again with one of the most interesting aspects of Lefort's thought and, at the same time, with a critical point in which the tension that innervates his definition of democracy resurfaces. This tension or aporia has already been highlighted in the previous sections, but it emerges most clearly at this point. By outlining in this way the symbolic democratic institution of the social, Lefort intends to set out his idea of a "global configuration",[30] acted out and at the same time

---

[29] Arato (2012) reads Lefort as the philosopher of the post-revolutionary paradigm of democratic transformation.

[30] The expression is used by Merleau-Ponty, who states that "every institution is a symbolic system that the subject incorporates as a functional style, as a global configuration, without needing to conceive it expressly" (Merleau-Ponty 1988, p. 59).

endured, in which the society and thought of today are inscribed, and of which those involved in it are not fully aware. In this way, however, it escapes the grip of the game of politics and conflict itself. It represents the symbolic background to which societies must somehow adapt and respond to appropriately. Beyond the difficulty inherent in a way of thinking that claims to be conscious of a symbolic dimension acted out by actors who are not fully conscious of it, this definition once again sees democracy as a transcendent horizon completely divorced from the actions of the subjects within it. Democracy again becomes the fulfillment of an unstoppable, centuries-old, and enduring *telos*.

This image is obviously at odds with the heart of Lefort's thought and his definition of the symbolic, whereby the latter is always the contingent result of political conflict. It is always *experience*: it is the fruit of the actions of men and is composed of them, in the same way as for Merleau-Ponty Being is the experience of Being and never a background that characterizes entities. From this point of view, the very image of the democratic, fragmented society without center and without community must be understood as the result of the present situation and of conflicting relations, as a hegemony. The democratic *institution* can and must be criticized, as otherwise it resolves itself into an acceptance and celebration of the existing, which can only be partially corrected at its margins. This is what Marcel Gauchet meant when in 1980, specifically in opposition to his master's theses, he wrote that rights are not politics (Gauchet 2002, pp. 2–26). The point is not to restore the One, but to always keep in mind that, just as Lefort taught us, every representation of the social is a political matter, an attempt at "founding", however contingent it may appear to be. The same is true of democracy, which therefore cannot be configured as a complete deconstruction, but only as continuous refoundation. Democracy, in short, does not do away with beliefs and illusions, it only insists that these should not be justified through transcendence or tradition.[31]

By interpreting Lefort's texts, we learn that democracy is the name of a society that accepts the interplay of conflict and ideologies and is aware

---

[31] This interpretation of democracy brings Lefort closer to radical democracy theorists like Laclau and Mouffe (Laclau 2005) or McCormick (2011) without eliminating the radical differences between them. On radical democracy see Deleixhe (2019), Breckman (2013), and Tønder and Thomassen (2005). J.D. Ingram (2006) grasps the tension between liberalism and radical democracy in Lefort's thought.

that any representation of itself is only the result of a contingent hegemony which, in turn, can only be a representation, the meaning created by a political discourse, an ideology. This takes place in a framework that depends on and is created by the actions of individuals and political conflict, but at the same time is not completely manageable by the people involved. Herein lies the meaning of ultimate indeterminacy.

REFERENCES

Abensour, Miguel. 1993. Les deux interprétations du totalitarisme chez Lefort. In *La démocratie à l'œuvre. Autour de Claude Lefort*, ed. C. Habib and C. Mouchard, 79–136. Paris: Éditions Esprit.

Agamben, Giorgio. 1993. *The Coming Community*. Minneapolis: University of Minnesota Press.

Arato, Andrew. 2012. Lefort, the Philosopher of 1989. *Constellations* 19/1: 23-29.

Ask Popp-Madsen, Benjamin. 2021. *Visions of Council Democracy. Castoriadis, Arendt, Lefort*. Edinburgh: Edinburgh University Press.

Audier, Serge. 2004. *Tocqueville Retrouvé: Genèse et enjeux du renouveau tocquevillien français*. Paris: Vrin.

Baczko, Bronislaw. 1993. Une lecture de Quinet. In *La démocratie à l'œuvre. Autour de Claude Lefort*, ed. C. Habib and C. Mouchard, 213–228. Paris: Éditions Esprit.

Bilakovics, Steven. 2013. Lefort and Tocqueville on the Possibility of Democratic Despotism. In *Claude Lefort. Thinker of the Political*, ed. M. Plot, 136–154. London: Palgrave Macmillan.

Blanchot, Maurice. 2006. *The Unavowable Community*. Barrytown: Station Hill Press.

Breckman, Warren. 2019. Retour sur «l'idéologie invisible» selon Lefort. *Raison Publique*, 23: 37–54.

Breckman, Warren. 2013. *The Adventures of the Symbolic. Post-Marxism and Radical Democracy*. New York: Columbia University Press.

Castoriadis, Cornelius. 1987. *The imaginary institution of the society*. Cambridge: Polity Press.

Castoriadis, Cornelius. 1988a. *Political and Social Writings Volume 1, 1946–1955: From the Critique of Bureaucracy to the Positive Content of Socialism*. Minneapolis: University of Minnesota Press.

Castoriadis, Cornelius. 1988b. *Political and Social Writings Volume 2, 1955–1960: From the Workers' Struggle Against Bureaucracy to Revolution in the Age of Modern Capitalism*. Minneapolis: University of Minnesota Press.

Castoriadis, Cornelius. 2018. *La Société bureaucratique. Écrits politiques, 1945–1997, V*. Paris: Éditions du Sandre.

Chevrier, Marc, Couture, Yves, and Vibert, Stéphane. 2015. *Démocratie et modernité. La pensée politique française contemporaine*. Rennes: Presses Universitaires de Rennes.

Christofferson, Michael, Scott. 2004. *French Intellectuals Against the Left: The Antitotalitarian Moment of the 1970s*. New York: Berghahn Books.

Couture, Jean-Yves. 2014. Problématiser les liens entre la démocratie et les droits de l'homme. Les perspectives de Castoriadis, Lefort et Gauchet. *Klesis. Revue philosophique*, XXIX: 50–64.

Couture, Jean-Yves. 2019. Prendre les droits de l'homme au sérieux. *Esprit*, CDLI: 62–74.

Dallmayr, Fred. 1993. Postmetaphysics and Democracy. *Political Theory* 21/1: 101–127.

Deleixhe, Martin. 2019. La démocratie radicale et la critique du marxisme. *Raisons politiques* 75/3 : 29–44.

Demelemestre, Gaëlle. 2012. Le concept lefortien du pouvoir comme lieu vide. Paradoxes de la société démocratique moderne. *Raison politiques* 46/2: 175–193.

Di Pierro, Mattia. 2020. «Istituzione politica» e «istituzione democratica» in Claude Lefort. In *Istituzione. Filosofia, politica, storia, Almanacco di Filosofia e Politica 2*, (ed.) M. Di Pierro, F. Marchesi, 151–164. Macerata: Quodlibet.

Esposito, Roberto. 2009. *Communitas. The Origin and Destiny of Community*. Redwood City: Stanford University Press.

Forti, Simona. 2024. *Totalitarianism. A Borderline Idea in Political Philosophy*. Stanford: Stanford University Press.

Furet, François. 1976. Au centre de nos représentations politiques. *Esprit*, 460/9 : 172–178.

Furet, François. 1981. *Interpreting the French Revolution*. Cambridge: Cambridge University Press.

Gauchet, Marcel. 2002. *La démocratie contre elle-même*. Paris: Gallimard.

Guellec, Laurence. 2001. La complication : Lefort lecteur de Tocqueville. *Raison politiques*, 1/1: 141–153.

Howard, Dick. 1993. La révolution américaine et l'idéologie révolutionnaire. In *La démocratie à l'œuvre. Autour de Claude Lefort*, ed. C. Habib, C. Mouchard, 229–241. Paris: Éditions Esprit.

Ingram, James. 2006. The Politics of Claude Lefort's Political: Between Liberalism and Radical Democracy. *Thesis Eleven* 87/1: 33–50.

Laclau, Ernesto. 2005. *On populist reason*. London-New York: Verso.

Lefort, Claude. 1976. *Un homme en trop. Réflexions sur « l'Archipel du Goulag »*. Paris: Seuil.

Lefort, Claude. 1977. Formation de l'État moderne, pouvoir, corps politique, nation. In *Archives Claude Lefort*, EHESS-CESPRA, CL. 9, envelope 4.

Lefort, Claude. 1979. *Éléments d'une critique de la bureaucratie*. 2nd edition. Paris: Gallimard.

Lefort, Claude. 1986. *The Political Forms of Modern Society. Bureaucracy, Democracy, Totalitarianism*. Cambridge: MIT Press.

Lefort, Claude. 1988. *Democracy and Political Theory*. Cambridge: Polity Press.

Lefort, Claude. 1994. *L'invention démocratique. Les limites de la domination totalitaire*. Paris: Fayard.

Lefort, Claude. 2000. *Writing. The Political Test*. Durham and London: Duke University Press.

Lefort, Claude. 2007a. *Complications. Communism and the Dilemma of Democracy*. New York: Columbia University Press.

Lefort, Claude. 2007b. *Le temps présent. Écrits 1945–2005*, Paris: Belin.

McCormick, John. 2011. *Machiavellian Democracy*. Cambridge: Cambridge University Press.

Merleau-Ponty, Maurice. 1988. *In Praise of Philosophy and Other Essays*. Evanston: Northwestern University Press.

Michelet, Jules. 1967. *History of the French Revolution*. Chicago: The University of Chicago Press.

Michelet, Jules. 1989. *History of the French Revolution*. Chicago: University of Chicago Press.

Molina, Esteban. 2005. *Le défi du politique. Totalitarisme et démocratie chez Claude Lefort*. Paris: L'Harmattan.

Mongin, Olivier. 2019. Aujourd'hui. *Esprit*, 451: 99–110.

Moyn, Samuel. 2012. The Politics of Individual Rights: Marcel Gauchet and Claude Lefort. In *French Liberalism. From Montesquieu to the Present Day*, (ed.) R. Geenens and H. Rosenblatt (291–310). Cambridge: Cambridge University Press.

Muldoon, James. 2018. *Council Democracy. Towards a Democratic Socialist Politics*. New York-London: Routledge.

Nancy, Jean-Luc. 1991. *The Inoperative Community*. Minneapolis: University of Minnesota Press.

Poltier, Hugues. 1997. *Claude Lefort. La découverte du politique*. Paris: Michalon.

Pranchère, Jean-Yves. 2019. Un monde habitable par tous. Claude Lefort et la question du social. *Esprit*, CDLI: 111–122.

Quinet, Edgar. 1987. *La révolution*. Paris: Belin.

Richir, Marc. 1976. L'aporie révolutionnaire. *Esprit*, 469/9: 179–186.

Simard, Augustin. 2015. Les deux corps du droit. Rôle et nature du droit dans la pensée de Claude Lefort. *Politique et Sociétés*, 34/1: 61–83.

Solzhenitsyn, Alexander. 1974. *The Gulag archipelago: 1918–1956. An experiment in literary investigation*. 3 vol. New York: Harper & Row.
Thériault, Joseph Yvon. 2015. L'Institution de la démocratie et la démocratie radicale. La leçon de Lefort. In *Démocratie et modernité. La pensée politique française contemporaine*, (ed.) M. Chevrier, Y. Couture, and S. Vibert, 229–239. Rennes: Presses Universitaires de Rennes.
Thibaud, Paul. 1976. Créativité sociale et révolution. *Esprit*, 460/9: 213–224.
Tocqueville, Alexis de. 2011. *The Ancien Régime and the French Revolution*. New York: Columbia University.
Tønder, Lars, and Thomassen, Lasse. 2005. *Radical Democracy. Politics Between Abundance and Lack*. Manchester: Manchester University Press.

Index

A
Abensour, Miguel, x, 7, 11, 64, 197, 199, 211, 232, 234
Alienation, 32, 42, 53, 55, 67–69, 73, 90–94, 100, 102, 105, 106
Alighieri, Dante, 14, 132
Althusser, Louis, 12, 148, 161, 198
Ancien régime, x, 118, 119, 122–124, 128, 139, 225, 227, 230, 235, 236
Anthropology, viii, 57, 60, 61, 66, 73, 74, 99, 192
Anti-Stalinism, 19
Arendt, Hannah, vii, x, 5–7, 76, 184
Aron, Raymond, 148, 155, 191, 232
Autonomy, 3, 6, 11, 28, 29, 34, 35, 41, 45, 64, 77, 104, 107, 120, 128–130, 134, 139, 153, 155, 221, 237

B
Bali, 63, 64
Baron, Hans, 135, 136, 149
Bateson, Gregory, 57, 63, 68, 73, 75
Body, theory of the, 119, 121
Bruni, Leonardo, 14, 131, 135, 140, 141, 156, 220
Bureaucratic society, 12, 22, 25–27, 29, 30, 33, 43, 45, 232–234

C
Capitalism, 13, 25, 26, 32, 41, 69, 71, 91, 96, 100, 102, 111–113, 117, 124
Castoriadis, Cornelius, viii, x, 20–31, 41–45, 67, 75, 97, 100, 105, 128, 130, 191, 197, 210, 232, 242
Chaulieu-Montal Tendency, 23, 25
Chiasma, 8–10, 82
Clastres, Pierre, viii, 7, 64–66, 75, 197, 199
Community, 11, 15, 58–66, 89, 93, 104, 107, 113–118, 120–123,

125, 127, 129, 131, 133–135, 139, 142, 158, 164, 165, 169, 172, 174–176, 181–183, 185, 220, 222, 223, 227–229, 236–238, 241, 246, 247
Conflict, viii, 11, 25, 26, 30, 37, 63, 74, 75, 102, 104–106, 108, 112, 131, 140, 141, 161–166, 168–170, 173–175, 181–183, 185, 187, 195, 210, 214, 220, 223, 224, 235, 237, 240, 244, 246–248

D

de La Boétie, Étienne, 142, 180
Deleuze, Gilles, viii, 4, 5, 12, 200, 212–214
Democracy, vii, viii, x, 1, 2, 6, 7, 10–15, 21, 27, 45, 74, 98, 106–108, 124, 129, 140, 142, 147, 148, 191, 219–231, 235–237, 239–241, 245–247
sauvage democracy, 7
Dialectic, viii, ix, 36, 52, 55, 56, 61, 62, 92–94, 102, 103, 140
dialectical materialism, 28, 52, 56
Disincorporation, 117, 122, 125, 129, 131, 161, 221, 227, 235
Division, viii, 9, 13, 15, 22, 26–29, 31, 39, 43, 45, 55, 63–66, 70–73, 75, 76, 81, 93–98, 102, 105, 116, 117, 119, 128, 137, 141, 152, 163, 166, 169, 170, 172, 173, 175, 181–187, 197, 198, 208, 211, 214, 220, 222, 223, 225, 230, 235–238, 240, 241, 244–246
social division, 27, 95, 97, 98, 115, 118, 162, 182, 207, 220, 236

E

Economicism, 6
Effect, 186
Egocrat, 235–237
Essentialism, 54, 55
Ethnology, viii, 12, 74, 77, 192
Evans-Pritchard, Edward E., 57, 66, 67, 73

F

Faction, 204
Fetishism, theory of, 54
Flesh, 9, 14, 15, 76, 181, 184, 186, 196, 198
chair, 9
Florence, 136, 138–140, 148, 155–157, 159, 165, 173, 207
Republic of Florence, 168
Form of history, 111, 116, 117
Form of society, 1, 14, 15, 97, 107, 111, 116, 117, 122, 124, 128, 131, 147, 187, 215, 219, 222, 231, 232, 234, 235, 238
Formulas, 75
Foucault, Michel, vii, x, 3, 5, 12, 30, 148, 199–214
Foundation, vii, 2, 3, 5, 13–15, 56, 71, 73, 74, 89, 92, 94, 97, 102, 111, 117, 118, 121, 124, 125, 128, 130–132, 142, 147, 153, 155, 157–160, 165, 169, 181, 183, 184, 186, 187, 199, 202, 211, 214, 215, 220, 221, 224, 227, 228, 235–237, 240–246
French Communist Party (PCF), 19, 20, 22, 23, 40, 52, 200
Furet, François, 230, 242–244

G

Garin, Eugenio, 135–138, 157

Gauchet, Marcel, 64, 66, 75, 76, 119, 128, 130, 183, 197, 199, 210, 211, 224, 232, 247
Gide, André, 19
Gift, theory of the, 195

H

Hegel, Friedrich, 52–55, 61, 70, 111, 132, 180, 194, 196
Heteronomy, 116
   Hegelian interpretation of Marx, 52
   Hyppolite, Jean, 52
Hobbes, Thomas, 14, 131, 132
Holistic theory of the social, 60
   total social fact, 60
Humanism, 14, 131, 135–139, 141, 142, 157, 159, 160, 165, 225, 242
Human rights, 224, 225, 239
Husserl, Edmund, 9, 61, 62, 79–81, 111, 203

I

Ideology, 2, 4, 7, 15, 23, 28, 31, 32, 35, 37, 56, 69–71, 75, 90, 93–99, 102, 106, 140, 154, 156, 157, 172, 174, 179, 198, 199, 206, 215, 231–233, 235, 241–244, 247, 248
Image of the body, 66, 115–119, 121, 133, 235
Imaginary, x, 14, 45, 67, 68, 72, 96–98, 122, 131, 172, 175–179, 221, 228, 235, 237
Immanence, viii, x, 3–5, 8, 10, 98, 131, 199, 208, 210, 211, 214, 222, 246
Indeterminacy, 2, 10, 15, 45, 59, 97, 99, 104, 131, 137, 139, 158, 159, 169, 180, 184, 186, 187, 198, 206–208, 211, 213–215, 220–222, 224, 225, 230, 234, 236–238, 240, 241, 246, 248
indetermination, 97, 187
Indirect ontology, 8, 83
Institution, vii, ix, xi, 2, 4, 6, 7, 9, 11, 14, 15, 42, 57–59, 61, 62, 70, 75, 77, 78, 80–84, 90, 96, 98, 100, 104, 105, 107, 116, 117, 121, 122, 124, 130–132, 137–139, 148, 151, 157–159, 163, 165, 168, 171, 180, 183, 185, 194, 195, 198–200, 208, 209, 211, 213, 214, 219, 221–223, 225–229, 231, 237, 239, 245, 246
   institution of the social, 11, 14, 63, 83, 125, 130–132, 181, 212, 219, 227, 239, 245
   Stiftung, 79, 80, 82, 83
Interpretation, ix, 1, 2, 4, 6, 8, 10, 11, 14, 15, 19, 29, 31, 32, 35, 38, 40, 45, 52–56, 66, 68, 70, 73, 75, 78, 81, 111, 113, 123, 131–135, 142, 148, 150, 151, 156, 158–161, 163, 164, 168, 172, 174, 184, 192, 194, 195, 198, 201, 202, 206, 208, 210–214, 223, 229, 232, 241, 247
Invisible ideology, 98, 241

J

Johnson-Forest Tendency (JFT), 3, 25, 29

K

Kantorowicz, Ernst, 119–121, 123–125
Kardiner, Abram, 57, 58, 73
Krahl, Hans Jürgen, 101
Kravchenko, Victor, 23, 233

L

Lacan, Jacques, 74, 172, 173, 204, 205
Laclau, Ernesto, 105, 172, 247
Les temps Modernes, 8, 19, 23, 40, 41, 45
Lévi-Strauss, Claude, 3, 12, 52, 57, 74, 77, 78, 81, 191–197, 204
Locke, John, 141

M

Machiavelli, Niccolò, ix, x, 10, 14, 15, 104, 130–132, 142, 147–157, 159–177, 179, 182–184, 186, 207, 210, 222, 225, 226
Marx, Karl, x, 12, 13, 19, 25, 31–33, 40, 41, 52–55, 61, 68, 70–73, 78, 91, 93, 99, 100, 103, 111–117, 131, 198, 223, 224
  marxism, 13, 19, 35, 52, 55, 68, 100, 103
Materialism, 2, 19, 20, 31, 36, 39, 52, 57
Mauss, Marcel, 52, 57, 59, 60, 73, 74, 78, 93, 192–196
Merleau-Ponty, Maurice, vii–x, 8, 9, 11, 19, 23, 35, 36, 39, 41, 44, 45, 52, 53, 56, 63, 73, 78–83, 103, 104, 161, 173, 180, 182, 186, 194, 195, 198, 221, 226, 246, 247
Michelet, Jules, 122–124, 230, 242, 243
Mise en forme, 61, 62, 75, 96
  shaping, 61, 230
Mise en scene, 75, 238
Mise en sens, 62, 64, 65, 238
Modernity, 11–15, 74, 108, 111, 117–119, 124–126, 128–132, 139, 141, 142, 147, 148, 160, 175, 184, 186, 225, 229, 231, 234, 241–243

Montaldi, Danilo, 25, 30, 37
Morin, Edgar, 105, 210

N

Nagy, Imre, 245
Nazism, 21, 233, 239
Negri, Antonio, 4, 101, 131, 161
Nuer, 66–68

O

Objective knowledge, 61, 77, 194
Openness, 84, 107, 128, 131, 169, 174, 221
Organic, 115, 121–125, 135, 176, 219, 235, 237
Origin, 70, 71, 75, 80, 84, 96, 113, 120, 128, 141, 157, 163, 176, 192, 202, 211, 220, 229, 235, 237
Otherness, 127
Overhanging thought, 35, 239
  pensée de surplomb, 56, 72

P

Parti Communiste Internationaliste (PCI), 19–21, 23, 25, 39, 41
People, viii, x, 7, 14, 20, 60, 61, 67, 104, 105, 107, 122, 123, 151, 160–164, 166–181, 183–186, 194, 220, 222, 223, 228, 230, 233, 235–239, 242–244
Phenomenological Marxism, 51
Phenomenology, viii, x, 4, 9–11, 13, 14, 39, 56, 73, 74, 81, 82, 195, 221
Philosophy of history, 36, 231
Political, the, vii, ix, xi, 2, 5, 6, 8, 10–12, 14, 15, 20, 21, 33, 35, 43, 73, 74, 76, 84, 116, 120, 123, 125, 128, 130, 140, 148,

159, 162, 165, 169, 175, 179, 181, 182, 184, 211, 214, 215, 219, 222, 225, 228, 232, 236, 240
le politique, 12, 75, 76, 181, 211, 214, 215
Politics, vii–x, 1, 2, 4–8, 10–12, 14, 15, 19, 21, 22, 25, 39, 43, 53, 60, 72, 73, 75, 76, 120, 121, 123, 125, 129–131, 135, 138–141, 150, 153–155, 159–161, 164, 166, 168–170, 172–175, 177–179, 181–184, 186, 200, 208, 211, 214, 224–226, 241–243, 247
la politique, 12, 75, 211
Positivist method, 72
Post-foundational, viii
Power, vii, viii, x, 2–5, 7, 11, 14, 20–23, 26, 27, 33, 37, 42–44, 53, 59, 64–66, 70, 72, 73, 75, 76, 90, 91, 93, 96–98, 100, 103–106, 114, 116–122, 124–133, 135, 136, 139–141, 150, 153, 157–161, 163–165, 167, 169–187, 192, 204, 208–212, 214, 219–227, 229, 230, 232, 233, 235–237, 240–242, 244–246
Praxis, xi, 27, 28, 30, 35, 36, 40, 56, 57, 68, 70, 76–78
Pre-capitalistic form, 113, 114, 116, 117, 125
Proletarian experience, 11, 36, 37, 39, 43, 56, 60, 91, 92
   experience, 40, 41, 69
Proletariat, 3, 11, 20–22, 24, 27–36, 38–45, 69, 92, 100–104, 106, 235, 236
Pseudo-Marxism, 31

Q
Quinet, Edgar, 123, 228, 242, 243

R
Rancière, Jacques, 5, 30, 172
Rationalist theory, 61
Reality, viii, ix, 4, 6, 8, 10, 20, 34–36, 38, 39, 41, 52–57, 60, 61, 67–73, 75, 77, 89, 91–99, 102, 104, 106, 107, 120, 121, 127, 150, 153, 158, 169, 174–179, 182–184, 193, 196–198, 203, 206, 208, 214, 221, 235, 240
reality-alienation dichotomy, 54, 55, 57
Religion, 53, 58–60, 66, 72, 75, 96, 116, 121–123, 125, 139, 160, 219, 225–227, 236, 243
Representation, x, 4, 38, 43, 57, 63, 68, 70–73, 75–77, 95–98, 106, 107, 115, 118, 119, 121–125, 128, 129, 160, 174, 179, 184, 185, 192, 195, 197, 198, 213, 214, 219–221, 223, 224, 228, 235, 236, 241–244, 247, 248
self-representation, 68, 73, 75, 76, 83, 84, 106, 116, 124, 127, 140, 161, 182, 183, 215, 222
Republicanism, 131, 142
Revolution, viii, 5, 12, 20, 21, 24, 26, 27, 32, 35, 42–44, 90, 97, 101, 102, 105, 106, 113, 123, 141, 142, 225, 227–230, 232, 234, 241–245
   French Revolution, 122, 226, 228–230, 242, 243
   Hungarian Revolution, 245
Richir, Marc, 199, 211, 244
Robespierre, Maximilien de, 227, 229, 230
Rome, 139, 140, 156, 163–165, 168, 170, 173, 181, 186, 187

Rousseau, Jean-Jacques, 14, 142

S
Salutati, Coluccio, 14, 131, 135, 140, 141, 156, 220
Sartre, Jean-Paul, 19, 23, 40, 41, 52, 103
Saussure, Ferdinand de, 78
Secularization, 124, 131, 225, 228
Social, viii–x, 2–6, 10, 11, 13–15, 20, 21, 23, 32–35, 39, 51, 54, 56–69, 71–73, 75–78, 83, 84, 89–102, 104–106, 112, 115, 121, 122, 124, 126–130, 132, 136, 140, 148, 160, 163–165, 172–175, 182–185, 187, 192–200, 208–214, 219, 221, 224, 225, 227–229, 233, 235–238, 240, 241, 246, 247
Socialisme ou Barbarie, 3, 11, 12, 25, 29, 31, 36, 41, 44, 100, 105, 191, 199, 210, 232
Society without history, 62
  stagnant society, 62
Soviet dissident, 19
Strauss, Leo, 150, 155, 160
Structuralism, 3, 5, 7, 8, 12, 51, 74, 76, 77, 81, 191, 192, 194, 195, 197–200, 211–213, 215
Structure, viii, 3, 8, 13, 20, 22, 23, 30, 42–44, 51–53, 57, 60, 66, 71, 72, 75–77, 80, 90, 92, 93, 102, 114, 116, 117, 121, 126, 130, 139, 151, 160, 175, 178, 182, 193–196, 198–200, 206, 213, 214, 220, 222, 236
Symbolic, x, 2, 11–15, 61, 68, 74–78, 81, 83, 84, 96, 99, 101, 105–107, 116, 117, 121, 123–128, 132, 139, 172, 175, 179, 181, 192, 194, 196, 199, 210, 211, 215, 220, 225–229, 231, 234, 235, 242, 243, 246, 247
symbolic dimension of the social, 72, 89, 97, 111, 117, 139, 199, 211, 212, 214, 234

T
Terror, 23, 24, 227, 232–234, 238, 239, 243
Theological-political, 121–124, 131, 132, 135, 139, 227, 243, 245
Tocqueville, Alexis de, 107, 123, 228–230, 243
Totalitarianism, x, 3, 6, 10–12, 15, 74, 107, 191, 231, 232, 234–241, 243
Totality, 8, 11, 58, 60, 61, 66, 68, 70, 73–75, 83, 91, 93, 99, 102, 104, 133, 185, 192, 202, 223, 235, 246
Transcendence, x, 10, 59, 78, 96, 120, 124, 128, 131, 208, 214, 215, 220, 225, 242, 247
Tronti, Mario, 101, 130
Trotskyism, 23, 24, 31
Trotsky, Leon, 19–21, 24, 232

U
USSR, 6, 12, 19–21, 23, 24, 26, 232, 234

W
Workerism (*operaismo*), 3, 25, 30

Printed in the United States
by Baker & Taylor Publisher Services